D1084828

Readings in Russian Poetics

Michigan Slavic Publications, Ann Arbor, Michigan

Readings in Russian Poetics: Formalist and Structuralist Views

Edited by
Ladislav Matejka
and
Krystyna Pomorska

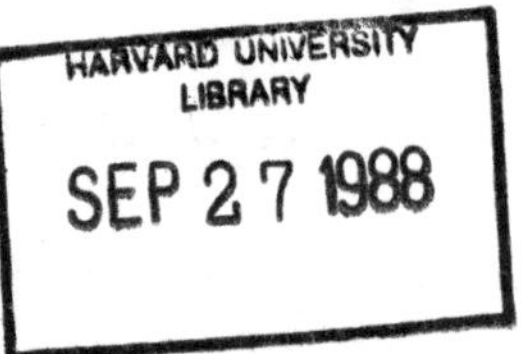

ISBN 0-930042-25-5

Reprinted with the permission
of the MIT Press

Michigan Slavic Contributions, 8

The primary objective of this volume is to acquaint English readers with the methodological struggles in which the leading Russian theorists of literature engaged during the 1920s and early 1930s. It is our belief that more than one aspect of their quest still retains crucial relevance for present-day endeavors to establish literary scholarship as an autonomous scientific discipline.

Part I comprises contributions to the general problems of literary theory and is introduced by Boris Èjxenbaum's "Theory of the 'Formal Method.' " This lucid retrospective essay, first published in 1925, surveys a decade of Russian scholarly effort to extricate literary inquiries from eclecticism and from methodological enthrallment to psychology, sociology, or political and cultural history. The principle that literary science should be specific and focused solely upon literary facts is viewed by Èjxenbaum as the fundamental tenet of the entire trend that became known as "Formalism" and on account of that very label was often misunderstood, misinterpreted, and vehemently attacked. On the one hand, therefore, he rejects accusations that the Formal method is a sort of decadent doctrine of art for art's sake, and on the other hand he defends this method against those who tried to convert it into a dogmatic system of terms, schemes, and classifications mechanically registering the elements of verbal art.

Although Èjxenbaum frequently refers to Roman Jakobson's role in the development of the Russian Formal method, he did not, and apparently could not, include in his survey Jakobson's fundamental study "On Realism in Art." This path-breaking excursus appears here as the second item. It was first published in Czech in 1921 and republished in 1927 in Ukrainian; its original Russian version, however, was issued for the first time in 1962 in *Michigan Slavic Materials*, No. 2, more than four decades after its origin. Jakobson's observation about the distinctive function of the two opposite participants in the communicative processes of verbal art, his emphasis on the mutual role of the language code and the art code to the given verbal manifestation, and in particular his approach to the interrelationship between synchrony and diachrony appear in striking contrast to the mechanistic simplifications of those who, in their preoccupation with the physical properties of the artifact, neglected its vital dependence on the entire system of both intrinsic and extrinsic factors.

The nature of extrinsic factors and the degree of their relevance to literary inquiries constitute the central issue of Boris Tomaševskij's "Literature and Biography" and Boris Èjxenbaum's "Literary Environment," both included in the first part of these readings. The problem of extrinsic factors in relationship with other factors of verbal art also reappears within the systematic framework of Jurij Tynjanov's study on literary evolution. Here the classificatory, taxonomical concern with the physical manifestation of verbal art is revealed as a misleading approach that is bound to miss the dynamic connection between the formal elements and their functions within the system as a whole.

A blunt rejection of taxonomical, as well as impressionistic, approaches to literature and a programmatic call for precision of methodological platform constitute the thesis of "Problems in the Study of Literature and Language," signed by both Jakobson and Tynjanov. This proclamation (1928) represents an explicit methodological shift toward structural conceptualization. From this vantage point, form is principally viewed only in its relationship to the complex of norms that ultimately determine the relevant values in any semiotic communication, including verbal art. Accordingly, the fundamental objective of literary scholarship is defined as a study of structural laws.

The first section of this book concludes with Jakobson's "Dominant," a retrospect translated from the manuscript of lectures on the Russian Formalists delivered at the Masaryk University in Brno during the spring term of 1935.

Jakobson here sees the new inquiries into the structural characteristics of verbal art as a third stage of Formalist research as opposed to its earlier stage of semantic emphasis and its still earlier form-oriented beginnings. Thus Formalism gradually underwent the conversion to Structuralism through its growing awareness of the delicate relationship between the material manifestation and the complex code of normative rules.

An essay on differentiating between the study of folklore and the study of literature, outlined by Roman Jakobson and Petr Bogatyrev, introduces the second section of the volume. The authors, who are much concerned with the clarity of analytic procedures, emphasize the fact that from the structural point of view these two types of verbal creativity, the oral and the written, are profoundly distinct from each other, notwithstanding their close genetic tie, and that they ought to be analyzed accordingly.

An early structural approach to the problems of oral tradition is illustrated by Vladimir Propp's "Fairy Tale Transformations," which masterfully reveals the specific character of oral narrative in terms of distinctive features applied to new typological observations. By virtue of similarities and dissimilarities, Propp's structural analysis implicitly illuminates the various problems of written verbal art as well.

Literary questions related to the language of poetry are discussed in the third section. It comprises a selection from Osip Brik's *Rhythm and Syntax* and the initial chapters of Tynjanov's *Problems of Verse Language.* Brik, a prominent Moscow art theoretician of the Formalist orientation approaches the language of poetry as a functional dialect marked by various kinds of interplay between the domain of rhythm and the domain of semantics. Tynjanov considers the arrangement of the verse language as a system within a system that implies that a work of art is a complex interaction of various factors that cannot be comprehended by any static inventory.

The nature of dialogue and monologue, which had already attracted analytic attention in the early stages of the Russian Formal method, provides a point of departure for V. N. Vološinov's and Mixail Baxtin's inquiries into prose. In the fourth section Vološinov is represented by a penetrating analysis of reported speech, and Baxtin, by his typology of verbal discourse. Vološinov's keen specification of the distinctive roles played by the participants in the communicative process discloses subtle semiotic functions in the various types of transmitted, transformed, and represented speech in verbal art and opens new horizons for literary investigation. Baxtin, in striking agreement with Vološinov's axioms, proceeds toward the typological observation of the entire range of literary components acting on verbal discourse in art.

The fifth section contains critical contributions concerned with specific literary works or specific writers. These include Nikolaj Trubeckoj's analytic discovery of the fifteenth-century travelogue by Afanasij Nikitin as a work of verbal art; Viktor Šklovskij's morphological exegesis of the mystery technique in Dickens's *Little Dorrit*; and Èjxenbaum's inquiry into the narrative craftsmanship of O. Henry.

The translations have been done by faculty members and graduate students (past and present) of the Department of Slavic

Languages and Literatures at the University of Michigan. Retrospective essays on linguistics and literary studies appear in the sixth section of this volume.

Ladislav Matejka
University of Michigan

Krystyna Pomorska
Massachusetts Institute of Technology

Part I

The Theory of the Formal Method*

Boris M. Èjxenbaum

3

Le pire, à mon avis, est celui qui représente la science comme faite.
A. de Condolle

The school of thought on the theory and history of literature known as the Formal method derived from efforts to secure autonomy and concreteness for the discipline of literary studies. It did not originate (as the name might suggest) out of ambition to create any particular "methodological" system. "Method" nowadays has unsuitably broadened and has come to stand for too much. It is not the methods of studying literature but rather literature as an object of study that is of prime concern to the Formalists.[1] In fact, we are not concerned with debating methodology. Our discussions have been, and can only be, about certain theoretical principles drawn from the study of the concrete material with its specific characteristics, not about one or another ready-made methodological or aesthetic system. The Formalists' writings on the theory of literature and the history of literature state these principles clearly enough. However, so many old misconceptions and so many new issues have accumulated over the past ten years that it would not be amiss now to attempt a kind of conspectus of them—as a historical summary, not as a dogmatic codification. It is vital to bring out how the work of the Formalists began, and how and in what respects it has evolved.

The factor of evolution in the history of the Formal method is extremely important. Our opponents and many of our followers overlook it. We are hedged round with eclectics and epigones who have turned the Formal method into some sort of rigid system, a "Formalism" that stands them in good stead for manufacturing terms, schemes, and classifications. This system is very handy for criticism but not at all characteristic of the Formal method. We did not, and do not, possess any such ready-made system or doctrine. In our scholarship we value theory only as a working hypothesis with the help of which facts are disclosed and take on meaning, that is, they are apprehended as immanent properties and become material for investigation. Therefore we are not concerned with definitions, for which the epigones yearn, nor do we construct general theories, which eclectics find so appealing. We establish concrete principles and adhere to them to the extent

*"Teorija 'formalnogo metoda,' " *Literatura: teorija, kritika, polemika* (Leningrad, 1927), pp. 116-148. Translated by I. R. Titunik. First published in Ukrainian in 1926.

they are proved tenable by the material. If the material requires their further elaboration or alteration, we go ahead and elaborate or alter them. In this sense we are relatively detached from our own theories, as indeed a science ought to be, seeing that there is a difference between theory and convictions. There are no ready-made sciences. The vitality of a science is not measured by its establishing truths but by its overcoming errors.

The purpose of this essay is not polemical. The initial stage of learned fracases and journalistic polemics is over and done with. To the sort of "polemic" that *Pečat´ i revoljucija* (1924, No. 5) saw fit to address to me, the reply now can only be new works of scholarship. My main purpose here is to demonstrate how the Formal method, as it has been gradually evolving and expanding its field of inquiry, goes well beyond what is usually called methodology and is turning into a special scientific discipline concerned with literature as a specific system of facts. Within the scope of this discipline the most diverse methods potentially can develop, provided only, at the same time, the specificity of the object of study remain the center of attention. Such in fact was the ambition of the Formalists at the very start, and that was the exact meaning of their struggle against the older traditions. The appellation "Formal method," which accrued to this school of thought and with which it is now indelibly stamped, must be understood with the qualification that it is a historical term and ought not be taken as defining the actual nature of the school. Neither "Formalism" as a theory of aesthetics nor "methodology" as a fully formulated scientific system is characteristic of us; what does characterize us is the endeavor to create an autonomous discipline of literary studies based on the specific properties of literary material. All that we require is theoretical and historical awareness of the facts of verbal art as such.

1

The representatives of the Formal method have been reproached repeatedly and from various quarters for an inexplicitness or inadequacy of basic principles—for ignoring the broad issues of aesthetics, psychology, philosophy, sociology, etc. These reproaches (aside from qualitative differences) are equally correct in the sense that they do properly grasp a feature that is characteristic of the Formalists, and not, of course, by accident: I mean, their disengagement not only from "aesthetics from above" but also from all ready-made or putatively ready-made general theories. This disengagement (especially from aesthetics) is a phenomenon more or less typical of all modern study of art. The modern study of art has put aside a number of general problems (such as the problem of beauty, the purpose of art) and has focused on the concrete problems of art science (*Kunstwissenschaft*). A fresh start has been made in advancing the question of what is to be understood by artistic "form" and its evolution, outside of any connection with the premises of general aesthetics, and this has sprung a whole series of concrete, theoretical, and historical issues. In this regard, the appearance of catchwords like Heinrich Wölfflin's *Kunstgeschichte ohne Namen* (history of art without names) and of experiments in the concrete analysis of styles and devices, such as K. Voll's "experiment in the comparative study of paintings," was very symptomatic. In Germany it was the theory and history of the fine arts—the study richest in experience and tradition—that took over the central position in art science and began exerting an influence both on the general theory of art and on individual disciplines—for instance, the study of literature.[2] In Russia, for what were clearly local historical reasons, it was literary scholarship that occupied an analogous position.

The Formal method attracted universal attention and became an issue of the day—not, of course, because of its methodological peculiarities but because of its attitude toward how to understand and study art. Formalist works put forward in no uncertain terms principles that cut athwart the seemingly hard-and-fast traditions and the "axioms" belonging not only to literary science but also to art science as a whole. Thanks to this sharp focus on principles, the distance between the particular problems of literary science and the general problems of the science of art narrowed. For all their concreteness, the concepts and principles on which the Formalists based their work naturally tended to point toward a theory of art in general. Therefore, the regeneration of poetics from a state of total disuse represented no simple matter of reestablishing particular problems but an attack on the whole domain of art science.

The situation had resulted from a whole series of historical events, the most important of which were the crisis in philosophical aesthetics and the radical change in art (in Russia a change most crucially and patently expressed in poetry). Aesthetics proved to be denuded, and art deliberately presented itself laid bare in the full primitive mode. The Formal method and

Futurism proved to have a historical interconnection. But the main historical meaning of the emergence of the Formalists comprises a topic in its own right—here I must follow a different line, inasmuch as my intention is to outline the evolution of the principles and problems of the Formal method and the position of the Formal method at the present moment.

At about the time the Formalists emerged, academic scholarship—with its utter disregard of theoretical problems and its nonchalant making-do with obsolete aesthetic, psychological, and historical "axioms"—had lost the sense of its own proper object of study to such a degree that its very existence became illusory. Academic scholarship hardly needed attack. There was no call to force open the door, because, as it turned out, there was none—we discovered, instead of a fortress, a through alley. The theoretical legacy of Potebnja and Veselovskij, once handed down to their students, was left to stagnate as so much dead capital—a fortune which they were afraid to tap and so caused it to depreciate. Authority and influence gradually passed from academic scholarship to the scholarship of what might be called "the journalistic style"—works by the critics and theorists of Symbolism. In point of fact, the books and articles by Vjačeslav Ivanov, Brjusov, A. Belyj, Merežkovskij, Čukovskij, and others had far greater influence in 1907-1912 than did the scholarly research and dissertations of the university professors. Behind that journalistic style of scholarship, for all its subjectivity and tendentiousness, there were theoretical principles and slogans that were drawing strength from the new movements in art and from the propaganda on their behalf. It was only to be expected that books like Andrej Belyj's *Symbolism* (1910) would mean incomparably more to the younger generation than gratuitous monographs written by literary historians devoid of any scientific verve, any standpoint on things.

That is why, when the time came for the historical confrontation between the two generations (a confrontation this time highly charged with fundamental issues), it was not academic scholarship that set the terms but rather a journalistic scholarship comprised of Symbolist theories and the methods of impressionistic criticism. We engaged in battle with the Symbolists in order to wrest poetics from their hands and, once having divested poetics of any ties with subjective, aesthetic, or philosophical theories, to redirect it to the route of a scientific investigation of facts. Having ourselves been educated on Symbolist works, we had the advantage of being able to see their mistakes all the more clearly. The revolt of the Futurists (Xlebnikov, Kručenyx, Majakovskij) against the poetic system of Symbolism, a revolt that had taken definite shape at about that time, lent support to the Formalists and imbued their struggle with an even greater relevance.

The basic motto uniting the original group of Formalists was the emancipation of the poetic word from philosophical and religious biases to which the Symbolists had increasingly fallen prey. Dissension among the theorists of Symbolism (1910-1911) and the appearance of the Acmeists prepared the ground for an all-out revolt. All compromises had to be cast aside. History demanded from us a genuine revolutionary élan—categorical theses, pitiless irony, a pugnacious refusal to come to terms on any basis whatsoever. In this state of affairs it was vital to counter the subjective-aesthetic principles that had served the Symbolists as inspiration with propaganda for an objective-scientific attitude toward facts. That is the source of the new spirit of scientific positivism that characterizes the Formalists: the rejection of philosophical premises, psychological or aesthetic interpretations, and so forth. The break with philosophical aesthetics and ideological theories of art was dictated by the very state of affairs. It was time to turn to the facts and, eschewing general systems and problems, to start from the center—from where the facts of art confront us. Art had to be approached at close range, and science had to be made concrete.

2

The organization of the Formal method was governed by the principle that the study of literature should be made specific and concrete. All efforts were directed toward terminating the earlier state of affairs, in which literature, as A. Veselovskij observed, was *res nullius*. That was what made the Formalists so intolerant of other "methods" and of eclectics. In rejecting these "other" methods, the Formalists actually were rejecting (and still reject) not methods but the gratuitous mixing of different scientific disciplines and different scientific problems. Their basic point was, and still is, that the object of literary science, as literary science, ought to be the investigation of the specific properties of literary material, of the properties that distinguish such material from material of any other kind, notwithstanding the fact that its secondary and oblique features make that material properly and legitimately exploitable, as auxiliary material, by other disciplines. The point was consummately formulated by Roman Jakobson:

> The object of study in literary science is not literature but "literariness," that is, what makes a given work a *literary* work. Meanwhile, the situation has been that historians of literature act like nothing so much as policemen, who, out to arrest a certain culprit, take into custody (just in case) everything and everyone they find at the scene as well as any passers-by for good measure. The historians of literature have helped themselves to everything—environment, psychology, politics, philosophy. Instead of a science of literature, they have worked up a concoction of homemade disciplines. They seem to have forgotten that those subjects pertain to their own fields of study—to the history of philosophy, the history of culture, psychology, and so on, and that those fields of study certainly may utilize literary monuments as documents of a defective and second-class variety among other materials.[3]

To establish this principle of specificity without resorting to speculative aesthetics required the juxtaposing of the literary order of facts with another such order. For this purpose one order had to be selected from among existent orders, which, while contiguous with the literary order, would contrast with it in terms of functions. It was just such a methodological procedure that produced the opposition between "poetic" language and "practical" language. This opposition was set forth in the first *Opojaz* publications (L. Jakubinskij articles), and it served as the activating principle for the Formalists' treatment of the fundamental problems of poetics. Thus, instead of an orientation toward a history of culture or of social life, toward psychology, or aesthetics, and so on, as had been customary for literary scholars, the Formalists came up with their own characteristic orientation toward linguistics, a discipline contiguous with poetics in regard to the material under investigation, but one approaching that material from a different angle and with different kinds of problems to solve. The linguists in their turn took an interest in the Formal method, inasmuch as the facts of poetic language, brought to light by its juxtaposition with practical language, might be regarded in the purely linguistic sphere of problems as facts of language in general. What came about was something analogous to the relationship of mutual utilization and delimitation, such as exists, for instance, between physics and chemistry. Against this background, the issues once raised by Potebnja and accepted on faith by his disciples revived and took on new meaning.

The comparison of poetic language with practical language was made in general terms by Lev Jakubinskij in his first article, "On Sounds in Verse Language."[4] The formulation of the difference between the two language systems ran as follows:

The phenomena of language ought to be classified according to the purpose for which the speaker uses his language resources in any given instance. If the speaker uses them for the purely practical purpose of communication, then we are dealing with the system of *practical language* (discursive thought), in which language resources (sounds, morphological segments, and so forth) have no autonomous value and are merely a *means* of communication. But it is possible to conceive and in fact to find language systems in which the practical aim retreats to the background (it does not necessarily disappear altogether), and language resources acquire autonomous value.

It was important to establish this difference not only as a foundation for building a poetics but also in order to grasp the meaning of the Futurists' trend toward a "transrational language" (*zaumnyj jazyk*) as the utmost baring of autonomous value, a phenomenon already observable in some aspects in children's language, in the glossolalia of religious sectarians, and so forth. The transrational experiments of the Futurists acquired considerable significance in principle as demonstration against the tendency of Symbolism to balk at going beyond the sound "orchestration" accompanying meaning and, as a consequence, to debase the role of sounds in verse. The issue of sounds in verse then took on particular point. Just at that juncture, the Formalists, joining forces with the Futurists, clashed with the theorists of Symbolism face to face. It was perfectly natural for the Formalists to have given battle on these grounds first: the issue of sounds had to be reexamined, above all with the aim of pitting a system of exact observations against the Symbolists' philosophical and aesthetic biases, and the pertinent scientific conclusions had to be drawn. That is what accounts for the makeup of our first volume of studies—a volume devoted entirely to the problem of sounds and of "transrational language."

Along with Jakubinskij, there was Viktor Šklovskij, who, in his article "On Poetry and Transrational Language,"[5] used a large variety of examples to demonstrate that "words are a human need even apart from meaning." Transrational quality was found to be a widespread fact of language and a phenomenon characteristic of poetry: "A poet doesn't set out to make a transrational utterance; transrational quality is usually hidden under the guise of some sort of content, often deceptive or illusory in nature—the sort of thing that makes poets admit that they themselves don't understand what their own poems are about." Šklovskij's article shifted the central question from the level of pure sound (acoustics in which connections between sound and the object or emotion depicted are apt to be posited and given impressionistic interpretations) to the level of articulation, the implementation of sound: "Beyond doubt, the articulatory aspect is a vital component in the enjoyment of a referenceless transrational utterance. It may very well be that a large part of the pleasure poetry gives us stems from its articulatory aspect—from a special dance of the organs of speech." The question of how to regard transrational language thus acquired the significance of a serious scientific problem, the illumination of which might elucidate many facts of verse speech in general. Šklovskij did in fact formulate the general issue:

> If we stipulate that a word in order to be a word must designate a concept and must in all circumstances be meaningful, then, of course, transrational language goes out of the picture as something external with regard to language. However, it is not all that goes out of the picture: the facts that have been cited make one wonder whether the words in a speech that is not only unmarked as transrational but is simply poetic do always have meaning, or, whether this impression is a false one and a consequence of our inattentiveness.

The natural conclusion from all these observations and principles was that poetic language is not just a language of "images," and that sounds in verse are not at all mere elements of external euphony serving only to "accompany" meaning, but that they do have autonomous value. The stage was set for a reexamination of Potebnja's general theory with its basic assertion that poetry is "thinking in images." This conception, which was the one accepted by the theorists of Symbolism, made it requisite to regard the sounds of verse as the "expression" of something standing behind a poem and to interpret them either as onomatopoeia or as "painting with sounds." Andrej Belyj's studies are especially illustrative of this. Belyj found in two lines of Puškin the complete "picture in sounds" of champagne being poured from a bottle into a glass and in Blok's repetition of cluster *rdt* the "tragedy of turning sober."[6] Such attempts, verging on parody, to "explain" alliterations were bound to provoke on our part energetic opposition in terms of basic theory and our endeavors to demonstrate concretely that sounds in verse exist outside any connection with imagery and have an independent speech function.

L. Jakubinskij's articles linguistically substantiated the autonomous value of sounds in verse. Osip Brik's article "Sound Repetitions"[7] brought actual material to the fore (excerpts from Puškin and Lermontov) and arranged it in various typological classes. After disputing the popular notion of poetic language as the language of "images," Brik came to the following conclusion:

However the interrelationship of sound and image may be regarded, one thing is certain: sounds and sound harmonies are not merely a euphonic extra but are the result of an autonomous poetic endeavor. The orchestration of poetic speech is not fully accounted for by a repertoire of overt euphonic devices, but represents in its entirety the complex product of the interaction of the general laws of euphony. Rhythm, alliteration, and so forth are only the obvious manifestation of particular instances of basic euphonic laws.

In contrast to Belyj's works, Brik's article contained no interpretations of what particular cases of alliteration were supposed to mean; the article limited itself to the supposition that repetition in verse is analogous to tautology in folklore, that is, that repetition in these instances plays some aesthetic role in its own right. "It is likely that we are dealing here with various manifestations of the same general poetic principle—the principle of simple combination, the material being either the sounds of the words, or their meaning, or both." This sort of predication of one device applied to a wide range of material was very characteristic of the early period of the Formalists' work. After Brik's article, the issue of sounds in verse lost its special point and assumed its place within the general system of the problems of poetics.

3

The Formalists had begun their work with the most militant and crucial issue of the time—the sounds of verse. Behind that particular question of poetics were theses of a more general nature, and these were indeed bound to emerge. The distinction between the poetic and the practical language systems, which had shaped the work of the Formalists from the very start, was bound to make its mark on the formulation of a whole series of basic questions. The conception of poetry as "thinking in images" and the equation "poetry = imagery" derived from it were blatantly out of keeping with the facts observed and in contradiction to the general principles the facts suggested. Rhythm, sounds, syntax—all these things from that point of view were secondary matters not necessarily characteristic of poetry, and they had to drop out of the system. The Symbolists, who had adopted Potebnja's general theory because it substantiated the predominance of the image symbol, were unable to overcome its much acclaimed correlative, "the harmony of form and content," despite its being blatantly contradictory to their own predilection for formal experimentations and despite its adulterating that predilection with "aestheticism." In departing from Potebnja's point of view, the Formalists simultaneously freed themselves from the traditional correlation of "form-content" and from the conception of form as an outer cover or as a vessel into which a liquid (the content) is poured. The facts testified that the specificity of art is expressed not in the elements that go to make up a work but in *the special way they are used.* By the same token, the concept of "form" took on a different meaning; it no longer had to be paired with any other concept, it no longer needed correlation.

In 1914, before the *Opojaz* alliance and during the days of the Futurists' public demonstrations, Šklovskij published a pamphlet, *The Resurrection of the Word.*[8] Relying in part on Potebnja and Veselovskij (the question of imagery had then not yet acquired crucial meaning), he advanced the principle of the palpableness (*oščutimosť*) of form as the specific criterion of perception in art:

> We do not experience the familiar, we do not see it, we recognize it. We do not see the walls of our rooms. We find it very difficult to catch mistakes when reading proof (especially if it is in a language we are very used to), the reason being that we cannot force ourselves to see, to read, and not just "recognize," a familiar word. If it is a definition of "poetic" perception or of "artistic" perception in general we are after, then we must surely hit upon this definition: "artistic" perception is a perception that entails awareness of form (perhaps not only form, but invariably form).

It should be evident that *perception* figures here not as a simple psychological concept (the perception of individual human beings) but as an element of art in itself, since it is impossible for art to exist without being perceived. A concept of form in a new meaning had now come into play—not just the outer covering but the whole entity, something concrete and dynamic, substantive in itself, and unqualified by any correlation. This signalized a decisive departure from the principles of Symbolism, which had held that something already "substantive" was supposed to emanate "through form." It also meant that "aestheticism"—a delectation with certain elements of form consciously divorced from "content"—had likewise been overcome.

This, however, did not yet constitute an adequate basis for concrete work. To supplement the points established by the recognition of a difference between poetic language and practical language and by the recognition that the specificity of art is expressed in a special usage of material, the principle of the palpableness of form had to be made concrete enough to foster the analysis of form itself—form understood as content. It had to be shown that the palpableness of form results from special artistic devices acting on perceivers so as to force them to experience form. Šklovskij's "Art as Device,"[9] a kind of manifesto of the Formal method, set the stage for the concrete analysis of form. Here the removal from Potebnja and Potebnjaism and by the same token from the principles of Symbolism was made perfectly explicit. The article opens with objections to Potebnja's basic stand on imagery and on the relationship of the image with what it is meant to explain. Šklovskij points out among other things that images are almost always static:

The more light you shed on a literary period, the more you become convinced that the images you had considered to be the creation of a certain particular poet had been borrowed by him from other poets, virtually unchanged. All that the work of poetic schools amounts to is the acquisition and demonstration of new devices for deploying and elaborating verbal materials; in particular, it amounts much more to deploying images than creating them. Images are handed down; and poetry involves far more reminiscence of images than thinking in them. In any case, imagistic thinking is not that factor whose change constitutes the essence of the momentum of poetry.

Further on, the difference between the poetic and the prosaic image is pointed out. The poetic image is defined as one of the means of poetic language—a device equal in the task it fulfills to other devices of poetic language: parallelism (simple and negative), comparison, repetition, symmetry, hyperbole, etc. The concept of the image was relegated to a position within the general system of poetic devices, and so it had lost its overriding importance for theory. Concomitantly, the principle of artistic economy, a principle deeply embedded in the theory of art, had been refuted. Šklovskij countered by advancing the device of "making it strange" (*ostranenie*) and the device of impeded form, "which augments the difficulty and the duration of perception, since the process of perception in art is an end in itself and is supposed to be prolonged." Art is conceived as a way of breaking down automatism in perception, and the aim of the image is held to be, not making a meaning more accessible for our comprehension, but bringing about a special perception of a thing, bringing about the "seeing," and not just the "recognizing," of it. Hence the usual connection between the image and the device of "making strange."

The break with Potebnjaism was definitively formulated in Šklovskij's "Potebnja."[10] He repeats once again that the use of images and symbols does not constitute the distinguishing feature of poetic language as against prosaic (practical) language:

> Poetic language is distinguished from prosaic language by the palpableness of its construction. The palpableness may be brought about by the acoustical aspect or the articulatory aspect or the semasiological aspect. Sometimes what is palpable is not the structure of the words but the use of words in a construction, their arrangement. One of the means of creating a palpable construction, the very fabric of which is experienced, is the poetic image, but it is only one of the means. . . . If scientific poetics is to be brought about, it must start with the factual assertion, founded on massive evidence, that there are such things as "poetic" and "prosaic" languages, each with their different laws, and it must proceed from an analysis of those differences.

These articles may be considered the summation of the initial period in the Formalists' work. The main accomplishment of that period consisted in establishing a number of theoretical principles to serve as working hypotheses for a further concrete investigation of facts; it also surmounted popularly held theories derived from Potebnjaism. As is evident from the articles cited, the basic efforts of the Formalists were directed neither toward the study of so-called "form" nor toward the construction of a special "method," but toward substantiating the claim that verbal art must be studied in its specific features, that it is essential for that purpose to take the different functions of poetic and practical languages as the starting point. As for "form," all that concerned the Formalists was to shift the meaning of that badly confused term in such a way as to obviate its persistent association with the concept of "content," a term even more badly confused than form and totally unscientific. It was important to do away with the traditional correlation and by so doing to enrich the concept of form with new meanings. As matters further evolved, it was the concept of "device" that had a far greater significance, because it stemmed directly from the recognition of the difference between poetic and practical languages.

The preliminary stage of the theoretical work had been passed. The general theories likely to aid in orienting ourselves within the context of the facts had been mapped out. Now we needed to come closer to the material and to make the problems involved concrete. At the center of things stood the issues of theoretical poetics, of which our early work had provided only a general outline. We had now to go beyond the issue of sounds in verse—the significance of which had actually been a matter of illustrating the general proposition of the difference between the poetic and the practical languages—and to take up the general theory of verse. We had to move from general considerations of the device to the study of plot, and so on. Side by side with the Potebnja question, there emerged the question of what to do about Veselovskij's ideas and his theory of plots.

Naturally enough, the Formalists were using literary works at this point only as material for testing and corroborating theoretical theses, to the exclusion of tradition, evolution, and so forth. It was vital to attain the widest possible purview of the material, to establish sui generis "laws," and to carry out a preliminary survey of the facts. Thus the Formalists kept clear of resorting to abstract premises, and on the positive side they managed to master the material without floundering among details.

Šklovskij's work on the theory of plot and the theory of the novel was particularly significant during this period. Using a wide variety of materials—fairy tales, oriental tales, Cervantes's *Don Quixote*, Tolstoj, Sterne's *Tristram Shandy*, and other material—Šklovskij demonstrated the existence of special devices of "plot formation" (*sjužetosloženie*) and their connection with the general devices of style. Leaving the details aside (their treatment properly belongs to specialized studies, and not in a general essay on the Formal method), I shall focus only on those points with a theoretical bearing exclusive of the problem of plot as such, which left their mark on the further evolution of the Formal method.

A whole series of such points are contained in the first of these works by Šklovskij, "The Connection of Devices of Plot Formation with General Devices of Style."[11] First, the very assertion of the actuality of special devices of plot formation—an assertion copiously illustrated with examples—altered the traditional notion of plot as a set of motifs and redirected it from the provenance of thematic concepts to that of compositional concepts.

Thus the concept of plot (*sjužet*) acquired a new meaning which did not coincide with that of story (*fabula*), and plot formation itself assumed its natural place in the sphere of formal study as a specific property of literary works. The concept of form became enriched with new features and at the same time as it gradually relinquished its previous abstractness, it relinquished its significance as a crucial polemical issue as well. It was becoming clear that for us the concept of form was beginning gradually to coincide with the concept of literature as such—that is, the concept of literary fact. Furthermore, the postulation of an analogy between devices of plot formation and devices of style held promise of major theoretical importance. The typically epic serial construction (*stupenčatoe postroenie*) could be grouped together with sound repetition, tautology, tautological parallelism, other kinds of repetitions, etc., as the general principle of verbal art's being structured step by step, with progress arrested.

Thus Roland's three attempts to break his sword against a rock (*Song of Roland*) and similar triple repetitions common in folktale plots are brought into conjunction as things of the same order as Gogol′'s use of synonyms, or such verbal constructs as *kudy-mudy*, *pljuški-mljuški* [cf. similar English reduplications like "even-steven," "actor-schmacter," and so on.] "All these instances of slowed-down serial construction are usually not classed together, as the attempt is made to provide each with a separate explanation." What is clearly at stake here is the endeavor to predicate a unity of device over a diversity of material. And that was the point at which a characteristic conflict with Veselovskij occurred, seeing that Veselovskij had been in the habit of resorting in such instances to a historical-genetic, not a theoretical, hypothesis, in attempting to explain epic repetitions by the mechanics of the original performance (amoebaean song). That kind of explanation, even if correct in genetic terms, does not elucidate the phenomenon in question as literary fact. Šklovskij did not reject the overall interrelationship between literature and communal culture which Veselovskij and other representatives of the ethnographic school had used to explain the properties of folktale motifs and plots; all he did was deny its capacity to explain those properties as literary fact. The genetic approach can elucidate only origin and nothing more, while for poetics the elucidation of literary function is vital. Precisely what the genetic point of view fails to reckon with is the device as a special kind of utilization of material; it fails to reckon with the selection of material from communal culture, its transformation, its constructional role; it fails, finally, to reckon with the fact that a detail of communal culture may disappear, and yet its literary function remains; it remains not as a mere relic but as a literary device, retaining its own meaning, even if totally unrelated to communal culture. Typically enough, Veselovskij lapses into contradiction with himself when he calls the adventure series of the Greek (Hellenistic) novel a purely stylistic device.

Veselovskij's "ethnographism" met with natural opposition on the Formalists' part, because it ignored the specificity of the literary device and supplanted a theoretical and evolutionary point of view with a genetic one.[12] It was only to be expected that the Formalists would be unable to agree with Veselovskij whenever he had had his say about general questions of literary evolution. The clash with the Potebnja doctrine had resulted in a clarification of the basic problems of theoretical poetics; the clash with the general outlook of Veselovskij and his followers could be expected to result in a definition of the Formalists' views on literary evolution and, by extension, their views on constructing a history of literature.

And, indeed, the process found its start in this very same article by Šklovskij. Confronted with Veselovskij's formula—a formula based on the same, broadly understood ethnographic principles—that "new form comes about in order to express new content," Šklovskij advanced a different point of view:

> A work of art is perceived against the background of, and by way of association with, other works of art. The form of a work of art is determined by its relationship with other forms existing prior to it. . . . Creation as a parallel with and contrast to some model is a description applicable not just to parody but to any work of art in general. *New form comes about not in order to express new content but in order to replace an old form that has already lost its artistic viability.*

In support of his thesis, Šklovskij brings to bear B. Christiansen's point about special "differential impressions" or "impressions of divergencies," making it the basis for the dynamism characteristic of art—a dynamism expressed in incessant violations of the canon being established. At the end of the article, he quotes Brunetière's statement declaring that "chief among all influences operative in the history of literature is the influence of *work on work*," and that "one ought not multiply causes uselessly or, on the pretext that literature is an expression of society, confuse the history of literature with the history of manners and morals. They are two completely different things."

Thus, Šklovskij's article mapped the way out of the sphere of theoretical poetics into the history of literature. The original concept of form took on the added complexity of new features of evolutionary dynamism, of incessant change. The transition to the history of literature had come about, not by way of simply expanding the range of topics for investigation, but as the result of an evolution in the concept of form. It was now evident that a literary work is not perceived in isolation—its form produces an impression against the background of other works, and not on its own. This meant that the Formalists had made a decisive move beyond the "formalism" conceived as a process of manufacturing schemes and classifications (the common notion of the Formal method held by ill-informed critics), which is so eagerly utilized by certain scholastics who always welcome any dogma with joy. This scholastic "formalism" has no connection, either historically or in principle, with the work of *Opojaz*—quite to the contrary of our being apologists for it, we are its most irreconcilable and convinced foes.

5

Before I turn to the Formalists' endeavors in literary history, I want to bring to a conclusion my survey of the theoretical principles and problems contained in the *Opojaz* works of the earliest period. In that article by Šklovskij already discussed, there is another concept that played a major role in the subsequent study of the novel: the concept of "motivation" (*motivirovka*). The determination of various devices of plot formation (serial construction, parallelism, framing, concatenation, and others) established the distinction between the elements of a work's construction and the elements comprising the material it uses (the story stuff, the choice of motifs, of protagonists, of themes, etc.). This distinction was then stressed especially heavily, because the main task was to establish the unity of any chosen structural device within the greatest possible diversity of material. Older scholarship had operated exclusively with material conceived as the "content" and had relegated everything else to "outer form," which it regarded a matter of interest only to fanciers of form, or even as a matter of no interest at all. That is the derivation of the naive and touching "aestheticism," by which our older critics and historians of literature discovered the "neglect of form" in

Tjutčev's poetry and simply "poor form" in writers like Nekrasov or Dostoevskij.

What saved the situation was the fact that form was forgiven these writers out of deference to the profundity of their ideas or attitudes. It was only natural that the Formalists, during their years of struggle and polemics against traditions of that sort, should have directed all their efforts toward promoting the significance of structural devices and subordinating everything else as *motivation.* In discussing the Formal method and its evolution, it is essential always to keep in mind that a great many of the principles advanced by the Formalists during those years of intense struggle with their opponents had value not only as scientific principles but also as slogans—slogans spiked with paradoxes in the interest of propaganda and opposition. To fail to take that fact into account and to treat the *Opojaz* works of 1916-1921 as works of an academic character is to ignore history.

The concept of motivation enabled the Formalists to approach literary works (in particular, novels and short stories) at even closer range and to observe the details of their construction. And that is just what Šklovskij did in his next two studies, *Plot Unfolding* and *Sterne's Tristram Shandy and the Theory of the Novel.*[13] In both of these works he scrutinized the relationship between device and motivation, using Cervantes's *Don Quixote* and Sterne's *Tristram Shandy* as material for a study of the construction of story and novel outside the context of literary historical problems. *Don Quixote* is viewed as a point of transition from story collections (like the *Decameron*) to the single-hero novel, structured on the device of concatenation, with a journey serving as motivation.

That *Don Quixote* was the novel singled out for special attention had to do with the fact that device and motivation are not so integrated in it as to produce a fully motivated novel with all parts fused together. The material is often merely interpolated and not infused; the devices of plot formation and the techniques of manipulating material to further the plot stand out sharply, whereas the later development of novel construction goes "the way of ever more tightly wedging fragments of material into the very body of the novel." In the course of analyzing "how *Don Quixote* is made," Šklovskij, among other things, points out the hero's pliability and infers that this very "type" of hero came about "under the impact of devising the construction of the novel." Thus, the predominance of the construction, of the plot over material, was stressed.

The most suitable material for illustrating theoretical problems of this sort is, understandably enough, art which is not fully motivated or which deliberately tears away motivation and bares its construction. The very existence of works with an intentionally bared construction necessarily stands these problems in good stead as confirmation of the importance of their treatment and the real fact of their pertinence. Moreover, it is precisely the light shed by these problems and principles that elucidates the works themselves. And that was exactly the case with Sterne's *Tristram Shandy*. Thanks to Šklovskij's study, this novel not only contributed illustrations for theoretical postulations but also acquired a new meaning of its own so that it attracted fresh attention. Against the background of a new-found interest in its construction, Sterne's novel became a piece of contemporary writing, and Sterne became a topic of discussion for people who, until then, had seen nothing in his novel except tedious chatter or curios, or who had viewed it from the angle of its much-made-of "sentimentalism," a "sentimentalism" for which Sterne was as little responsible as Gogol′ was for "realism."

Observing in Sterne a deliberate baring of constructional devices, Šklovskij argues that the very design of construction is emphasized in Sterne's novel: Sterne's awareness of form, brought out by way of his violation of form, is what in fact constitutes the content of the novel. At the end of his study, Šklovskij formulates the distinction between plot (*sjužet*) and story-stuff (*fabula*):

> The concept of *plot* is too often confused with the depiction of events–with what I tentatively propose terming "story-stuff." The story-stuff actually is only material for filling in the plot. Therefore, the plot of *Evgenij Onegin* is not the hero's romance with Tat′jana but the plot-processing of this story-stuff worked out by introducing intermittent digressions. . . . The forms of art are to be explained by their artistic immanence, not by real-life motivation. When an artist holds back the action of a novel, not by employing intruders, for example, but simply by transposing the order of the parts, he makes us aware of the aesthetic laws underlying both devices of composition.

It was in connection with the construction of the short story that my article "How Gogol′'s 'Overcoat' Is Made"[14] was written. The article couples the problem of plot with the problem of *skaz*, that is, the problem of a construction based on a narrator's manner of narrating. I tried to show that Gogol′'s text "is composed of animated locutions and verbalized emotions," that "words and sentences were chosen and linked together in Gogol′ on the principle of expressive *skaz*, in which a special role belongs to articulation, miming, sound gestures, etc." From that point of view the composition of *The Overcoat* proved on analysis to be built on a successive alternation of comic *skaz* (with its anecdotes, play on words, etc.) and sentimental-melodramatic declamation, thus imparting to the story the character of a grotesque. In this connection, the ending of *The Overcoat* was interpreted as an apotheosis of the grotesque—something like the mute scene in *The Inspector General.* Traditional arguments about Gogol′'s "romanticism" or "realism" proved to be unnecessary and irrelevant.

The problem of the study of prose fiction was therefore moved off dead center. A distinction had been established between the concept of plot, as that of construction, and the concept of story-stuff, as that of material; the typical devices of plot formation had been clarified thanks to which the stage was now set for work on the history and theory of the novel; concomitantly, *skaz* had been advanced as the constructional principle of the plotless story. These studies exercised an influence detectable in a whole series of investigations produced in later years by persons not directly connected with *Opojaz.*

6

As the theoretical problems broadened and deepened, a natural division of specialization set in—one all the more reasonable since *Opojaz* had added to its membership persons previously unaffiliated with it or only then beginning their work. The basic dividing line ran between prose fiction and verse. Contrary to the Symbolists, who were then attempting to liquidate, both in theory and practice, the boundaries between poetry and prose fiction and were using all their ingenuity to educe, for this purpose, meter from prose, the Formalists advocated a clear-cut discrimination between these two kinds of verbal art.

The preceding section of this essay has shown how intensive the Formalists' work was in the study of prose fiction. We were the pioneers in that field, not counting certain Western works which coincided with ours in individual details of concrete observation (e.g., Wilhelm Dibelius's *Englische Romankunst*, 1910) but were far removed from our theoretical problems and principles. We felt ourselves almost completely detached from tradition in our work on prose fiction.

Things were somewhat different in the case of poetry. Vast numbers of works by Western and Russian theorists, the Symbolists' practical and theoretical experiments, debates over the concepts of rhythm and meter, and the whole corpus of specialized literature to which those debates gave rise between 1910 and 1917, and finally, the appearance of the Futurists' new verse forms—all this did not so much facilitate as complicate the study of verse and even the formulation of the problems involved. Instead of addressing themselves to the basic issues, many investigators devoted their efforts to special problems in metrics or to the task of sorting out the systems and views already amassed. Meanwhile, no theory of verse, in the broad sense of the word, was to be had; there was no theoretical illumination of the problem of verse rhythm or of the connection between rhythm and syntax or of sounds in verse (the Formalists had only identified a certain linguistic groundwork), or of verse vocabulary and semantics, and so on. In other words, the problem of verse, as such, remained essentially up in the air. An approach was needed which would steer away from particular problems of metrics and would engage verse from some more fundamental point of view. What was needed, first of all, was a restatement of the problem of rhythm in such a way that the problem would not hinge on metrics and would encompass the more substantive aspects of verse language.

In this chapter, as in the preceding one, I shall limit my topic, focusing on the problem of verse only to the extent that its elaboration led to new theoretical views of verbal art or of verse speech. The start was made by Osip Brik's "On Rhythmic-Syntactic Figures."[15] Brik's report demonstrated the actual existence in verse of constant syntactic formations inseparably bound with rhythm. Therefore the concept of rhythm relinquished its abstract character and touched on the very fabric of verse—*the phrase unit.* Metrics retreated to the background, retaining a significance as the rudiments, the alphabet, of verse. This step was as important for the study of verse as the coupling of plot with construction had been for the study of prose fiction. The discovery of rhythmic-syntactic figures conclusively discredited the notion that rhythm is an external increment, something confined to the surface of speech. The theory of verse was led down a line of inquiry which treated rhythm as the structural base from which all elements of verse—nonacoustical as well as acoustical—

derived definition. The stage was set for a more sophisticated theory of verse under which metrics would have to occupy the position of propaedeutics. The Symbolists and the theorists of the Belyj school, despite all their efforts, had failed to come up with this line of inquiry precisely because the issues of metrics as such persisted as their focal point.

However, Brik's work only hinted at the possibility of this new line of inquiry. His report, as was also true of his first article, "Sound Repetitions," went no further than bringing out examples and ordering them in groups. One could proceed from Brik's work either in the direction of new problems or (equally as well) in the direction of simple classification and cataloging, or the systematization of material, something which had no essential connection with the Formal method at all. The latter is exactly the type of work to which V. Žirmunskij's book *Composition of Lyric Verse*[16] belongs. Not sharing *Opojaz*'s theoretical principles, Žirmunskij found the Formal method of interest only as one of a set of possible scientific rubrics—as the technique of breaking material down into various groupings under various labels. With such a conception of the Formal method, nothing else could have been expected of him than what he in fact produced.

His procedure is to take some egregious feature as the criterion and to sort out the material in groups from that standpoint. Hence, the invariable classificatory and handbook character of all Žirmunskij's theoretical writings. Work of this type had no fundamental meaning in the overall evolution of the Formal method; it only marked a tendency (evidently a bit of historical inevitability) to add an academic aura to the Formal method. It is not surprising, therefore, that Žirmunskij, as things developed, entirely withdrew from *Opojaz*, with whose principles he has repeatedly disagreed in his later works (see especially his preface to the translation of O. Walzel's *Problem of Form in Poetry*, 1923).

There was a certain connection between Brik's work on rhythmic-syntactic figures and my book *Verse Melodics*,[17] a study which had been shaped by an interest in the sound aspect of verse and in that respect was connected with a whole series of Western works (Sievers, Saran, and others). I started from the position that, since stylistic differentiation was usually based on vocabulary, "we thereby sidestep verse as such and really deal with poetic language in general. . . . It is essential to find something connected with the verse *phrase unit* that, at the same time, would not lead us away from verse as such—something located on the border between phonetics and semantics. That 'something' is syntax." Rhythmic-syntactic phenomena in my study were examined, not in and of themselves, but in connection with the problem concerning the constructional significance of intonation in verse and speech. I thought it particularly important to emphasize the concept of the *dominant* (that which underlies the organization of any poetic style) and to discriminate between a concept of "melodics," as a system of intonation, and the concept of the general "musicality" of verse. Taking that as my starting point, I proposed distinguishing three basic styles in lyric poetry: declamatory (oratorical), *chantant* (*napevnyj*), and discursive (*govornoj*). The whole book was devoted to the study of the melodic properties of the *chantant* style, using as material lyric verse by Žukovskij, Tjutčev, Lermontov, and Fet. Avoiding hard and fast schemes, I made this point in the conclusion to my book:

> What I consider most important in scholarship is not erecting schemes but being able to see facts. Theory is essential for this, because it is precisely in the light of theory that facts become visible, that is, really become facts. Theories may perish or change, but the facts discovered and established with their help abide.

The tradition of specialized metrical studies remained in force among the theorists affiliated with Symbolism (A. Belyj, V. Brjusov, S. Bobrov, V. Čudovskij, and others), but gradually it went the way of meticulous statistical computations and lost its relevance to fundamental principles. A role of considerable importance to the problem was played by B. Tomaševskij in a series of metrical investigations ending with his textbook *Russian Versification.*[18] The net effect was the subordination of metrics (as an auxiliary discipline with a very restricted range of problems) and the advancement of the theory of verse, in its full scope, to the fore. An early article of Tomaševskij's, "Puškin's Iambic Pentameter,"[19] in which the attempt was made to go beyond metrics into language, had already evinced the ambition (which had marked the whole preceding development of the Formal method) to expand and enrich the idea of verse rhythm by connecting it with the structure of verse language. It was here that the basic charge against Belyj and his school was made: "The task that rhythm carries out is not conformity with factitious paeons but the distribution of expiratory energy over a single wave—the verse line." This ambition was again expressed with the greatest explicitness in another article by Tomaševskij, "The Problem of

Verse Rhythm."[20] In this article the earlier opposition of meter and rhythm is expanded to the whole range of linguistic elements in the makeup of a verse line: alongside rhythm of the word-accent variety are placed "phrasal-intonational" rhythm and "harmonic" rhythm (alliterations and the like). Therefore, the concept of *verse* becomes the concept of a *special type of speech* which—instead of being forced into one or another metrical pattern, resisting it and producing "rhythmic deviations" (the point of view Žirmunskij adheres to in his *Introduction to Metrics*)[21]—functions wholly in the creation of a poem. According to Tomaševskij,

> Verse speech is speech *organized* in its sound aspect. But inasmuch as sound aspect is a *complex* phenomenon, only some one particular element of sound is canonized. Thus in classical metrics the canonized element is the word stress, which classical metrics proceeded to subject to codification as a norm under its rules. . . . But once the authority of traditional forms is even slightly shaken, the compelling thought arises that these primary features do not exhaust the nature of verse, that verse is viable also in its secondary features of sound, that there is such a thing as a recognizable rhythm along with meter, that verse can be written with only its secondary features observed, that *speech can sound like verse even without its observing a meter.*

The importance of "rhythmic impulse," a concept which had already figured in Brik's work, is affirmed by Tomaševskij as the general rhythmic operational mode:

> Rhythmic devices can participate in various degrees in the creation of a rhythmic impression of artistic value: in individual works some one device or another may predominate; some one procedure or another may be the *dominant.* Focus on one rhythmic device or another determines the character of the work's concrete rhythm, and, with this in mind, verse may be classified as tonic-metrical verse (e.g., the description of the battle in *Poltava*), intonational-melodic verse (Žukovskij's poetry), and harmonic verse (typical of Russian Symbolism in its later years).

Verse form, so understood, is not in opposition to any "content" extrinsic to it; it is not forced to fit inside this "form" but is conceived of as the genuine content of verse speech. Thus the very concept of form, as in our previous works, emerges with a new sense of sufficiency.

7

New problems in the general theory of verse rhythm and verse language were put forward in Roman Jakobson's book *On Czech Verse.*[22] Against the theory of "the unqualified correspondence of poetry with the spirit of the language, the nonresistance of form to material," Jakobson advanced the theory of "the organized coercion of language by poetic form." A characteristic corrective entered in the discrimination between the sound system of practical language and the sound system of poetic language: it was pointed out that the dissimilation of liquids, which, according to Jakubinskij, is absent in poetic language as against practical language,[23] is actually possible in both, but in practical language it is "conditioned," whereas in poetic language it is, so to speak, "made purposeful, i.e., the two are essentially different phenomena." Moreover, Jakobson pointed out the difference in principle between emotive language and poetic language (a topic already discussed as far back as his first work, *Recent Russian Poetry*):

> Poetry may employ the methods of emotive language, but only *for its own purposes.* This resemblance between the two language systems and this employment by poetic language of the means customary in emotive language often suggest an identification of poetic language with emotive language. Such an identification is fallacious, for it fails to take into account the cardinal *functional* difference between the two language systems.

In this connection, Jakobson invalidates attempts by Grammont and other investigators of verse to explain sound constructs by resorting to onomatopoeia or to emotive ties established between sounds and images or ideas: "A sound construct is not always a construct of sound imagery, and a construct of sound imagery does not always make use of the methods of emotive language." Jakobson's study may be regarded as highly characteristic of the Formal method because it constantly exceeds the limits of its special, particular topic (the prosody of Czech verse), shedding light on general questions in the theory of poetic language and theory of verse. For example, at the end a complete essay on Majakovskij, supplementing Jakobson's earlier work on Xlebnikov, is appended.

In my own study of Anna Axmatova (1923) I also made a point of reexamining the basic theoretical issues related to the theory of verse: the connection of rhythm with syntax and intonation, sounds in verse in connection with articulation, and, last, the vocabulary of verse and its semantics. Referring to a study by Jurij Tynjanov (then being written), I advanced the idea that "a word incorporated into verse is, as it were, wrenched from ordinary speech, surrounded with a new aura of meaning, and perceived against a background composed not of speech in general but precisely of speech in poetry." I also postulated that the formation of lateral meanings, disrupting the usual associations of words, is the chief property of verse semantics.

In about the same period the original connection of the Formal method with linguistics slackened considerably. The division of fields of inquiry had been worked out to such an extent that we no longer needed special support from linguistics, particularly from psychologically oriented linguistics. As a matter of fact, certain works by linguists pertaining to the study of poetic style were causing us to react with objections to fundamental terms. The appearance at the moment of Tynjanov's *The Problem of Verse Language*[24] had the effect of underscoring the difference between psychological linguistics and the study of poetic language and style. This work, with its revelation of the close connection between the meaning of words and the verse structure, gave our concept of verse rhythm a new and fresher content and applied the Formal method to a line of study which inquired not only into the acoustical and syntactic properties of verse speech but into its semantic properties as well. In his preface Tynjanov declares:

> The study of *verse* has recently made great strides forward; the near future will undoubtedly see its development into an entire field, even though the drafting stage of the study may still be fresh in everybody's mind. But alongside that study there is the issue of poetic language and style. Studies in this area have been separated from the study of verse; the impression has been created that poetic language and style are unconnected with verse, have no relationship with it. The concept of "poetic language," advanced only recently, is now undergoing a crisis brought on by the extensiveness, the amorphousness, of the scope and content of the concept in its reliance on a psychological-linguistic base.

Among the general issues of poetics posed and illuminated afresh by this study, the question, how to understand "material," had a crucial significance. The accepted practice had been to oppose this concept to the concept of "form," with the result that both concepts suffered a loss of meaning in serving merely as a substitute for the old opposition of "form" versus "content." In point of fact, as already stated, the concept of form in the Formalists' usage, having accrued a sense of complete sufficiency, had merged with the idea of the work of art in its entirety. Thus it did not require any opposition other than with another category of forms of the nonartistic variety. Tynjanov points out that the material of verbal art is not uniform either in kind or in value, that "one factor may be put forward at the expense of the others, as a result of which these others are deformed and sometimes are reduced to the level of a neutral prop." The conclusion is that "the concept of material does not extend beyond form—it too is formal; its confusion with extraconstructional factors is a mistake." In this context form takes on complexity via the features of dynamism:

> The unity of a work is not a matter of a closed, symmetrical whole (*celost'*) but of an evolving, dynamic integratedness (*celostnost'*); between its elements there can be no static equal or plus signs, but there are always the dynamic signs of correlation and integration. The form of a literary work must be recognized as dynamic.

Rhythm is presented in Tynjanov's study as the basic structural factor of verse, permeating all its elements. The *unity and the compactness of the rhythmic series,* the one in direct relationship with the other, are established as the objective sign of verse rhythm. The fundamental difference between verse and prose is affirmed anew:

> An orientation in verse toward prose is an emplacement of the unity and compactness of its series in an unusual object and, therefore, does not entail effacing the essence of verse but rather puts verse in relief with new force. . . . Once incorporated into the domain of verse, any element of prose turns another, functionally projected facet of itself in the verse line and thus displays two factors at once: the structure-emphasizing factor—the factor of verse—and the factor of the deformation of an unusual object.

Further on the semantic issue is raised: "Isn't it true that in verse we have a deformed semantics, which, for that very reason, cannot be studied with speech when isolated from its structural government?" The answer to this question takes up the entire second part of Tynjanov's work, which establishes the tight relationship between the factors of rhythm and semantics. The decisive circumstance for the verbal items is their membership in rhythmic unities: "These members prove to have a stronger and closer connection than is true in ordinary speech; a *correlation by position* comes into play," one which is absent in prose.

Thus the Formalists' departure from Potebnja's theory and the conclusions associated with it received a new substantiation, and new prospects were opened for the theory of verse. Tynjanov's work showed us the possibility of encompassing new problems and also the advancing evolution. It became unmistakably clear, even to those outside *Opojaz,* that the essence of our work lay, not in erecting some rigid "Formal method," but in studying the specific properties of verbal art, and that the point was not the method but the object of study. Tynjanov again formulated this idea:

> The object of a study claiming to be the study of *art* must be to identify that specific set of things which distinguishes art from all other domains of intellectual activity, and which makes them its material or tools. Each work of art involves a complex interaction of many factors; consequently, the task to be carried out in investigation and research is the determination of the specific character of this interaction.

8

Above I noted that point in our development when, alongside theoretical problems, there arose, naturally enough, the issue of the movement and succession of forms, i.e., the issue of literary evolution. It arose in connection with our reexamination of Veselovskij's views on folktale motifs and devices, and the answer given then ("New form comes about not in order to express new content but in order to replace old form") derived from our new way of understanding form. Form conceived as content itself, incessantly changing shape in relation to previous models, naturally required our approaching it without abstract, hard-and-fast classificatory schemes, but instead our taking into account its concrete historical meaning and significance. A kind of duplex perspective took shape: one dimension was that of theoretical study (Šklovskij's *Plot Unfolding* or my *Verse Melodics*, for example) focused on some particular problem of theory and having the greatest possible variety of material; the other dimension was that of historical study, the study of literary evolution as such. The conjunction of these two dimensions of study, an organic consequence of the development of the Formal method, confronted us with a series of new and very complex problems, many of which have remained until now unelucidated and even partially undefined.

The fact of the matter is that the Formalists' original endeavor to pin down some particular constructional device and trace its unity through voluminous material had given way to an endeavor to qualify further the generalized idea, to grasp the concrete *function* of the device in each given instance. This concept of functional value gradually moved out to the forefront and overshadowed our original concept of the device. Such a process of making further qualifications of one's own general concepts and principles is characteristic of the entire evolution of the Formal method. We maintain no general, dogmatic positions that would bind our hands and keep us from getting at the facts. We do not vouch for the schemata we construct if other people try to apply them to facts unknown to us—the facts may require changes or elaborations or corrections in our schemata. Work on concrete material is what started us talking about function and by that very fact led us to a new level of complexity in the concept of the device. Theory itself required our branching out into history.

Here again we came into conflict with the traditions of academic scholarship and certain tendencies in literary criticism. During our student days, the academic history of literature had confined itself by and large to the biographical and psychological study of individual writers—only, needless to say, "the greats." There was not even any trace of the earlier attempts at compiling histories of Russian literature in its entirety, attempts that revealed an intention to systematize a huge quantity of historical material. Nevertheless, the tradition of such compilations (like A. N. Pypin's *History of Russian Literature*) did retain scientific authority, all the more so because the succeeding generation was reluctant to undertake such vast pursuits. Meanwhile, these compilations had relied heavily on such vague generalities as the concepts of "realism" and "romanticism" (with the added qualification that realism is better than romanticism); evolution was taken to mean a steady advancement toward perfection, like human progress (hence, from romanticism to realism); succession was understood as a decorous transfer of a legacy from father to son; literature, as such, played no role whatever—it had been supplanted by material taken from the history of social movements, from biography, and so on.

This primitive historicism, with its effect of leading away from literature, naturally provoked a reaction against any kind of historicism on the part of the Symbolist theorists and the literary critics. A whole literature of impressionistic sketches and "silhouettes" developed, and the rage set in for "modernizing" writers of the past and turning them into "eternal companions." The history of literature was implicitly (and sometimes even explicitly) declared useless.

We had to demolish those academic traditions and liquidate those tendencies in journalistic criticism. We had to pit against those forces a new concept of literary evolution and of literature itself—a concept divorced from ideas of progress and decorous succession, from the concepts of realism and romanticism, from any material extrinsic to literature as a specific order of things. As for the critics, we had to proceed by pointing out concrete historical facts, the mobility and mutability of form, the need to take into account the concrete functions of particular devices, in short, by pointing out the difference between a literary work as a definite historical fact and the free interpretation of it from the standpoint of present-day literary needs, tastes, or interests. Thus the governing spirit of our literary historical work had to be the spirit of destruction and negation—as it had been during our theoretical debut—that afterward had assumed a more moderate character once the individual problems involved had been resolved.

That explains why our first pronouncements on literary history took the form of something close to spontaneous theses exhibited in connection with some piece of concrete material. A particular issue would unexpectedly develop into a general problem—theory merged with history. Tynjanov's *Dostoevskij and Gogol'*[25] and Šklovskij's *Rozanov*[26] were two highly characteristic examples.

Tynjanov's main task was to prove that Dostoevskij's *Village of Stepančikovo* may be regarded a parody and that behind the overt features of the story there is the background of Gogol' and his *Correspondence with Friends.* In Tynjanov's hands, however, this particular issue swelled to the proportions of a whole theory of parody—parody as a device of style (parody-stylization) and as one manifestation of the dialectical change of schools having particular literary historical significance. In this connection, the question of how to understand "succession" and "tradition" emerged, and consequently the basic problems of literary evolution were raised:

> When people talk about "literary tradition" or "succession". . . . they usually imagine a kind of straight line joining a younger representative of a given literary branch with an older one. As it happens, things are much more complex than that. It is not a matter of continuing on a straight line, but rather one of setting out and pushing off from a given point—a struggle. . . . Each instance of literary succession is first and foremost a struggle involving a destruction of the old unity and a new construction out of the old elements.

Our idea of literary evolution took on new complexity once the factors of struggle and periodic revolts were pointed out, and it relinquished its older meaning of a decorous progression. Dostoevskij's literary relationship with Gogol' assumed in this context the character of a complex struggle.

Running through Šklovskij's pamphlet on Rozanov was what

was almost a digression from the main topic—a whole theory of literary evolution reflecting the lively discussion of that problem then taking place in the *Opojaz* circle. Šklovskij pointed out that literature moves ahead in a broken line:

> Not one but several literary schools exist during each literary epoch. They exist in literature simultaneously, but one of them forms the canonized crest. The others exist without being canonized and without resonance, as, for instance, in Puškin's time, the Deržavin tradition existed in the poetry of Kjuxelbeker and Griboedov simultaneously with the tradition of Russian vaudeville verse and a host of other traditions, for example, the tradition of the pure adventure novel as represented by Bulgarin.

Once the older art has been canonized, new forms are created in a lower stratum, the "junior line," which

> forces its way into the position occupied by the older one, and so we get the vaudevillist Belopjatkin becoming Nekrasov (Osip Brik's study), Tolstoj, the direct heir of the eighteenth century, creating a new novel (Boris Èjxenbaum), Blok canonizing the themes and tempos of the "gypsy song" and Čexov's bringing *Budil'nik* [The Alarm Clock—the name of a Russian comic newspaper] into Russian literature. Dostoevskij raises the devices of the dime novel to the level of the literary norm. Each new school of literature is a revolution—something like the emergence of a new class. But that, of course, is only an analogy. The defeated line is not annihilated, it does not cease to exist. It only topples from the crest, drops below for a time of lying fallow, and may again rise as an ever present pretender to the throne. Moreover, in practice, things are complicated by the fact that the new hegemony is usually not a pure instance of a restoration of earlier form, but one involving the presence of features from other junior schools, even features (but now in a subordinate role) inherited from its predecessor on the throne.

A discussion of the dynamism of genres is also presented, and Rozanov's books are interpreted as the inception of a new genre, as a new type of novel, with no motivation binding its parts together: "On the level of thematics, they are characterized by the canonization of new themes; on the compositional level, by laying the device bare."

In connection with the general theory, the idea of the "dialectical self-generation of new forms" is introduced, an idea with implications both for an analogy with the development of other orders of culture and also for the substantiation of the autonomy of literary evolution. In oversimplified form, this theory was quickly embraced on all sides, and, as always happens, it took the shape of a simple and static schema of the kind criticism finds very handy. In actual fact, all we had here was a general outline of evolution outfitted with a whole set of complex qualifications.

The Formalists proceeded from this general outline to a more closely argued elaboration of literary historical problems and facts, giving their original theoretical premises a new concreteness and complexity.

9

Naturally, with our understanding of literary evolution as the dialectical change of forms, we do not resort to the material that occupied a central position in literary historical criticism of the old type. We study literary evolution to the extent that it bears a specific character, and within such limits as allow us to call it autonomous, not directly dependent on other orders of culture. In other words, we limit the factors so as not to wallow in an endless quantity of vague "connections" and "correspondences," which, in any case, cannot elucidate the evolution of literature as such. We do not incorporate into our work issues involving biography or the psychology of creativity—assuming that those problems, very serious and complex in their own right, ought to have their place in other disciplines. We are concerned with finding in evolution the features of immanent historical laws. Therefore, we leave aside whatever, from that point of view, may be said to be "fortuitous," not relevant to history. What interests us is the very process of evolution, the very *dynamics* of literary forms in so far as it may be observed in the facts of the past. The central problem of literary history for us is the problem of evolution outside individual personality—the study of literature as a *social phenomenon sui generis.* In this connection, the issue that takes on enormous importance for us is the formation and the successive change of genres, including "second- rate" and "popular" literature, insofar as that literature plays a role in the process. All that is required here is to make a distinction between that type of popular literature which prepared the ground for the formation of new genres and that type which comes about in the process of their dissolution and which may be regarded as material for the study of historical inertia.

On the other hand, it is not the past *per se*, the past as discrete historical fact, that interests us—we are not in the business of simply restoring epochs that for some reason or other appeal to us. History gives us what the contemporary situation cannot—a full measure of material. But that is precisely why we approach history with a certain supply of theoretical problems and principles suggested in part by the facts of contemporary literature. Hence, the Formalists' distinguishing characteristic of maintaining close contact with the contemporary literary scene and of making criticism approach scholarship (in contrast to the Symbolists, who made scholarship approach criticism, and to the earlier historians of literature, who for the most part kept their distance from the contemporary scene). Thus the history of literature for us is not so much a special *subject*, as against theory, but a special *method*, a special dimension of study. That is what explains the nature of our literary historical works of always having a bearing not only on historical but also on theoretical conclusions—on the posing of new theoretical problems and the verification of old ones.[27]

What remains for me now is a general summing up. The evolution of the Formal method, which I have attempted to delineate, presents a picture of the consecutive development of theoretical principles above and beyond, so to speak, the individual role of any single one of us. Indeed, *Opojaz* realized in practice a genuine type of collective endeavor. This came about, in all likelihood, for the very reason that we understood our concern from the outset to be *historical*, and not our personal concern. Herein is our major link with our age. Science itself is evolving, and we are evolving together with it. Now I shall briefly indicate the basic factors in the evolution of the Formal method over the past ten years.

1. From an initial summary opposition between poetic language and practical language, we arrived at a differentiation within the concept of practical language in terms of its functions (Jakubinskij) and at a discrimination between the methods of poetic language and the methods of emotive language (Jakobson). Associated with this evolution is our special interest in studying oratory—precisely that kind of speech, from the practical sphere, that is closest to poetic speech but differs with respect to function—and we have begun discussing the necessity of revitalizing rhetoric along with poetics. (See the articles on Lenin's language in *Lef*, No. 1(5), 1924, by Šklovskij, Ѐjxenbaum, Tynjanov, Jakubinskij, Kazanskij, and Tomaševskij.)

2. From the general concept of form in its new meaning, we arrived at the concept of device, and hence at the concept of function.

3. From the concept of verse rhythm in its opposition with meter, we arrived at the concept of rhythm as the structural factor of verse in its total integrity and therefore to the concept of

verse as a special form of speech possessing its own special linguistic (syntactic, lexical, and semantic) qualities.

4. From the concept of plot as construction, we arrived at the concept of material as motivation, and hence at that of material as an element participating in the construction in dependence on the character of the form-organizing *dominant.*

5. From the predication of the unity of a device over diverse material, we arrived at a differentiation within device in terms of function, and hence at the issue of the evolution of forms, that is, at the problem of literary historical study.

We are facing a whole series of new problems. The clear evidence of this fact is seen in Tynjanov's recent article "Literary Fact."[28] It poses the question of the nature of the relationship between life and literature—a problem "solved" by a great many people with all the facility of dilettantism. Examples are used in the article to show how cultural life becomes literature, and, conversely, how literature retreats into cultural life: "During the period of the dissolution of a genre, it shifts from center to periphery, and, from literary backyards and domestic life, a new phenomenon emerges to take its place."

There was good reason for my having entitled this essay "The Theory of the Formal Method" and for having produced what is evidently a sketch of its evolution. We possess no theory of such a kind as could be deployed as a rigid, ready-made system. Theory and history have merged for us, not only in what we preach, but also in what we practice. We are too well trained by history itself to imagine that we could do without history. The moment we ourselves are obliged to acknowledge that ours is a theory which is all-encompassing, able to cope with all contingencies of past and future, and therefore neither in need of nor amenable to evolution, we shall at the same time be obliged to acknowledge that the Formal method has ceased to exist and that the spirit of scientific inquiry has abandoned it. So far that has not happened.

Notes

1. By "Formalists" I mean that group of theorists who banded together in the *Obščestvo izučenija poètičeskogo jazyka* (*Opojaz*) [Society for the Study of Poetic Language], and who began issuing their own publication in 1916.

2. R. Unger notes the powerful influence Wölfflin's work had on representatives of the "aesthetic" trend in contemporary German historical study,

men such as O. Walzel and F. Strich. See Wölfflin's article "Moderne Strömungen in der deutschen Literaturwissenschaft," in *Die Literatur*, 2 November 1923. See also Walzel's *Gehalt und Gestalt im Kunstwerk des Dichters* (Berlin, 1923).

3. *Novejšaja russkaja poèzija. Nabrosok pervyj* [Recent Russian Poetry, Sketch 1] (Prague, 1921), p. 11.

4. "O zvukax stixotvornogo jazyka" in *Sborniki po teorii poètičeskogo jazyka, Vypusk pervyj* (Petrograd, 1916).

5. "O poèzii i zaumnom jazyke."

6. See Andrej Belyj's articles in the collection of essays, *Skify* (1917), and in *Vetv'* (1917), and my article, "O zvukax v stixe" [On Sound in Verse] (1920), reprinted in the collection of my essays, *Skvoz' literaturu* (1924).

7. Zvukovye povtory," in *Sborniki po teorii poètičeskogo jazyka, Vypusk II* (Petrograd, 1917).

8. *Voskrešenie slova.*

9. "Iskusstvo kak priem," in *Sborniki po teorii poètičeskogo jazyka, Vypusk II*, 1917.

10. "Potebnja," in *Poètika: Sborniki po teorii poètičeskogo jazyka* (Petrograd, 1919).

11. "Svjaz' priemov sjužetosloženija s obščimi priemami stilja," in *Poètika, 1919.*

12. Somewhat later than the period now being discussed, Veselovskij's view of "syncretism" as a phenomenon belonging only to archaic poetry, engendered by the communal culture of the time, came under criticism in a work by B. Kazanskij, "Ideja istoričeskoj poètiki" [The Idea of Historical Poetics], in *Poètika I*, Leningrad, "Academia," 1926. Kazanskij affirmed the existence of syncretic tendencies, strikingly pronounced during certain periods in each of the arts and refuted the "ethnographic" point of view.

13. *Razvertyvanie sjužeta* and *Tristram Šendi Sterna i teorija romana* (published separately by Opojaz in 1921).

14. "Kak sdelana 'Šinel' Gogolja," in *Poètika*, 1919.

15. "O ritmiko-sintaktičeskix figurax" (a report delivered to Opojaz in 1920 and not only never published but even, I believe, never fully completed).

16. *Kompozicija liričeskix stixotvorenij.* Opojaz 1921.

17. *Melodika stixa.* Opojaz 1922.

18. *Russkoe stixosloženie* 1924.

19. "Pjatistopnyj jamb Puškina." First printed in 1919 and reprinted in the collection of essays *Očerki po poètike Puškina* (Berlin, 1923).

20. "Problema stixotvornogo ritma," in *Literaturnaja mysl, Vypusk II*, 1922.

21. *Vvedenie v metriku.* 1925.

22. *O češskom stixe (Sborniki po teorii poètičeskogo jazyka, Vypusk V*, 1923). [See also Brown University Slavic Reprint VI, 1969.]

23. By this time Jakubinskij himself had pointed out the excessive inclusiveness of the concept "practical language" and the necessity of breaking it down in terms of functions (colloquial, scientific, oratorical, etc.). See his article, "O dialogičeskoj reči" [On Dialogic Speech] in the collection of essays *Russkaja reč* 1923.

24. *Problema stixotvornogo jazyka.* Academia 1924.

25. *Dostoevskij i Gogol'*. Opojaz 1921.

26. *Rozanov*. Opojaz 1921.

27. Between 1921 and 1924 a whole series of works of the type I have been talking about appeared. I shall list the main ones.

Jurij Tynjanov: "Stixovye formy Nekrasova" [Nekrasov's Verse Forms]; "Dostoevskij i Gogol'" [Dostoevskij and Gogol']; "Vopros o Tjutčeve" [The Tjutčev Question]; "Tjutčev i Gejne" [Tjutčev and Heine]; "Arxaisty i Puškin" [The Archaists and Puškin]; "Puškin i Tjutčev" [Puškin and Tjutčev]; "Oda kak deklamacionnyj žanr" [The Ode as a Declamatory Genre].

Boris Tomaševskij: *Gavrilliada* (a critical edition of Puškin's *Gavrilliada*, chapters on composition and genre); Puškin—čitatel francuzskix poètov" [Puškin, Reader of the French Poets]; "Puškin" (on contemporary problems of the historical study of literature); "Puškin i Bualo" [Puškin and Boileau]; "Puškin i Lafonten" [Puškin and La Fontaine].

Boris Èjxenbaum: *Molodoj Tolstoj* [The Young Tolstoj]; *Lermontov;* "Problemy poètiki Puškina" [Problems of Puškin's Poetics]; "Put' Puškina k proze" [Puškin's Approach to Prose]; "Nekrasov."

One should add to this list historical works on literature not directly connected with Opojaz but following the same line of study. For example: V. Vinogradov: "Sjužet i kompozicija povesti Gogolja 'Nos' " [The Plot and Composition of Gogol''s Story 'Nose']; "Sjužet i arxitektonika romana Dostoevskogo *Bednye ljudi*" [The Plot and Architectonics of Dostoevskij's Novel, *Poor Folk*].

The following items have to do with the poetics of the Natural School: "Gogol' i Žjul' Žanen" [Gogol' and Jules Janin]; "Gogol' i real'naja škola" [Gogol' and the Realist School]; "Ètjudy o stile Gogolja" [Studies on Gogol''s Style].

V. Žirmunskij: *Bajron i Puškin* [Byron and Puškin].

S. Baluxatyj: *Dramaturgija Čexova* [Čexov's Dramaturgy].

A. Cejtlin: "Povesti o bednom činovnike Dostoevskogo" [Dostoevskij's Tales of a Poor Clerk].

K. Šimkevič: "Nekrasov i Puškin" [Nekrasov and Puškin].

Furthermore, certain members of seminars given under our direction at the university and at the Institute for the History of Arts have produced a series of works, published as the collection *Russkaja proza* [Russian Prose], Academia 1926, on Dal', Marlinskij, Senkovskij, Vjazemskij, Vel'tman, Karamzin, on the genre of the journey, and other topics.

This is not the place to discuss these studies in any detail. I need say only that they all typically draw on "second-rate" writers (the *entourage*), meticulously elucidate traditions, follow changes in genres and styles, and so on. As part and parcel of this work, many forgotten names and facts have been made viable again, popular estimates of reputations have been proved wrong, traditional ideas have been altered, and, most importantly, the very process of evolution has gradually been made clearer. The work of studying this material has only just begun. A set of new problems lies before us: the further qualification of our theoretical and historical concepts of literature, the incorporation of new material, the postulation of new issues, and so on.

28. "Literaturnyj fakt." *Lef*, No. 2 (6), 1925.

Until recently, the history of art, particularly that of literature, has had more in common with causerie than with scholarship. It obeyed all the laws of causerie, skipping blithely from topic to topic, from lyrical effusions on the elegance of forms to anecdotes from the artist's life, from psychological truisms to questions concerning philosophical significance and social environment. It is such a gratifying and easy task to chat about life and times using literary works as a basis, just as it is more gratifying and easier to copy from a plaster cast than to draw a living body. In causerie we are slipshod with our terminology; in fact, variations in terms and equivocations so apt to punning often lend considerable charm to the conversation. The history of art has been equally slipshod with respect to scholarly terminology. It has employed the current vocabulary without screening the words critically, without defining them precisely, and without considering the multiplicity of their meanings. For example, historians of literature unconscionably confused the idealism denoting a specific philosophical doctrine with a looser idealism denoting behavior, motivated by other than narrow considerations of material gain. Still more hopeless was the web of confusion surrounding the term "form," brilliantly exposed by Anton Marty in his works on general grammar. It was the term "realism," however, which fared especially badly. The uncritical use of this word, so very elusive in meaning, has had fateful consequences.

What is realism as understood by the theoretician of art? It is an artistic trend which aims at conveying reality as closely as possible and strives for maximum verisimilitude. We call realistic those works which we feel accurately depict life by displaying verisimilitude. Right off we are faced with an ambiguity, namely:

1. *Realism may refer to the aspiration and intent of the author; i.e., a work is understood to be realistic if it is conceived by its author as a display of verisimilitude, as true to life* (meaning *A*).
2. *A work may be called realistic if I, the person judging it, perceive it as true to life* (meaning *B*).

In the first case, we are forced to evaluate on an intrinsic basis; in the second case, the reader's individual impression is the decisive criterion. The history of art has hopelessly confused these two interpretations of the term "realism." An objective and irrefutable validity is ascribed to individual, private local points of

*"O xudožestvennom realizme," *Readings in Russian Poetics.* Michigan Slavic Materials, 2 (Ann Arbor, 1962), pp. 30-36. Translated from the Russian by Karol Magassy. First published in Czech in 1921.

view. The question as to whether a given work is realistic or not is covertly reduced to the question of what attitude I take toward it. Thus meaning *B* imperceptibly replaces meaning *A*.

Classicists, sentimentalists, the romanticists to a certain extent, even the "realists" of the nineteenth century, the modernists to a large degree, and, finally, the futurists, expressionists, and their like have more than once steadfastly proclaimed faithfulness to reality, maximum verisimilitude—in other words, realism—as the guiding motto of their artistic program. In the nineteenth century, this motto gave rise to an artistic movement. It was primarily the late copiers of that trend who outlined the currently recognized history of art, in particular, the history of literature. Hence, one specific case, one separate artistic movement was identified as the ultimate manifestation of realism in art and was made the standard by which to measure the degree of realism in preceding and succeeding artistic movements. Thus, a new covert identification has occurred, a third meaning of the word "realism" has crept in (meaning *C*) *one which comprehends the sum total of the features characteristic of one specific artistic current of the nineteenth century.*

In other words, to the literary historians the realistic works of the last century represent the highest degree of verisimilitude, the maximum faithfulness to life.

Let us now analyze the concept of verisimilitude in art. While in painting and in the other visual arts the illusion of an objective and absolute faithfulness to reality is conceivable, "natural" (in Plato's terminology), verisimilitude in a verbal expression or in a literary description obviously makes no sense whatever. Can the question be raised about a higher degree of verisimilitude of this or that poetic trope? Can one say that one metaphor or metonymy is conventional or, so to say, figurative. The methods of projecting three-dimensional space onto a flat surface are established by convention; the use of color, the abstracting, the simplification, of the object depicted, and the choice of reproducible features are all based on convention. It is necessary to learn the conventional language of painting in order to "see" a picture, just as it is impossible to understand what is spoken without knowing the language. This conventional, traditional aspect of painting to a great extent conditions the very act of our visual perception. As tradition accumulates, the painted image becomes an ideogram, a formula, to which the object portrayed is linked by contiguity. Recognition becomes instantaneous. We no longer see a picture.

The ideogram needs to be deformed. The artist-innovator must impose a new form upon our perception, if we are to detect in a given thing those traits which went unnoticed the day before. He may present the object in an unusual perspective; he may violate the rules of composition canonized by his predecessors. Thus Kramskoj, one of the founders of the so-called realist school of Russian painting, recounts in his memoirs his efforts to deform to the utmost the principles of composition as advocated by the Academy. The motivation behind this "disorder" was the desire for a closer approximation of reality. The urge to deform an ideogram usually underlies the *Sturm und Drang* stage of new artistic currents.

Everyday language uses a number of euphemisms, including polite formulas, circumlocutions, allusions, and stock phrases. However, when we want our speech to be candid, natural, and expressive, we discard the usual polite etiquette and call things by their real names. They have a fresh ring, and we feel that they are "the right words." But as soon as the name has merged with the object it designates, we must, conversely, resort to metaphor, allusion, or allegory if we wish a more expressive term. It will sound more impressive, it will be *more striking.* To put it in another way, when searching for a word which will revitalize an object, we pick a farfetched word, unusual at least in its given application, a word which is forced into service. Such an unexpected word may, depending on current usage, be either a figurative or a direct reference to the object. Examples of this sort are numerous, particularly in the history of obscene vocabulary. To call the sex act by its own name sounds brazen, but if in certain circles strong language is the rule, a trope or euphemism is more forceful and effective. Such is the verb *utilizirovat'* [to utilize] of the Russian hussar. Foreign words are accordingly more insulting and are readily picked up for such purposes. A Russian may use the absurd epithets *gollandskij* [Dutch] or *moržovyj* [walruslike] as abusive modifiers of an object which has nothing to do with either Holland or walruses; the impact of his swearing is greatly heightened as a result. Instead of the infamous oath involving copulation with the addressee's mother, the Russian peasant prefers the fantastic image of copulating with the addressee's soul—and, for further emphasis, uses the negative parallelism: *tvoju dušu ne mat'* [your soul not your mother].

The same applies to revolutionary realism in literature. The words of yesterday's narrative grow stale; now the item is described by features that were yesterday held to be the least descriptive, the least worth representing, features which were scarcely noticed. "He is fond of dwelling on unessential details" is the classic judgment passed on the innovators by conservative critics of every era. I leave it to the lover of quotations to collect similar judgments pronounced on Puškin, Gogol′, Tolstoj, Andrej Belyj, and others by their contemporaries. To the followers of a new movement, a description based on unessential details seems more real than the petrified tradition of their predecessors. But the perception of those of a more conservative persuasion continues to be determined by the old canons; they will accordingly interpret any deformation of these canons by a new movement as a rejection of the principle of verisimilitude, as a deviation from realism. They will therefore uphold the old canons as the only realistic ones. Thus, in discussing meaning A of the term "realism" (i.e., the artistic intent to render life as it is), we see that the definition leaves room for ambiguity:

A_1: *The tendency to deform given artistic norms conceived as an approximation of reality;*

A_2: *The conservative tendency to remain within the limits of a given artistic tradition, conceived as faithfulness to reality.*

Meaning B presupposes that my subjective evaluation will pronounce a given artistic fact faithful to reality; thus, factoring in the results obtained, we find:

B_1: *I rebel against a given artistic code and view its deformation as a more accurate rendition of reality;*

B_2: *I am conservative and view the deformation of the artistic code, to which I subscribe, as a distortion of reality.*

In the latter case, only those artistic facts which do not contradict my artistic values may be called realistic. But inasmuch as I hold my own values (the tradition to which I belong) to be the most realistic, and because I feel that within the framework of other traditions my code cannot be fully realized even if the tradition in question does not contradict it, I find in these traditions only a partial, embryonic, immature, or decadent realism. I declare that the only genuine realism is the one on which I was brought up. Conversely, in the case of B_1, my attitude to all artistic formulas contradicting a particular set of artistic values unacceptable to me would be similar to my attitude in the case of B_2 toward forms which are *not* in opposition. I can readily ascribe a realistic tendency (realistic as understood by A_1) to forms which were never conceived as such. In the same way, the Primitives were often interpreted from the point of view of B_1. While their incompatibility with the norms on which we were raised was immediately evident, their faithful adherence to their own norms and tradition was lost from view (i.e., A_2 was interpreted as A_1). Similarly, certain writings may be felt and interpreted as poetry, although not at all meant as such. Consider Gogol′'s pronouncement about the poetic qualities of an inventory of the Muscovite crown jewels, Novalis's observation about the poetic nature of the alphabet, the statement of the Futurist Kručenyx about the poetic sound of a laundry list, or that of the poet Xlebnikov claiming that at times a misprint can be an artistically valid distortion of a word.

The concrete content of A_1, A_2, B_1, and B_2 is extremely relative. Thus a contemporary critic might detect realism in Delacroix, but not in Delaroche; in El Greco and Andrej Rublev, but not in Guido Reni; in a Scythian idol, but not in the Laocoön. A directly opposite judgment, however, would have been characteristic of a pupil of the Academy in the previous century. Whoever senses faithfulness to life in Racine does not find it in Shakespeare, and vice versa.

In the second half of the nineteenth century, a group of painters struggled in Russia on behalf of realism (the first phase of *C*, i.e., a special case of A_1). One of them, Repin, painted a picture, "Ivan the Terrible Kills His Son." Repin's supporters greeted it as realistic (*C*, a special case of B_1). Repin's teacher at the Academy, however, was appalled by the lack of realism in the painting, and he carefully itemized all the instances of Repin's distortion of verisimilitude by comparison with the academic canon which was for him the only guarantee of verisimilitude (i.e., from the standpoint of B_2). But the Academy tradition soon faded, and the canons of the "realist" Itinerants (*peredvižniki*) were adopted and became social fact. Then new tendencies arose in painting, a new *Sturm und Drang* began; translated into the language of manifestos, a new truth was being sought.

To the artist of today, therefore, Repin's painting seems unnatural and untrue to life (i.e., from the standpoint of B_2). In turn, Repin failed to see anything in Degas and Cézanne except grimace and distortion (i.e., from the standpoint of B_2). These examples bring the extreme relativity of the concept of "realism" into sharp relief. Meanwhile, those art historians who, as we have already indicated, were primarily associated with the later imitators of "realism" by virtue of their aesthetic code (the second phase of *C*), arbitrarily equated *C* and B_2, even though *C* is in fact simply a special case of *B*. As we know, meaning *B* covertly replaces *A*, so that the whole difference between A_1 and A_2 is lost, and the destruction of ideographs is understood only as a means of creating new ones. The conservative, of course, fails to recognize the self-sufficient aesthetic value of deformation. Thus, supposedly having *A* in mind (actually A_2), the historian of art addresses himself to *C*. Therefore, when a literary historian brilliantly delcares that "Russian literature is typically realistic," his statement is tantamount to saying, "Man is typically twenty years old."

As the tradition equating realism with *C* became established, new realist artists (in the A_1 sense) were compelled to call themselves neorealists, realists in the higher sense of the word, or naturalists, and they drew a line between quasi- or pseudo-realism (*C*) and what they conceived to be genuine realism (i.e., their own). "I am a realist, but only in the higher sense of the word," Dostoevskij declared. And an almost identical declaration has been made in turn by the Symbolists, by Italian and Russian Futurists, by German Expressionists, and so on and on. These neorealists have at various times completely identified their aesthetic platforms with realism in general, and, therefore, in evaluating the representatives of *C*, they had to expel them from the ranks of realism. Thus posthumous criticism has periodically questioned the realism of Gogol′, Dostoevskij, Tolstoj, Turgenev, and Ostrovskij.

The manner in which *C* itself is characterized by historians of art, especially historians of literature, is very vague and approximate. We must not forget that the imitators were those who decided which characteristics typified realism. A closer analysis will no doubt replace *C* with a number of more precise values and will reveal that certain devices which we indiscriminately associate with *C* are by no means typical of all the representatives of the so-called realist school; the same devices are in fact also found outside the realist school.

We have already mentioned the characterization of progressive realism in terms of unessential details. One such device—cultivated, incidentally, by a number of the representatives of the *C* school (in Russia, the so-called Gogolian school) and for that reason sometimes incorrectly identified with *C*—is *the condensation of the narrative by means of images based on contiguity*, i.e., *the use of the normal designative term.* This "condensation" is realized either in spite of the plot or by eliminating the plot entirely. Let us take a crude example from Russian literature, that of the suicides of Poor Liza and of Anna Karenina. Describing Anna's suicide, Tolstoj primarily writes about her handbag. Such an unessential detail would have made no sense to Karamzin, although Karamzin's own tale (in comparison with the eighteenth-century adventure novel) would likewise seem but a series of unessential details. If the hero of an eighteenth-century adventure novel encounters a passer-by, it may be taken for granted that the latter is of importance either to the hero or, at least, to the plot. But it is obligatory in Gogol′ or Tolstoj or Dostoevskij that the hero first meet an unimportant and (from the point of view of the story) superfluous passer-by, and that their resulting conversation should have no bearing on the story. Since such a device is frequently thought to be realistic, we will denote it by *D*, stressing that this *D* is often found within *C*.

A pupil is asked to solve a problem: "A bird flew out of its cage; how soon will it reach the forest, if it flies at such and such a speed per minute, and the distance between the cage and the forest is such and such?" "What color is the cage?" asks the child. This child is a typical realist in the *D* sense of the word.

Or, an anecdote of the type known as the Armenian riddle: "It hangs in the drawing room and is green; what is it?" The answer: "A herring."–"Why in a drawing room?"–"Well, why couldn't they hang it there?" "Why green?"–"It was painted green."–"But why?"–"To make it harder to guess." This desire to conceal the answer, this deliberate effort to delay recognition, brings out a new feature, the newly improvised epithet. Exaggeration in art is unavoidable, wrote Dostoevskij; in order to show an object, it is necessary to deform the shape it used to have; it must be tinted, just as slides to be viewed under the microscope are tinted. You color your object in an original way and think that it has become more palpable, *clearer*, more real (A_1). In a Cubist's picture, a single object is multiplied and shown from several points of view; thus it is made more tangible. This is a device used in painting. But it is also possible to motivate and justify this device in the painting itself; an object is doubled when reflected in a mirror. The same is true of literature. The herring is green because it has been painted; a startling epithet results, and the trope becomes an epic motif. Why did you paint it? The author will always have an answer, but, in fact, there is only one right answer: "To make it harder to guess."

Thus a strange term may be foisted on an object or asserted as a particular aspect of it. Negative parallelism explicitly rejects metaphorical substitution for its proper term: "I am not a tree, I am a woman," says the girl in a poem by the Czech poet Šrámek. This literary construction can be justified; from a special narrative feature, it can become a detail of plot development: "Some said, 'These are the footprints of an ermine'; others reported, 'No, these are not the footprints of an ermine; it was Čurila Plenkovič passing by.' " Inverted negative parallelism rejects a normally used term and employs a metaphor (in the Šrámek poem quoted earlier: "I am not a woman, I am a tree," or the following from a play by another Czech poet, Čapek: "What is this?–A handkerchief.–But it is not a handkerchief. It is a beautiful woman standing by the window. She's dressed all in white and is dreaming of love."

In Russian erotic tales, copulation is frequently stated in terms of inverted parallelism; the same is true of wedding songs, with the difference that in the latter, the constructions using metaphors are not usually justified, while in the former these metaphors find motivation as the means by which the cunning hero can seduce the fair maid, or as an interpretation of human copulation by an animal incapable of comprehending it. From time to time, the consistent motivation and justification of poetic constructions have also been called realism. Thus the Czech novelist Čapek-Chod in his tale, "The Westernmost Slav," slyly calls the first chapter, in which "romantic" fantasy is motivated by typhoid delirium, a "realistic chapter."

Let us use *E* to designate such realism, i.e., *the requirement of consistent motivation and realization of poetic devices.* This *E* is often confused with *C*, *B*, etc. By failing to distinguish among the variety of concepts latent in the term "realism," theoreticians and historians of art–in particular, of literature–are acting as if the term were a bottomless sack into which everything and anything could be conveniently hidden away.

This objection may be made: no, not everything. No one will call Hoffmann's fantastic tales realistic. But does this not indicate that there is somehow a single meaning in the word "realism," that there is, after all, some common denominator?

My answer is: No one will call a "key" a "lock," but this does not mean that the word "lock" has only one meaning. We cannot equate with impunity the various meanings of the word "realism" just as we cannot, unless we wish to be called mad, equate a hair lock with a padlock. It is true that the various meanings of some words (for example, "bill") are far more distinct from one another than they are in the case of the word "realism," where we can imagine a set of facts about which we could simultaneously say, this is realism in the meaning *C*, *B*, or A_1, etc., of the word. Nevertheless, it is inexcusable to confuse *C*, *B*, A_1, etc. A term once used in American slang to denote a socially inept person was "turkey." There are probably "turkeys" in Turkey, and there are doubtless men named Harry who are blessed with great amounts of hair. But we may not jump to conclusions concerning the social aptitudes of the Turks nor the hairiness of men named Harry. This "commandment" is self-evident to the point of imbecility, yet those who speak of artistic realism continually sin against it.

Diaries as well as curiosity about unpublished documents and biographical "findings" mark an unhealthy sharpening of interest in documentary literary history, that is, history that is concerned with mores, personalities, and with the interrelationship between writers and their milieu. Most of the "documents" are relevant, not to literature or its history, but rather to the study of the author as a man (if not to the study of his brothers and aunts).

In contrast to these biographical studies, there is a concurrent development of critical literature concentrating on the specific poetic elements in verbal art (the contributions of the *Opojaz* and other branches of "Formalism"). Thus at first glance there would appear to be a profound split among literary scholars. These two currents seem to have diverged in a definitive way, and no reconciliation seems possible. To a certain extent this is true: many biographers cannot be made to comprehend an artistic work as anything but a fact of the author's biography; on the other hand, there are those for whom any kind of biographical analysis is unscientific contraband, a "back-door" approach.

Consider Puškin's poem, *Ja pomnju čudnoe mgnoven'e* [I Recall a Wondrous Instant]. Is this an artistic reference to the personal relation of Puškin to A. Kern? Or is it a free lyrical composition which uses the image of Kern as an indifferent "emblem," as structural material having no relationship to biography? Is it possible to take a neutral position on this question? Or would this be sitting down between two chairs? The question itself is very clear: do we need the poet's biography in order to understand his work, or do we not?

Before we can answer this question, however, we must remember that creative literature exists, not for literary historians, but for readers, and we must consider how the poet's biography operates in the reader's consciousness. Here we shall not regard "biography" as a self-sufficient class of historical writing (from this point of view Puškin's biography is no different from the biographies of generals and engineers); instead, we shall consider the "literary functions" of biography as the traditional concomitant of artistic work.

There have been eras during which the personality of the artist was of no interest at all to the audience. Paintings were signed with the donor's name, not the artist's; literary works bore the name of the customer or the printer. There was a great tendency

*"Literatura i biografija," *Kniga i revoljucija*, 4 (1923), pp. 6-9. Translated by Herbert Eagle.

toward anonymity, thus leaving a wide field of investigation for present-day archaeologists and textologists. The name of the master had as much significance as the trademark of a company has today. Thus Rembrandt had no qualms about signing the paintings of his pupil, Maas.

However, during the individualization of creativity—an epoch which cultivated subjectivism in the artistic process—the name and personality of the author came to the forefront. The reader's interest reached beyond the work to its creator. This new relationship toward creativity began with the great writers of the eighteenth century. Before that time the personality of the author was hidden. Bits of gossip and anecdotes about authors did penetrate society, but these anecdotes were not combined into biographical images and considered equally along with authors and personages not connected with literature. In fact, the less gifted the writer, the more numerous the anecdotes about him. Thus anecdotes have come down to us concerning, for example, the Abbé Cotin, a minor eighteenth-century poet—but no one knows his works. At the same time, our information about Molière or about Shakespeare is quite meager, though it is true that nineteenth-century biographers later "created" the biographies of these writers and even projected their plays onto these imagined biographies. However, such biographies did not prevent others from just as successfully attributing the tragedies of Shakespeare to Bacon, Rutland, or others. From a biographical standpoint, Shakespeare remains the "iron mask" of literature.

On the other hand, eighteenth-century writers, especially Voltaire, were not only writers but also public figures. Voltaire made his artistic work a tool for propaganda, and his life, bold and provocative, served this same end. The years of exile, the years of reigning at Ferney, were used as weapons for the ideological battle and for preaching. Voltaire's works were inseparably linked with his life. His audience not only read his work but even went on pilgrimages to him. Those who admired his writings were worshipers of his personality; the adversaries of his writings were his personal enemies. Voltaire's personality linked his literary works together. When his name was mentioned, his literary works were not what first came to mind. Even today, when most of his tragedies and poems have been completely forgotten, the image of Voltaire is still alive; those forgotten works shine with reflected light in his unforgettable biography. Equally unforgettable is the biography of his contemporary, Rousseau, who left his *Confessions* and thus bequeathed to posterity the history of his life.

Voltaire and Rousseau, like many of their contemporaries, were prolific in many genres, from musical comedies to novels and philosophical treatises, from epigrams and epitaphs to theoretical articles on physics and music. Only their lives could have united these various forms of verbal creation into a system. This is why their biographies, their letters and memoirs, have become such an integral part of their literary heritage. In fact, the knowledge that their biographies were a constant background for their works compelled Voltaire and Rousseau to dramatize certain epic motifs in their own lives and, furthermore, to create for themselves an artificial legendary biography composed of intentionally selected real and imaginary events. The biographies of such authors require a Ferney or a Jasnaja Poljana: they require pilgrimages by admirers and condemnations from Sorbonnes or Holy Synods.

Following in the footsteps of these eighteenth-century writers, Byron, the poet of sharp-tempered characters, created the canonical biography for a lyrical poet. A biography of a Romantic poet was more than a biography of an author and public figure. The Romantic poet *was* his own hero. His *life* was poetry, and soon there developed a canonical set of actions to be carried out by the poet. Here, the traditions of the eighteenth century served as a model. The end of that century had produced the stereotype of the "dying poet": young, unable to overcome the adversities of life, perishing in poverty, the fame he merited coming too late. Such were the legendary biographies of two poets, Malfilâtre and Gilbert, later popularized by the Romantics (for example, Alfred de Vigny). The late eighteenth-century poets Parny and Bertin wrote their elegies with a definite orientation toward autobiography. They arranged those elegies in such a way as to convince the reader that their poems were fragments of a real romance, that their Eleonoras and Eucharidas were actual people. Delille in France and our own Xvostov appended footnotes to the feminine names they used, such as "the poet's name for his wife."

The necessity for such "real" commentary was dictated by the style of the period. Readers demanded the complete illusion of life. They made pilgrimages to the final resting places of the heroes of even the most unbelievable novels. For example, near Moscow one can still visit "Liza's Pond," in which Karamzin's sugary heroine drowned herself. They say that at Lermontov's house in Pjatigorsk artifacts which belonged to Princess Mary are exhibited.

The readers' demand for a living hero results in the perennial question: from whom is the character drawn? This is the question which Lermontov contemptuously brushed aside in the introduction to *A Hero of Our Time.* In this connection we should consider the usual commentary to Griboedov's *Gore ot uma* [Woe from Wit]; the Moscow "old-timers" assigned all of Griboedov's heroes to actual people—as is typical of old-timers.

Once the question of copying characters from life has arisen, writers actually *do* begin to copy from life—or at least they pretend to do so. The author becomes a witness to and a living participant in his novels, a living hero. A double transformation takes place: heroes are taken for living personages, and poets become living heroes—their biographies become poems.

In the Puškin era, when the genre of "friendly epistles" flourished, poets paraded before their audience as characters. Now Puškin writes to Baratynskij from Bessarabia, now Jazykov writes to Puškin. And then all three of them become the themes of lyrical poems.

The lyricism of Puškin's long poems is clearly the result of an orientation toward autobiography. The reader had to feel that he was reading, not the words of an abstract author, but those of a living person whose biographical data were at his disposal. Thus the author had to make literary use of his own biography. So Puškin used his southern exile as a poetic banishment. Motifs of exile, of wanderings, run throughout his poetry in many variations. We must assume that Puškin poetically fostered certain facts of his life. For example, he jealously expunged references to *deva junaja* [the young maid] from poems already completed and well-known in print, and from those widely circulated in manuscript. At the same time, he wrote to his friends in an ambiguous and enigmatic tone about unrequited love. In conversation, he became prone to mysteriously incoherent outpourings. And behold, the poetic legend of a "concealed love" was created with its ostentatious devices used for concealing love, when it would have been much simpler to keep silent. However, Puškin was concerned about his "biography," and the image of a young exile with a hidden and unrequited love, set against the background of Crimean nature, fascinated him. He needed this image as a frame for his southern poems. Nonetheless, present-day biographers have dealt mercilessly with this stylish legend. They have been determined to learn at any cost the identity of the woman whom Puškin so hopelessly loved (or pretended to love). Thus they have destroyed the very core of the legend—the unknown. In place of "young maids," they have proposed various respectable society women.

The interrelationships of life and literature became confused during the Romantic era. Romanticism and its mores constitute a problem to which careful investigations have been devoted. It is sometimes difficult to decide whether literature recreates phenomena from life or whether the opposite is in fact the case: that the phenomena of life are the result of the penetration of literary clichés into reality. Such motifs as the duel, the Caucasus, etc., were invariant components both of literature and of the poet's biography.

The poets used their lives to realize a literary purpose, and these literary biographies were necessary for the readers. The readers cried: "Author! author!"–but they were actually calling for the slender youth in a cloak, with a lyre in his hands and an enigmatic expression on his face. This demand for a potentially existing author, whether real or not, gave rise to a special kind of anonymous literature: literature with an invented author, whose biography was appended to the work. We find a literary precedent for this genre in Voltaire's mystifications. He published stories under the name of Guillaume Vadé and appended a letter written by Catherine Vadé (the imaginary first cousin of the imagined author) describing the last days of her cousin Guillaume.

In this connection, we should also consider the stories of Belkin and Rudyj Pan′ko. At the basis of these mystifications lies the very same demand of the public: "Give us a living author!" If the author wanted to hide, then he had to send forth an invented narrator. Biography became an element of literature.

The biographies of real authors, for example of Puškin and Lermontov, were cultivated as oral legends. How many interesting anecdotes the old-timers "knew" about Puškin! Read the reminiscences of the Kišenev inhabitants about the poet. You will find tales that even Puškin wouldn't have dreamt of. In these tales, a tragic love and an exotic lover (a gypsy or a Greek) are absolutely necessary. As fiction, however, all this is far more superior to the recently published anecdote in the notes of Naščokin-Bartenevskij concerning Puškin and the Countess Finkel′mon.

Thus, legends about poets were created, and it was extremely important for the literary historian to occupy himself with the restoration of these legends, i.e., with the removal of later layers and the reduction of the legend to its pure "canonical" form. These biographical legends are the literary conception of the poet's life, and this conception was necessary as a perceptible background for the poet's literary works. The legends are a premise which the author himself took into account during the creative process.

The biographical commentary to a literary work often consists of the curriculum vitae, the genealogy, of the characters mentioned in the work. However, in referring to a given character, the author did not assume that the reader knew the curriculum vitae of that character. However, he did assume that the reader knew the character's anecdotal representation, consisting of actual and invented material, created in the reader's milieu. When Puškin was writing *Mozart and Salieri*, what was important was not the actual historical relationship between these two composers (and here their biographies, based on documents and investigations, would not help anyway), but the fact that there existed a legend about the poisoning of Mozart by Salieri, and that rumors were current that Beaumarchais had poisoned his wives. The question of whether these rumors and legends had any foundation in fact was irrelevant to their function.

In exactly the same way, the poet considers as a premise to his creations not his actual curriculum vitae, but his ideal biographical legend. Therefore, only this biographical legend should be important to the literary historian in his attempt to reconstruct the psychological milieu surrounding a literary work. Furthermore, the biographical legend is necessary only to the extent that the literary work includes references to "biographical" facts (real or legendary) of the author's life.

However, the poet did not always have a biography. Toward the middle of the nineteenth century, the poet-hero was replaced by the professional poet, the businessman-journalist. The writer wrote down his manuscript and gave it to a publisher; he did not allow any glimpses of his personal life. The human face of the author peered out only in pasquinades, in satirical pamphlets, or in monetary squabbles which burst out noisily in public whenever contributors were not satisfied with their royalties. Thus the phenomenon of writers without biographies appeared. All attempts to invent biographies for these writers and to project their work onto these biographies have consistently ended in farce. Nekrasov, for example, appears on the literary scene without a biography, as do Ostrovskij and Fet. Their works are self-contained units. There are no biographical features shedding light on the meaning of their works. Nevertheless, there are scholars who want to imagine literary biographies even for these authors.

It is, of course, obvious that these authors do have *actual* biographies, and that their literary work enters into these biographies as a fact of their lives. Such actual biographies of private individuals may be interesting for cultural history, but not for the history of literature. (I say nothing of those literary historians who classify literary phenomena on the basis of the circumstances of the writer's birth.) No poetic image of the author—except perhaps as a deliberately invented narrator who is introduced into the story itself (like Puškin's Belkin)—can be found in this period. Works did not depend on the presence of a biographical background.

This "cold" nineteenth-century writer, however, did not represent an exclusive type which was to replace "biographically oriented" literature forever. At the very end of the century interest in the author began to arise once again, and this interest has continued to grow to the present day. First, there appeared a timid interest in "good people." We suffered through a period when the writer was necessarily considered "a good person"; we suffered through images of wretched victims, images of oppressed consumptive poets. We suffered through them to the point of nausea.

In the twentieth century there appeared a special type of writer with a demonstrative biography, one which shouted out: "Look at how bad and how impudent I am! Look! And don't turn your head away, because all of you are just as bad, only you are fainthearted and hide yourselves. But I am bold; I strip myself stark naked and walk around in public without feeling ashamed." This was the reaction to the "sweetness" of the "good man."

Fifteen years ago someone came out with a "calendar of writers," in which the autobiographies of the men of letters fashionable at that time were collected. These writers all vied with one another in crying out that they had no formal education because they had been expelled from high school and from trade school, that they had only torn trousers and a few buttons—and all this because they absolutely didn't care about anything.

However, alongside this petty naughtiness in literature, there emerged a new intimate style. Many writers, of course, still persisted in concealing their private lives from the public. Sologub, for one, systematically refused to provide any information whatsoever about himself. But other and rather different trends were also present in literature. Vasilij Rozanov created a distinctive intimate style. The pages of his books were like "falling leaves," and he strolled through them uncombed, whole, completely himself. He produced a special literature of intimate conversations and confidential confessions. We know, by his own admission, that he was a mystifier. It is the business of cultural historians to judge to what extent the face he carefully drew in his fragments and aphorisms was his own. As a literary legend, Rozanov's image has been drawn, by him, definitively and with complete consistency. This image shows little resemblance either to the "heroic poets" of the beginning of the nineteenth century or to the "good persons" with progressive convictions of the end of the century. However, it is impossible to deny that this image was viable and artistically functional during the years of Rozanov's literary work. Furthermore, the autobiographical devices of Rozanov's literary manner have survived him and are still present today in novelistic or fragmentary memoirs.

Parallel to this prosaic element in the Symbolist movement, there also developed a biographical lyricism. Blok was certainly a poet with a lyrical biography. The numerous memoirs and biographical works on Blok which appeared within a year of his death testify to the fact that his biography was a living and necessary commentary to his works. His poems are lyrical episodes about himself, and his readers always informed themselves (perhaps at third-hand) about the principal events of his life. It would be inaccurate to say that Blok put his life on display. Nonetheless, his poems did arouse an insurmountable desire to know about the author, and they made his readers avidly follow the various twists and turns of his life. Blok's legend is an inescapable concomitant to his poetry. The elements of intimate confession and biographical allusion in his poetry must be taken into account.

Symbolism was superseded by Futurism, which intensified to a hyperbolic clarity those features which had previously appeared only in hidden, mystically masked forms of Symbolism. Intimate confessions and allusions were transformed into demonstrative declarations delivered in a monumental style. Whereas Blok's biography appeared only as a legendary concomitant to his poetry, the Futurist legendary biographies were boldly inserted into the works themselves.

Futurism took the Romantic orientation toward autobiography to its ultimate conclusions. The author really became the hero of his works. We need mention here only the construction of Majakovskij's books: they are an open diary in which intimate feelings are recorded. This type of construction, in fact, intersects the path of the future biographer, who will have to try to construct a different, extraliterary, biography. Today the writer shows his readers his own life and writes his own biography, tightly binding it to the literary cycles of his work. If, for example, Gor'kij drives away importunate idlers, then he does this knowingly, as a demonstration: he knows that this very fact will be taken into account in his biography. Just consider how many of today's poets reminisce about themselves and their friends, how many of them produce memoir literature—memoirs transformed into artistic structures.

Obviously, the question of the role of biography in literary history cannot be solved uniformly for all literatures. There are writers with biographies and writers without biographies. To attempt to compose biographies for the latter is to write satires or denunciations on the alive or the dead as well. On the other hand, for a writer with a biography, the facts of the author's life must be taken into consideration. Indeed, in the works themselves the juxtaposition of the texts and the author's biography plays a structural role. The literary work plays on the potential reality of the author's subjective outpourings and confessions. Thus the biography that is useful to the literary historian is not the author's curriculum vitae or the investigator's account of his life. What the literary historian really needs is the biographical legend created by the author himself. Only such a legend is a *literary fact.*

As far as "documentary biographies" are concerned, these belong to the domain of cultural history, on a par with the biographies of generals and inventors. With regard to literature and its history, these biographies may be considered only as external (even if necessary) reference material of an auxiliary nature.

Literary Environment*

Boris M. Èjxenbaum

1

We do not apprehend all the facts at once; it isn't always the same facts we take in, and not always the same correlations of facts we need bring out. Not everything we know or could get to know makes a connection in our minds under some specific conceptual sign, that is, turns from sheer contingency into a fact of a certain particular meaning. The immensity of the past, stored as documents and various kinds of personal papers, finds its way onto the printed page only piecemeal (and not always as the same material), in so far as theory gives us the right and the possibility of incorporating a part of that store into a system under some conceptual sign. Without theory no historical system would be possible, because there would be no principle for selecting and conceptualizing facts.

However, every theory is a working hypothesis fostered by our interest in the facts themselves: theory is essential for sorting out the pertinent facts and ordering them in a system—it is for that and no more. The very need for some particular set of facts, the very prerequisite of having some particular conceptual sign—these are conditions dictated by contemporary life with its specific problems. History is, in effect, a science of complex analogies, a science of double vision: the facts of the past have meanings for us that differentiate them and place them, invariably and inevitably, in a system under the sign of contemporary problems. Thus one set of problems supplants another, one set of facts overshadows another. History in this sense is a special method of studying the present with the aid of the facts of the past.

The successive change of problems and conceptual signs leads to the reassortment of traditional material and the inclusion of new facts excluded from an earlier system because of the latter's innate limitations. The incorporation of a new set of facts (under the sign of some particular correlation) strikes us as being the discovery of those facts, since their existence outside a system (their "contingent" status) had been from a scientific point of view equivalent to their nonexistence.

Just such an issue has now arisen to confront literary scholarship—and also literary criticism, at any rate in so far as theory overlaps criticism and scholarship. The literary situation of the present day has brought to the fore a set of facts needing conceptualization and incorporation in a system. In other

*"Literaturnyj byt," *Moj vremennik* (Leningrad, 1929), pp. 49-58. Translated by I. R. Titunik.

words, it is necessary to pose new problems and construct new theoretical hypotheses, in the light of which these facts, newly brought out by life, may take on meaning.

In recent years literary specialists and critics have focused attention primarily on questions of literary "technology" and on elucidating the specific features of literary evolution—the inner dialectics of styles and genres. It was the natural consequence of our having experienced a boom in literature that culminated in literary revolution (Symbolism and Futurism). Exactly that literary boom was what the enormous corpus of theoretical writings produced over the past fifteen years registered and ramified. Curiously, and symptomatically, the *history* of literature, in the strict sense of the term, was left aside, and not merely left aside—its very scientific value came under suspicion. This is understandable if one considers that the questions really pertinent then, those requiring analysis and generalization, had to do with "how to write in general" and "what to write next." The technological and (as regards the study of evolutive trends) theoretical endeavors of literary scholarship were prompted by the very situation in which literature found itself: it was necessary to sum up the results of the boom we had experienced and to shed light on the questions confronting the new literary generation. The scrutiny of how a literary work "was made" or could be made was meant to answer the first question; the establishment of intrinsic, concrete "laws" of literary evolution pertained to the second.

Both these processes were successfully carried out to the extent necessary for the generation entering literature ten years ago, and the product of that work has now become largely the property of university studies, having entered into the curriculum. History (as always happens) handed these matters over to the second-stringers who, with rare zeal (and often on equally rare paper) but without any verve, devote themselves to the business of devising terminology and displaying their erudition.

The present-day state of our literature poses new questions and has brought new facts to the fore. Literary evolution, only recently so engrossed with the dynamics of forms and styles, seems to have come to a halt. The literary struggle has lost the specificity it formerly had: earlier polemics on purely literary topics have petered out; there are no clear-cut alliances among periodicals; there are no sharply defined literary schools; finally, there is no commanding criticism and no dependable reader. Each writer writes as if solely in his own name, and literary groupings, if there really are any, take shape on extraliterary grounds—grounds that may be designated *literary-environmental.* Concurrently, technical issues have clearly given way to other issues, at whose center stands the problem of the literary profession, the "literary trade." The question, "how to write," has been supplanted, or at any rate given a new complexity, by the question, "*how to be a writer.*" In other words, the problem of literature per se has been overshadowed by the problem of the writer.

It may be positively stated that the crisis involves, not literature in and of itself, but literature's social mode of being. The writer's professional status has changed, the reader-writer relationship has changed, the customary conditions and forms of literary endeavor have changed; a decisive shift has occurred in the very sphere of literary environment, bringing to light a whole series of facts concerning the dependence of literature and the dependence of its evolution on conditions forming outside literature. The social realignment and the changeover to a different economic order brought about by the Soviet revolution have deprived the writer of a whole number of what at any rate used to be the mainstays of his profession (a dependable stratum of well-versed readers, a wide variety of journalistic and publishing enterprises, etc.), while at the same time forcing him to become a professional to an even greater degree than was formerly necessary. The writer's situation has come to resemble that of the artisan who works on a demand basis or who hires himself out; but meanwhile the very concept of literary "demand" remains undefined or proves contradictory to the writer's views of his literary rights and duties. A special type of writer has come on the scene—the dilettante in a professional capacity. Without worrying over the real issues at stake or his own fate as a writer, he grinds out hack work in response to demand. The situation is complicated by the confrontation of two literary generations, the older of which had regarded the meaning and the aim of the literary profession differently than the younger does now. Consequently, we have something like the situation of Russian literature in the early 1860s, but this time in far more complex and less familiar terms.

Given this situation, one is not surprised that issues pertaining to literary environment should now take on special point and relevance, and that the very way writers are identified with groups should follow literary-environmental lines. The facts that now loom large have to do not so much with evolution (as previously understood at any rate) but with *genesis*, and, that being the case, literary scholarship finds itself faced with the rise of a new theoretical problem: *the problem of the interrelationship between the facts of literary evolution and those of literary environment.* This problem had not entered into the formation of the earlier literary-historical system simply because the situation had not brought those facts to the fore. The process of a scientific elucidation of them is now on the agenda, because the literary evolution now taking place before our eyes cannot otherwise be understood.

In other words, we confront the revived question as to what a literary-historical fact is. The history of literature needs fresh substantiation as a scientific discipline indispensable to the elucidation of contemporary literary problems. The impotence of criticism today and its partial reversion to earlier, obsolete principles are explainable in large measure by the poverty of literary-historical awareness.

2

The traditional literary-historical system was forged without regard to the fundamental distinction between the concepts of genesis and evolution, these having been taken instead for synonyms. Likewise, it made do without attempting to establish what was meant by literary-historical fact. The consequence was a naive theory about "lineal descent" and "influence," and an equally naive psychological biographism.

To overcome this system, literary specialists of the recent past turned away from the material of traditional literary history (including the biographical) and concentrated on the general problems of literary evolution. Their most common procedure was to take some literary-historical fact and use it as an illustration of general theoretical postulations. Literary-historical topics as such retreated to the background. If the older writings of historians of literature were often notable for their indiscriminate mixing of disparate and inscrutably associated facts, then in the newer writings we witness the opposite tendency: the categorical dismissal of everything not directly related to the problem of literary evolution per se. This was not merely a polemical matter. It was a necessity, even more, a historical duty: that was what the driving spirit of science had to be for the new generation, the generation that had traveled the road from Symbolism to Futurism.

It is not only literature that evolves; literary scholarship also evolves along with literature. The driving spirit of scientific inquiry changes direction in accordance with changes in the relationship of immediate literary facts and problems. The moment has come to focus on the reassortment of old material and the incorporation of new facts in the literary-historical system. The history of literature is posited anew—not merely as a topic but as a scientific principle.

The concern with literary-environmental material does not in the least signify a turning away from literary fact or the problems of literary evolution, as some people seem to think. It means only incorporating the genetic facts into the theoretical-evolutionary system, as that system had been worked out in recent years—at the very least, incorporating those genetic facts which can and should be interpreted as having a historical bearing, as being connected with the facts of *evolution* and *history*. When it was a matter of studying the general laws of literary evolution, particularly in their application to problems of literary technology, the importance of various and sundry historical connections and interrelationships was a secondary or even an irrelevant issue. Now it is exactly that issue which has become central.

Literary-environmental material, material so keenly perceived today, remains unutilized, despite the fact that it would seem to be exactly the right material for founding contemporary literary-sociological studies. The trouble is that the problem of the nature of literary-historical fact has never been raised in these studies, and consequently neither the reassortment of old material nor the incorporation of new material has come about. Instead of utilizing under a new conceptual sign the earlier observations of the specific features of literary evolution (and those observations, after all, not only do not contradict but actually support an authentic sociological point of view), our literary "sociologists" have taken up the metaphysical quest for the prime principles of literary evolution and literary forms. They have had two possibilities at hand, both already amply applied and proved incapable of producing any literary-historical system: (1) the analysis of works of literature from the point of view of the writer's class ideology (a purely psychological approach, for which art is the least appropriate, the least characteristic material) and (2) the cause-and-effect derivation of literary forms and styles from the general socioeconomic and agricultural-industrial forms of the epoch (e.g., Lermontov's poetry and the grain export in the 1830s)—an approach that inevitably deprives literary scholarship of both its autonomy and its concreteness and is furthest removed from anything "materialistic." It is of no mean significance that Engels, in letters written in 1890, warned against taking this tack and expressed his indignation over endeavors of just this sort:

> The materialistic conception of history now has a host of sympathizers for whom it constitutes a pretext for not studying history. . . . The phraseology of historical materialism (and *anything* can be made into a phrase) serves many Germans of the younger generation only as an expedient way of marshaling their own and relatively quite modest knowledge of history and bravely forging onward. . . . What these gentlemen lack is dialectics. They are forever spying a cause here, an effect there. They do not see that this is an empty abstraction and that such metaphysical polar oppositions exist in the real world only during times of crisis, that the whole grand process comes about through an interaction.

It is no surprise that the literary-sociological endeavors of recent years not only have failed to lead to new results but even represent a step backward—a reversion to literary-historical impressionism. No genetic study, however far it may go, can lead us to the prime principle (assuming that the aims envisaged are scientific, not religious). Science in the long run does not explain phenomena but rather establishes only their properties and relationships. History is incapable of answering a single "why" question; it can only answer the question, "what does this mean?"

Literature, like any other specific order of things, is not generated from facts belonging to other orders and therefore *cannot be reduced* to such facts. The relations between the facts of the literary order and facts extrinsic to it cannot simply be causal relations but can only be the relations of correspondence, interaction, dependency, or conditionality. These relations change in conjunction with changes in the literary fact (see Jurij Tynjanov, *Literaturnyj fakt* [Literary Fact] in *Lef*, 1925, No. 2), now functioning in the evolution and taking an active part in determining the literary-historical process (dependency or conditionality), now assuming a more passive character, with the genetic order remaining extraliterary and as such receding into the sphere of factors belonging to the general history of culture (correspondence or interaction). Thus, for example, at certain times periodicals and the environment created by the activities of editing and publishing take on meaning as literary fact, while at other times the same meaning is conferred on societies, circles, salons. Therefore the very selection of the literary-environmental material and the principles for its incorporation must be determined by the nature of the connections and correlations under the sign of which literary evolution at any given point in time comes about.

Since literature is not reducible to any other order of things and cannot be the simple derivative of any other order, there is no reason to believe that all its constituent elements can be genetically conditioned. Literary-historical fact is a complex construct in which the fundamental role belongs to *literariness*—an element of such specificity that its study can be productive only in immanent-evolutionary terms. Puškin's iambic tetrameter, for instance, cannot possibly be connected (not only in causal terms but in terms of conditionality as well) either with the general socioeconomic conditions during the reign of Nicholas I or even with the characteristics of the literary environment of the time. Yet Puškin's turning to periodical prose and thus the very evolution of his creative art at that moment were conditioned by the general professionalization of literary endeavors in the early 1830s and the new significance of journalism as literary fact. This connection is not, of course, a causal connection; it merely represents the utilization of new literary-environmental conditions, conditions previously not part of the picture—the expansion of the reading public beyond the circle of the court and the aristocracy, the appearance on the scene, along with booksellers, of a special variety of professional publisher (Smirdin, for instance), the transition from miscellanies (almanacs) of a more or less amateur standing to periodical publications of the commercial type (Senkovskij's *Biblioteka dlja čtenija*), and so forth. In this context, literary-historical meaning also accrued to the heated polemic over the issue of the writing profession and the "mercantile trend of our literature" as Ševyrev remarked in his famous article, *Slovestnost' i torgovlja* [Literature and Commerce], in which the topic of discussion was (in current terminology) "demand" and "hack work".

These facts lead us back to an even earlier time—to the commercial success of the miscellany, *Poljarnaja zvezda* (1823), and of Puškin's *Baxčisarajskij Fontan* [Fountain of Bakhchisaray] (1824), which came as such a surprise to the booksellers. There even ensued a whole "extraliterary" polemic over the Puškin poem, a polemic in which both literary men (Bulgarin and Vjazemskij) and booksellers took part. An honorarium was still a rare exception for periodicals in 1826. Bulgarin, upon learning that Pogodin's *Moskovskij Vestnik* intended paying honoraria, wrote him, "Your announcement that you will pay 100 rubles per octavo is preposterous." Puškin aptly characterized the change in the state of literary affairs when he wrote Barant in 1836: "Literature began as an important branch of our industry not more than some twenty years ago. Before that it was looked upon exclusively as an elegant and aristocratic occupation."

Along with the growing industrialization of literature, the writer of the 1830s also emerged from his earlier dependence on the class in power and became a professional. The periodicals of the 1850s and 1860s were outright forms of professional writers' organizations influencing the very evolution of literature. Periodicals stood at the center of literary life, the writers themselves becoming editors and publishers. Attitudes toward literary professionalism acquired crucial meaning and differentiated one group of writers from another. Now the reverse process proved to have a bearing on literature as a characteristic and significant factor: the emergence from the literary profession into a "second profession," as was the case with Tolstoj and Fet. Tolstoj's estate of Jasnaja Poljana stood in opposition to the editorial offices of *Sovremennik*, where literary life was in full swing: it presented a glaring contrast in mode of life; it was a challenge on the part of the landowner-writer to the professional writer, the "literary man" (such as Saltykov became, for example). It may be claimed that *War and Peace* was a challenge not only to the periodical fiction of the time but also to the "despotism of the periodicals," about which Ivan Aksakov complained to Leskov in 1874: "I guess all one need do is to acquaint the readers with the beginning of one's work through the periodicals and then make it available separately. That's what Count Lev Tolstoj did with his novel."

These are isolated instances illustrating the concept of literary environment and the problem of its relationship to the facts of evolution. The forms and potentialities of literary endeavor as a profession change according to the social conditions of an age. Writing, once it becomes a profession, declasses the writer, but on the other hand it places him in dependence on the consumer, the "customer." The petty press develops (as happened in the 1860s), the feuilleton comes to the fore, and the high genres are demoted. In reaction, literature, abiding by the laws of its evolutionary dialectics, makes a circumlocution. On the scene, side by side with Nekrasov, comes a man like Fet, whose "class identity" is a means of carrying on a literary struggle against journalistic poetry. Side by side with Saltykov or Dostoevskij is Tolstoj about whose "class identity" Fet bears witness in the early 1860s: "In its blind infatuation, the literature of the gentry has reached the point where it is in opposition to the vital interests of the gentry, a situation that has aroused the fresh, untrammeled instincts of Lev Tolstoj to such a pitch of indignation."

For the history of literature, the concept of class is not important either in itself (as it would be in the economic sciences) or for the definition of a writer's "ideology," which is often devoid of any literary significance. It *is* important in its literary and literary-environmental function, and consequently it is important at such time as "class identity" comes to the fore, bringing that function to bear. The "class identity" of a writer was not a characteristic feature of Russian eighteenth-century poetry with its pervasive dutifulness; nor was it, from a different angle, characteristic of or even relevant to Russian literature of the late nineteenth century, which developed within the milieu of the intelligentsia. Just as social demand does not always coincide with literary demand, so the class struggle does not always coincide with the literary struggle or with literary alignments. One must be cautious and conscientious when dealing with the terms and concepts of other disciplines, however closely related to one's own they may be. The enormous efforts made in the past to emancipate literary scholarship from rendering service to the history of culture, philosophy, psychology, etc., were not made for the sake of putting it to the service of the juridical and economic sciences and thus letting it drag on a pitiful existence as applied "publicistics."

The situation of the present day has brought us to considering literary-environmental material, but not so as to turn us away from literature and lay to rest all that was done during recent years (I am referring, of course, to literary scholarship); rather, the effect of this new interest is to posit anew the question as to how the literary-historical system is to be constructed and to bring us to an understanding of what the evolutionary processes taking place before our eyes mean. The writer nowadays is trying to feel out the potentialities of his profession. These potentialities are unclear because the very functions of literature are themselves tangled in a tricky knot. The issue is critical: while out-and-out professionalism is taking the writer down the road of the petty press and the translation game, the tendency is growing for the writer to free himself from professionalism by developing a "second profession," and not just for the sake of earning his keep but also so that he can feel professionally independent. We literary specialists and critics have the responsibility of helping disentangle the knot and avoiding tying it still tighter by fabricating artificial alignments of writers, running "ideologies" to the ground, and foisting on literature publicistic imperatives. The ways and means of that kind of criticism have been exhausted. It's time to start talking about literature.

On Literary Evolution*

Jurij Tynjanov

(Dedicated to Boris Èjxenbaum)

1. Within the cultural disciplines literary history still retains the status of a colonial territory. On the one hand, individualistic psychologism dominates it to a significant extent, particularly in the West, unjustifiably replacing the problem of literature with the question of the author's psychology, while the problem of literary evolution becomes the problem of the genesis of literary phenomena. On the other hand, a simplified causal approach to a literary order leads to a sharp break between the literary order itself and the point of observation, which always turns out to be the major but also the most remote social orders. The organization of a closed literary order and the examination of the evolution within it sometimes collides with the neighboring cultural, behavioral, and social orders in the broad sense. Thus such an effort is doomed to incompleteness. The theory of value in literary investigation has brought about the danger of studying major but isolated works and has changed the history of literature into a *history of generals.* The blind rejection of a history of generals has in turn caused an interest in the study of mass literature, but no clear theoretical awareness of how to study it or what the nature of its significance is.

Finally, the relationship between the history of literature and living contemporary literature—a relationship useful and very necessary to science—is not always necessary and useful to the development of literature. The representatives of literature are ready to view the history of literature as the codification of certain traditional norms and laws and to confuse the historical character of a literary phenomenon with "historicism." As a result of this conflict, there has arisen an attempt to study isolated works and the laws of their construction on an extrahistorical plane, resulting in the abolition of the history of literature.

2. In order to become finally a science, the history of literature must claim reliability. All of its terminology, and first of all the very term, "the history of literature," must be reconsidered. The term proves to be extremely broad, covering both the material history of belles lettres, the history of verbal art, and the history of writing in general. It is also pretentious, since "the history of literature" considers itself a priori a discipline ready to enter into "the history of culture" as a system equipped with a scientific methodology. As yet it has no right to such a claim.

*"O literaturnoj èvoljucii," *Arxaisty i novatory* (Leningrad, 1929), pp. 30-47. Translated by C. A. Luplow. The first Russian version was published in 1927.

Meanwhile, the historical investigations of literature fall into at least two main types, depending on the points of observation: the investigation of the genesis of literary phenomena, and the investigation of the evolution of a literary order, that is, of literary changeability.

The point of view determines not only the significance but also the nature of the phenomenon being studied. In the investigation of literary evolution, the moment of genesis has its own significance and character, which are obviously not the same as in the investigation of the genesis per se.

Furthermore, the study of literary evolution or changeability must reject the theories of naive evaluation, which result from the confusion of points of observation, in which evaluation is carried over from one epoch or system into another. At the same time, evaluation itself must be freed from its subjective coloring, and the "value" of a given literary phenomenon must be considered as having an "evolutionary significance and character."

The same must also apply to such concepts as "epigonism," "dilettantism," or "mass literature," which are for now evaluative concepts.[1]

Tradition, the basic concept of the established history of literature, has proved to be an unjustifiable abstraction of one or more of the literary elements of a given system within which they occupy the same plane and play the same role. They are equated with the like elements of another system in which they are on a different plane, thus they are brought into a seemingly unified, fictitiously integrated system.

The main concept for literary evolution is the *mutation* of systems, and thus the problem of "traditions" is transferred onto another plane.

3. Before this basic problem can be analyzed, it must be agreed that a literary work is a system, as is literature itself. Only after this basic agreement has been established is it possible to create a literary science which does not superficially examine diverse phenomena but studies them closely. In this way the problem of the role of contiguous systems in literary evolution is actually posited instead of being rejected.

The analysis of the separate elements of a work, such as the composition, style, rhythm, and syntax in prose, and the rhythm and semantics in poetry, provides sufficient evidence that these elements, within certain limits, can be abstracted as a *working hypothesis*, although they are interrelated and interacting. The study of rhythm in poetry and prose was bound to show that the role of a given element is different in different systems.

The interrelationship of each element with every other in a literary work and with the whole literary system as well may be called the constructional *function* of the given element.

On close examination, such a function proves to be a complex concept. An element is on the one hand interrelated with similar elements in other works in other systems, and on the other hand it is interrelated with different elements within the same work. The former may be termed the *auto-function* and the latter, the *syn-function.*

Thus, for example, the lexicon of a given work is interrelated with both the whole literary lexicon and the general lexicon of the language, as well as with other elements of that given work. These two components or functions operate simultaneously but are not of equal relevance.

The function of archaisms, for example, depends wholly on the system within which they are used. In Lomonosov's system, in which lexical coloring plays a dominant role, such archaisms function as "elevated" word usage. They are used for their lexical association with Church Slavic. In Tjutčev's work archaisms have a different function. In some instances they are abstract, as in the pair: *fontan-vodomet* [fountain-spout]. An interesting example is the usage of archaisms in an ironical function: *"Pušek grom i musikija"* [Thunder of guns and musicke] is used by a poet who otherwise employs a word such as *musikijskij* [musicall] in a completely different function. The auto-function, although it is not decisive, makes the existence of the syn-function possible and at the same time conditions it. Thus up to the time of Tjutčev, in the eighteenth and nineteenth centuries, there existed an extensive parodic literature in which archaisms had a parodic function. But the semantic and intonational system of the given work finally determines the function of a given expression, in this case determining the word usage to be "ironic" rather than "elevated."

It is incorrect to isolate the elements from one system outside their constructional function and to correlate them with other systems.

4. Is the so-called "immanent" study of a work as a system possible without comparing it with the general literary system? Such an isolated study of a literary work is equivalent to abstracting isolated elements and examining them outside their work. Such

abstracting is continuously applied to contemporary works and may be successful in literary criticism, since the interrelationship of a contemporary work with contemporary literature is in advance an established, although concealed, fact. (The interrelationship of a work with other works by the same author, its relationship to genre, and so on, belong here.)

Even in contemporary literature, however, isolated study is impossible. The very existence of a fact *as literary* depends on its differential quality, that is, on its interrelationship with both literary and extraliterary orders. Thus, its existence depends on its function. What in one epoch would be a literary fact would in another be a common matter of social communication, and vice versa, depending on the whole literary system in which the given fact appears.

Thus the friendly letter of Deržavin is a social fact. The friendly letter of the Karamzin and Puškin epoch is a literary fact. Thus one has the literariness of memoirs and diaries in one system and their extraliterariness in another.

We cannot be certain of the structure of a work if it is studied in isolation.

Finally, the auto-function, that is, the interrelationship of an element with similar elements in other systems, conditions the syn-function, that is, the constructional function of the element.

Thus, whether or not an element is "effaced" is important. But what is the effacement of a line, meter, plot structure, and so on? What, in other words, is the "automatization" of one or another element?

The following is an example from linguistics. When the referential meaning of a word is effaced, that word becomes the expression of a relationship, a connection, and thus it becomes an auxiliary word. In other words, its function changes. The same is true of the "automatization" of a literary element. It does not disappear. Its function simply changes, and it becomes auxiliary. If the meter of a poem is "effaced," then the other signs of verse and the other elements of the work become more important in its place, and the meter takes on other functions.

Thus the short feuilleton verse of the newspaper uses mainly effaced, banal meters which have long been rejected by poetry. No one would read it as a "poem" related to "poetry." Here the effaced meter is a means of attaching feuilleton material from everyday life to literature. Meter thus has an auxiliary function, which is completely different from its function in a poetic work.

This also applies to parody in the verse feuilleton. Parody is viable only in so far as what is being parodied is still alive. What literary significance can the thousandth parody of Lermontov's "When the golden cornfield sways..." or Puškin's "The Prophet" have today? The verse feuilleton, however, uses such parody constantly. Here again we have the same phenomenon: the function of parody has become auxiliary, as it serves to apply extraliterary facts to literature.

In a work in which the so-called plot is effaced, the story carries out different functions than in a work in which it is not effaced. The story might be used merely to motivate style or as a strategy for developing the material. Crudely speaking, from our vantage point in a particular literary system, we would be inclined to reduce nature descriptions in old novels to an auxiliary role, to the role of making transitions or retardation; therefore we would almost ignore them, although from the vantage point of a different literary system we would be forced to consider nature descriptions as the main, dominant element. In other words, there are situations in which the story simply provides the motivation for the treatment of "static descriptions."

5. The more difficult and less studied question of literary genres can be resolved in the same way. The novel, which seems to be an integral genre that has developed in and of itself over the centuries, turns out to be not an integral whole but a variable. Its material changes from one literary system to another, as does its method of introducing extraliterary language materials into literature. Even the features of the genre evolve. The genres of the "short story" and the "novella" were defined by different features in the system of the twenties to forties than they are in our time, as is obvious from their very names. We tend to name genres according to secondary features or, crudely speaking, by size. For us the labels, short story, novella, and novel, are adequate only to define the quantity of printed pages. This proves not so much the "automatization" of genres in our literary system as the fact that we define genres by other features. The size of a thing, the quantity of verbal material, is not an indifferent feature; we cannot, however, define the genre of a work if it is isolated from the system. For example, what was called an ode in the 1820s or by Fet was so labeled on the basis of features different from those used to define an ode in Lomonosov's time.

Consequently, we may conclude that the study of isolated genres outside the features characteristic of the genre system with which they are related is impossible. The historical novel of Tolstoj is not related to the historical novel of Zagoskin, but to the prose of his contemporaries.

6. Strictly speaking, one cannot study literary phenomena outside of their interrelationships. Such, for example, is the problem of prose and poetry. We tacitly consider metrical prose to be prose, and nonmetrical free verse to be poetry, without considering the fact that in another literary system we would thus be placed in a difficult position. The point is that prose and poetry are interrelated and that there is a mutually shared function of prose and poetry. (Note the interrelationship of prose and poetry in their respective development, as established by Boris Èjxenbaum.)

The function of poetry in a particular literary system was fulfilled by the formal element of meter; but prose displays differentiation and develops, and so does poetry. The differentiation of one interrelated type leads to, or better, is connected with, the differentiation of another interrelated type. Thus metrical prose arises, as in the works of Andrej Belyj. This is connected with the transfer of the verse function in poetry from meter onto other features which are in part secondary and resultant. Such features may be rhythm, used as the feature of verse units, a particular syntax or particular lexicon, and so on. The function of prose with regard to verse remains, but the formal elements fulfilling this function are different. In the course of centuries the further evolution of forms may consolidate the function of verse with regard to prose, transfer it onto a whole series of other features, or it may infringe upon it and make it unessential. And just as in contemporary literature the interrelationship of genres is hardly essential and is established according to secondary signs, so a period may come in which it will be unessential whether a work is written in prose or poetry.

7. The evolutionary relationship of function and formal elements is a completely uninvestigated problem. An example is given above of how the evolution of forms results in a change of function. There are also many examples of how a form with an undetermined function creates or defines a new one, and there are also others in which a function seeks its own form. I will give an example in which both occurred together.

In the archaist trend of the 1820s the function of the combined elevated and folk verse epos arises. *The interrelationship of literature with the social order led to the large verse form.* But there were no formal elements, and the demands of the social system turned out to be unequal to the demands of literature. Then the search for formal elements began. In 1824 Katenin advocated the octave as the formal element of the poetic epopea. The passionate quarrels concerning the seemingly innocent octave were appropriate to the tragic "orphanhood" of function without form. The epos of the archaists failed. Six years later Ševyrev and Puškin used the form in a different function: to break with the whole iambic tetrameter epos and create a new, "debased" (as opposed to "elevated"), prosaicized epos, such as Puškin's *Little House in Kolomna.*

The relationship between form and function is not accidental. The comparable combination of a particular lexicon with a particular meter by Katenin and then twenty or thirty years later by Nekrasov, who probably did not know about Katenin, was not accidental.

The variability of the functions of a given formal element, the rise of some new function of a formal element, and the attaching of a formal element to a function are all important problems of literary evolution; but there is no room to study or resolve these problems here. I would like to say only that the whole problem of literature as a system depends on further investigation.

8. The assumption that the interrelationship of literary phenomena occurs when a work enters into a synchronic literary system and there "acquires" a function is not entirely correct. The very concept of a continuously evolving synchronic system is contradictory. A literary system is first of all a *system of the functions of the literary order which are in continual interrelationship with other orders.* Systems change in their composition, but the differentiation of human activities remains. The evolution of literature, as of other cultural systems, does not coincide either in tempo or in character with the systems with which it is interrelated. This is owing to the specificity of the material with which it is concerned. The evolution of the structural function occurs rapidly; the evolution of the literary function occurs over epochs; and the evolution of the functions of a whole literary system in relation to neighboring systems occurs over centuries.

9. Since a system is not an equal interaction of all elements but places a group of elements in the foreground—the "dominant"—and thus involves the deformation of the remaining elements, a work enters into literature and takes on its own literary function through this dominant. Thus we correlate poems with the verse

category, not with the prose category, not on the basis of all their characteristics, but only of some of them. The same is true concerning genres. We relate a novel to "the novel" on the basis of its size and the nature of its plot development, while at one time it was distinguished by the presence of a love intrigue.

Another interesting fact from an evolutionary point of view is the following. A work is correlated with a particular literary system depending on its deviation, its "difference" as compared with the literary system with which it is confronted. Thus, for example, the unusually sharp argument among the critics of the 1820s over the genre of the Puškin narrative poem arose because the Puškin genre was a combined, mixed, new genre without a ready-made "name." The sharper the divergence or differentiation from a particular literary system, the more that system from which the derivation occurs is accentuated. Thus, free verse emphasized the verse principle of *nonmetrical* features, while Sterne's novel emphasized the compositional principle of *nonplot* features (Šklovskij). The following is an analogy from linguistics: "The variability of the word stem makes it the center of maximum expressiveness and thus extricates it from the net of prefixes which do not change" (Vendryes).

10. What constitutes the interrelationship of literature with neighboring orders? What, moreover, are these neighboring orders? The answer is obvious: social conventions.

Yet, in order to solve the problem of the interrelationship of literature with social conventions, the question must be posited: *how and by what means* are social conventions interrelated with literature? Social conventions are by nature many-sided and complex, and only the function of all their aspects is specific in it. Social conventions are correlated with literature first of all in its verbal aspect. This interrelationship is realized through language. That is, literature in relation to social conventions has a verbal function.

We use the term "orientation." It denotes approximately the "creative intention of the author." Yet it happens that "the intention may be good, but the fulfillment bad." Furthermore, the author's intention can only be a catalyst. In using a specific literary material, the author may yield to it, thus departing from his first intention. Thus Griboedov's *Wit Works Woe* was supposed to be "elevated" and even "grandiose," according to the author's terminology. But instead it turned out to be a political publicistic comedy of the archaist school. *Evgenij Onegin* was first meant to be a "satiric narrative poem" in which the author would be "brimming over with bitterness." However, while working on the fourth chapter, Puškin had already said, "Where is my satire? There's not a trace of it in *Evgenij Onegin.*"

The structural function, that is, the interrelationship of elements within a work, changes the "author's intention" into a catalyst, but does nothing more. "Creative freedom" thus becomes an optimistic slogan which does not correspond to reality, but yields instead to the slogan "creative necessity."

The literary function, that is, the interrelationship of a work with the literary order, completes the whole thing. If we eliminate the teleological, goal-oriented allusion, the "intention," from the word "orientation," what happens? The "orientation" of a literary work then proves to be its verbal function, its interrelationship with the social conventions.

The "orientation" of the Lomonosov ode, its verbal function, is oratorical. The word is oriented on *pronunciation.* And to carry further the associations with actual life, the orientation is on declamation in the large palace hall. By the time of Karamzin, the ode was literarily "worn out." The "orientation" had died out or narrowed down in significance and had been transferred onto other forms related to life. Congratulatory odes, as well as others, became "uniform verses," i.e., what are purely real-life phenomena. Ready-made literary genres did not exist. Everyday verbal communication took their place. The verbal function, or orientation, was seeking its forms and found them in the romance, the joking play with rhymes, *bouts rimés,* charades, and so on. And here the moment of genesis, the presence of certain forms of everyday speech, received evolutionary significance. These speech phenomena were found in the salon of Karamzin's epoch. And the salon, a fact of everyday life, at this time became a literary fact. In this way the forms of social life acquired a literary function.

Similarly, the semantics of the intimate domestic circle always exists, but in particular periods it takes on a literary function. Such, too, is the application of *accidental results.* The rough drafts of Puškin's verse programs and the drafts of his "scenarios" became his finished prose. This is possible only through the evolution of a whole system—through the evolution of its orientation.

An analogy from our own time of the struggle between two orientations is seen in the mass orientation of Majakovskij's poetry ("the ode") in competition with the romance, chamber-style orientation of Esenin ("the elegy").

11. The verbal function must also be taken into consideration in dealing with the problem of the reverse expansion of literature into actual life. The *literary personality*, or the *author's personality*, or at various times the *hero*, becomes the verbal orientation of literature. And from there it enters into real life. Such are the lyric heroes of Byron in relationship to his "literary personality," i.e., to the personality which came to life for the readers of his poems and which was thus transferred into life. Such is the "literary personality" of Heine, which is far removed from the real biographical Heine. In given periods, biography becomes oral, apocryphal literature. This happens naturally, in connection with the speech orientation of a given system. Thus, one has Puškin, Tolstoj, Blok, Majakovskij, and Esenin as opposed to the absence of a literary personality in Leskov, Turgenev, Fet, Majkov, Gumilev, and others. This corresponds to the absence of a speech orientation on "the literary personality." Obviously, special real-life conditions are necessary for the expansion of literature into life.

12. Such is the immediate social function of literature. It can be established and investigated only through the study of closely related conditions, without the forcible incorporation of remote, though major, causal orders.

Finally, the concept of the "orientation" of a speech function is applicable to a literary order but not to an individual work. A separate work must be related to a literary order before one can talk about its orientation. The law of large numbers does not apply to small numbers. In establishing the distant causal orders for separate works and authors, we study not the evolution of literature but its modification, not how literature changes and evolves in correlation with other orders, but how neighboring orders deform it. This problem too is worth studying, but on a completely different plane.

The direct study of the author's psychology and the construction of a causal "bridge" from the author's environment, daily life, and class to his works is particularly fruitless. The erotic poetry of Batjuškov resulted from his work on the poetic language—note his speech, "On the Influence of Light Poetry on Language"—and Vjazemskij refused to seek its genesis in Batjuškov's psychology. The poet, Polonskij, who was never a theoretician but who as a poet and master of his craft understood this, wrote of Benediktov,

It is very possible that the severity of nature, the forests, the fields . . . influenced the impressionable soul of the child and future poet, but how did they influence it? This is a difficult question, and no one will resolve it without straining the point. It is not nature, which is the same for everyone, that plays the major role here.

Sudden changes in artists which are unexplainable in terms of their personal changes are typical. Such are the sudden changes in Deržavin and Nekrasov, in whose youth "elevated" poetry went side by side with "low" satiric poetry, but later under objective conditions were merged, thus creating new phenomena. Clearly, the problem here is not one of individual psychological conditions, but of objective, evolving functions of the literary order in relation to the adjacent social order.

13. It is therefore necessary to reexamine one of the most complex problems of literary evolution, the problem of "influence." There are deep psychological and personal influences which are not reflected on the literary level at all, as with Čaadaev and Puškin. There are influences which modify and deform literature without having any evolutionary significance, as with Mixajlovskij and Gleb Uspenskij. Yet what is most striking of all is the fact that you can have an extrinsic indication of an influence where no such influence has occurred. I have already cited the examples of Katenin and Nekrasov. There are other examples as well. The South American tribes created the myth of Prometheus without the influence of classical mythology. These facts point to a convergence or coincidence. They have proved to be so significant that they completely obscure the psychological approach to the problem of influence and make chronology ("Who said it first?") unessential. "Influence" can occur at such a time and in such a direction as literary conditions permit. In the case of functional coincidence, whatever influences him provides the artist with elements which permit the development and strengthening of the function. If there is no such "influence," then an analogous function may result in analogous formal elements without any influence.

14. It is now time to pose the problem of the main term with which literary history operates, namely, "tradition." If we agree that evolution is the change in interrelationships between the elements of a system—between functions and formal elements—then evolution may be seen as the "mutations" of systems. These changes vary from epoch to epoch, occurring sometimes slowly, sometimes rapidly. They do not entail the sudden and complete renovation or the replacement of formal elements, but rather the

new function of these formal elements. Thus the very comparison of certain literary phenomena must be made on the basis of functions, not only forms. Seemingly dissimilar phenomena of diverse functional systems may be similar in function, and vice versa. The problem is obscured here by the fact that each literary movement in a given period seeks its supporting point in the preceding systems. This is what may be called "traditionalism."

Thus, perhaps, the functions of Puškin's prose are closer to the functions of Tolstoj's prose than the functions of Puškin's verse are to those of his imitators in the 1830s or those of Majkov.

15. To summarize, the study of literary evolution is possible only in relation to literature as a system, interrelated with other systems and conditioned by them. Investigation must go from constructional function to literary function; from literary function to verbal function. It must clarify the problem of the evolutionary interaction of functions and forms. The study of evolution must move from the literary system to the nearest correlated systems, not the distant, even though major, systems. In this way the prime significance of major social factors is not at all discarded. Rather, it must be elucidated to its full extent through the problem of the evolution of literature. This is in contrast to the establishment of the direct "influence" of major social factors, which replaces the study of *evolution* of literature with the study of the *modification* of literary works—that is to say, of their deformation.

Notes

1. One need only examine the mass literature of the 1820s and 1830s to be convinced of their colossal evolutionary difference. In the 1830s, years of the automatization of preceding traditions, years of work on dusty literary material, "dilettantism" suddenly received a tremendous evolutionary significance. It is from dilettantism, from the atmosphere of "verse notes written on the margins of books," that a new phenomenon emerged—Tjutčev, who transformed poetic language and genres by his intimate intonations. The relationship of social conventions to literature, which seems to be its degeneration from an evaluative point of view, transforms the literary system. In the 1820s, the years of the "masters" and the creation of new poetic genres, dilettantism and mass literature were called "graphomania." The poets, who from the point of view of evolutionary significance were the leading figures of the 1830s, appeared to be determined as the "dilettantes" (Tjutčev, Poležaev) or the "epigones" and "pupils" (Lermontov) in their struggle with the preceding norms. In the period of the 1820s, however, even the secondary poets appeared like leading masters; note, for example, the universality and grandioseness of

the genres used by such mass poets as Olin. It is clear that the evolutionary significance of such phenomena as dilettantism or epigonism is different from period to period. Supercilious, evaluative treatment of these phenomena is the heritage of the old history of literature.

Problems in the Study of Literature and Language*

Jurij Tynjanov
Roman Jakobson

1. The immediate problems facing Russian literary and linguistic science demand a precision of the theoretical platform. They require a firm dissociation from the increasing tendency to paste together mechanically the new methodology and the old discarded methods; they necessitate a determined refusal of the contraband offer of naive psychologism and other methodological hand-me-downs in the guise of new terminology.

Furthermore, academic eclecticism, scholastic "formalism"—which replaces analysis by terminology and the classification of phenomena—and the repeated attempts to shift literary and linguistic studies from a systematic science to episodic and anecdotal genres should be rejected.

2. The history of literature (art), being simultaneous with other historical series, is characterized, as is each of these series, by an involved complex of specific structural laws. Without an elucidation of these laws, it is impossible to establish in a scientific manner the correlation between the literary series and other historical series.

3. The evolution of literature cannot be understood until the evolutionary problem ceases to be obscured by questions of episodic, nonsystemic origin, whether literary (for example, so-called "literary influences") or extraliterary. The literary and extraliterary material used in literature may be introduced into the orbit of scientific investigation only when it is considered from a functional point of view.

4. The sharp opposition of synchronic (static) and diachronic cross sections has recently become a fruitful working hypothesis, both for linguistics and for the history of literature; this opposition reveals the nature of language (literature) as a system at each individual moment of its existence. At the present time, the achievements of the synchronic concept force us to reconsider the principles of diachrony as well. The idea of the mechanical agglomeration of material, having been replaced by the concept of system or structure in the realm of synchronic study, underwent a corresponding replacement in the realm of diachronic study as well. The history of a system is in turn a system. Pure synchronism now proves to be an illusion: every synchronic system has its past and its future as inseparable structural elements of the system: (*a*) archaism as a fact of style; the linguistic and literary background recognized as the rejected

*"Problemy izučenija literatury i jazyka," *Novyj Lef.* 12 (1928), pp. 36-37. Translated by Herbert Eagle.

old-fashioned style; (*b*) the tendency in language and literature recognized as innovation in the system.

The opposition between synchrony and diachrony was an opposition between the concept of system and the concept of evolution; thus it loses its importance in principle as soon as we recognize that every system necessarily exists as an evolution, whereas, on the other hand, evolution is inescapably of a systemic nature.

5. The concept of a synchronic literary system does not coincide with the naively envisaged concept of a chronological epoch, since the former embraces not only works of art which are close to each other in time but also works which are are drawn into the orbit of the system from foreign literatures or previous epochs. An indifferent cataloguing of coexisting phenomena is not sufficient; what is important is their hierarchical significance for the given epoch.

6. The assertion of two differing concepts—*la langue* and *la parole*—and the analysis of the relationship between them (the Geneva school) has been exceedingly fruitful for linguistic science. The principles involved in relating these two categories (i.e., the existing norm and the individual utterances) as applied to literature must now be elaborated. In this latter case, the individual utterance cannot be considered without reference to the existing complex of norms. (The investigator, in isolating the former from the latter, inescapably deforms the system of artistic values under consideration, thus losing the possibility of establishing its immanent laws.)

7. An analysis of the structural laws of language and literature and their evolution inevitably leads to the establishment of a limited series of actually existing structural types (types of structural evolution).

8. A disclosure of the immanent laws of the history of literature (language) allows us to determine the character of each specific change in literary (linguistic) systems. However, these laws do not allow us to explain the tempo of evolution or the chosen path of evolution when several, theoretically possible, evolutionary paths are given. This is owing to the fact that the immanent laws of literary (linguistic) evolution form an indeterminate equation; although they admit only a limited number of possible solutions, they do not necessarily specify a unique solution. The question of a specific choice of path, or at least of the dominant, can be

solved only by means of an analysis of the correlation between the literary series and other historical series. This correlation (a system of systems) has its own structural laws, which must be submitted to investigation. It would be methodologically fatal to consider the correlation of systems without taking into account the immanent laws of each system.

The Dominant*

Roman Jakobson

The first three stages of Formalist research have been briefly characterized as follows: (1) analysis of the sound aspects of a literary work; (2) problems of meaning within the framework of poetics; (3) integration of sound and meaning into an inseparable whole. During this latter stage, the concept of the *dominant* was particularly fruitful; it was one of the most crucial, elaborated, and productive concepts in Russian Formalist theory. The dominant may be defined as the focusing component of a work of art: it rules, determines, and transforms the remaining components. It is the dominant which guarantees the integrity of the structure.

The dominant specifies the work. The specific trait of bound language is obviously its prosodic pattern, its verse form. It might seem that this is simply a tautology: verse is verse. However, we must constantly bear in mind that the element which specifies a given variety of language dominates the entire structure and thus acts as its mandatory and inalienable constituent dominating all the remaining elements and exerting direct influence upon them. However, verse in turn is not a simple concept and not an indivisible unit. Verse itself is a system of values; as with any value system, it possesses its own hierarchy of superior and inferior values and one leading value, the dominant, without which (within the framework of a given literary period and a given artistic trend) verse cannot be conceived and evaluated as verse. For example, in Czech poetry of the fourteenth century the inalienable mark of verse was not the syllabic scheme but rhyme, since there existed poems with unequal numbers of syllables per line (termed "measureless" verses), which nevertheless were conceived as verses, whereas unrhymed verses were not tolerated during that period. On the other hand, in Czech Realist poetry of the second half of the nineteenth century, rhyme was a dispensable device, whereas the syllabic scheme was a mandatory, inalienable component, without which verse was not verse; from the point of view of that school, free verse was judged as unacceptable *arrhythmia.* For the present-day Czech brought up on modern free verse, neither rhyme nor a syllabic pattern is mandatory for verse; instead, the mandatory component consists of intonational integrity—intonation becomes the dominant of verse. If we were to compare the measured regular verse of the Old Czech *Alexandriade*, the rhymed verse of the Realist period, and

*From the unpublished Czech text of lectures on the Russian Formalist school delivered at Masaryk University in Brno in the spring of 1935. Translated from the Czech by Herbert Eagle.

the rhymed measured verse of the present epoch, we would observe in all three cases the same elements—rhyme, a syllabic scheme, and intonational unity—but a different hierarchy of values—different specific mandatory, indispensable elements; it is precisely these specific elements which determine the role and the structure of the other components.

We may seek a dominant not only in the poetic work of an individual artist and not only in the poetic canon, the set of norms of a given poetic school, but also in the art of a given epoch, viewed as a particular whole. For example, it is evident that in Renaissance art such a dominant, such an acme of the aesthetic criteria of the time, was represented by the visual arts. Other arts oriented themselves toward the visual arts and were valued according to the degree of their closeness to the latter. On the other hand, in Romantic art the supreme value was assigned to music. Thus, for example, Romantic poetry oriented itself toward music: its verse is musically focused; its verse intonation imitates musical melody. This focusing on a dominant which is in fact external to the poetic work substantially changes the poem's structure with regard to sound texture, syntactic structure, and imagery; it alters the poem's metrical and strophical criteria and its composition. In Realist aesthetics the dominant was verbal art, and the hierarchy of poetic values was modified accordingly.

Moreover, the definition of an artistic work as compared to other sets of cultural values substantially changes, as soon as the concept of the dominant becomes our point of departure. For example, the relationship between a poetic work and other verbal messages acquires a more exact determination. Equating a poetic work with an aesthetic, or more precisely with a poetic, function, as far as we deal with verbal material, is characteristic of those epochs which proclaim self-sufficient, pure art, *l'art pour l'art.* In the early steps of the Formalist school, it was still possible to observe distinct traces of such an equation. However, this equation is unquestionably erroneous: a poetic work is not confined to aesthetic function alone, but has in addition many other functions. Actually, the intentions of a poetic work are often closely related to philosophy, social didactics, etc. Just as a poetic work is not exhausted by its aesthetic function, similarly aesthetic function is not limited to the poetic work; an orator's address, everyday conversation, newspaper articles, advertisements, a scientific treatise—all may employ aesthetic considerations, give expression to aesthetic function, and often use words in and for themselves, not merely as a referential device.

In direct opposition to the straight monistic point of view is the mechanistic standpoint, which recognizes the multiplicity of functions of a poetic work and judges that work, either knowingly or unintentionally, as a mechanical agglomeration of functions. Because a poetic work also has a referential function, it is sometimes considered by adherents of the latter point of view as a straightforward document of cultural history, social relations, or biography. In contrast to one-sided monism and one-sided pluralism, there exists a point of view which combines an awareness of the multiple functions of a poetic work with a comprehension of its integrity, that is to say, that function which unites and determines the poetic work. From this point of view, a poetic work cannot be defined as a work fulfilling neither an exclusively aesthetic function nor an aesthetic function along with other functions; rather, a poetic work is defined as a verbal message whose aesthetic function is its dominant. Of course, the marks disclosing the implementation of the aesthetic function are not unchangeable or always uniform. Each concrete poetic canon, every set of temporal poetic norms, however, comprises indispensable, distinctive elements without which the work cannot be identified as poetic.

The definition of the aesthetic function as the dominant of a poetic work permits us to determine the hierarchy of diverse linguistic functions within the poetic work. In the referential function, the sign has a minimal internal connection with the designated object, and therefore the sign in itself carries only a minimal importance; on the other hand, the expressive function demands a more direct, intimate relationship between the sign and the object, and therefore a greater attention to the internal structure of the sign. In comparison with referential language, emotive language, which primarily fulfills an expressive function, is as a rule closer to poetic language (which is directed precisely toward the sign as such). Poetic language and emotional language often overlap each other, and therefore these two varieties of language are often quite erroneously identified. If the aesthetic function is the dominant in a verbal message, then this message may certainly use many devices of expressive language; but these components are then subject to the decisive function of the work, i.e., they are transformed by its dominant.

Inquiry into the dominant had important consequences for

Formalist views of literary evolution. In the evolution of poetic form it is not so much a question of the disappearance of certain elements and the emergence of others as it is the question of shifts in the mutual relationship among the diverse components of the system, in other words, a question of the shifting dominant. Within a given complex of poetic norms in general, or especially within the set of poetic norms valid for a given poetic genre, elements which were originally secondary become essential and primary. On the other hand, the elements which were originally the dominant ones become subsidiary and optional. In the earlier works of Šklovskij, a poetic work was defined as a mere sum of its artistic devices, while poetic evolution appeared nothing more than a substitution of certain devices. With the further development of Formalism, there arose the accurate conception of a poetic work as a structured system, a regularly ordered hierarchical set of artistic devices. Poetic evolution is a shift in this hierarchy. The hierarchy of artistic devices changes within the framework of a given poetic genre; the change, moreover, affects the hierarchy of poetic genres, and, simultaneously, the distribution of artistic devices among the individual genres. Genres which were originally secondary paths, subsidiary variants, now come to the fore, whereas the canonical genres are pushed toward the rear. Various Formalist works deal with the individual periods of Russian literary history from this point of view. Gukovskij analyzes the evolution of poetry in the eighteenth century; Tynjanov and Èjxenbaum, followed by a number of their disciples, investigate the evolution of Russian poetry and prose during the first half of the nineteenth century; Viktor Vinogradov studies the evolution of Russian prose beginning with Gogol′; Èjxenbaum treats the development of Tolstoj's prose against the background of contemporaneous Russian and European prose. The image of Russian literary history substantially changes; it becomes incomparably richer and at the same time more monolithic, more synthetic and ordered, than were the *membra disjecta* of previous literary scholarship.

However, the problems of evolution are not limited to literary history. Questions concerning changes in the mutual relationship between the individual arts also arise, and here the scrutiny of transitional regions is particularly fruitful; for example, an analysis of a transitional region between painting and poetry, such as illustration, or an analysis of a border region between music and poetry, such as the *romance*.

Finally, the problem of changes in the mutual relationship between the arts and other closely related cultural domains arises, especially with respect to the mutual relationship between literature and other kinds of verbal messages. Here the instability of boundaries, the change in the content and extent of the individual domains, is particularly illuminating. Of special interest for investigators are the transitional genres. In certain periods such genres are evaluated as extraliterary and extrapoetical, while in other periods they may fulfill an important literary function because they comprise those elements which are about to be emphasized by belles lettres, whereas the canonical literary forms are deprived of these elements. Such transitional genres are, for example, the various forms of *littérature intime*—letters, diaries, notebooks, travelogues, etc.—which in certain periods (for example, in the Russian literature of the first half of the nineteenth century) serve an important function within the total complex of literary values.

In other words, continual shifts in the system of artistic values imply continual shifts in the evaluation of different phenomena of art. That which, from the point of view of the old system, was slighted or judged to be imperfect, dilettantish, aberrant, or simply wrong or that which was considered heretical, decadent, and worthless may appear and, from the perspective of a new system, be adopted as a positive value. The verses of the Russian late-Romantic lyricists Tjutčev and Fet were criticized by the Realist critics for their errors, their alleged carelessness, etc. Turgenev, who published these poems, thoroughly corrected their rhythm and style in order to improve them and adjust them to the extant norm. Turgenev's editing of these poems became the canonical version, and not until modern times have the original texts been reinstated, rehabilitated, and recognized as an initial step toward a new concept of poetic form. The Czech philologist J. Král rejected the verse of Erben and Čelakovský as erroneous and shabby from the viewpoint of the Realistic school of poetry, whereas the modern era praises these verses precisely for those features which had been condemned in the name of the Realistic canon. The work of the great Russian composer Musorgskij did not correspond to the requirements of musical instrumentation current in the late nineteenth century, and the contemporaneous master of compositional technique, Rimskij-Korsakov, refashioned them in accordance with the prevalent taste of his epoch; however, the new generation has promoted the path-breaking values saved by Musorgskij's "unsophisticatedness" but temporarily suppressed Rimskij-Korsakov's corrections and has naturally removed those retouchings from such compositions as "Boris Godunov."

The shifting, the transformation, of the relationship between individual artistic components became the central issue in Formalist investigations. This aspect of Formalist analysis in the field of poetic language had a pioneering significance for linguistic research in general, since it provided important impulses toward overcoming and bridging the gap between the diachronic historical method and the synchronic method of chronological cross section. It was the Formalist research which clearly demonstrated that shifting and change are not only historical statements (first there was A, and then A_1 arose in place of A) but that shift is also a directly experienced synchronic phenomenon, a relevant artistic value. The reader of a poem or the viewer of a painting has a vivid awareness of two orders: the traditional canon and the artistic novelty as a deviation from that canon. It is precisely against the background of that tradition that innovation is conceived. The Formalist studies brought to light that this simultaneous preservation of tradition and breaking away from tradition form the essence of every new work of art.

Part II

On the Boundary between Studies of Folklore and Literature
Roman Jakobson
Petr Bogatyrev

Fairy Tale Transformations
Vladimir Propp

On the Boundary between Studies of Folklore and Literature*

Roman Jakobson
Petr Bogatyrev

1. Regardless of how close the genetic ties between folklore and literature may be, there are essential structural differences between these two forms of verbal creativity.

a. There is a difference in content between the concept of "the birth of a literary work" and the concept of "the birth of a folklore work." The point at which an author puts down his completed piece of writing is the moment of birth of a literary work; this is the type of creativity most often encountered by the student of literature. By analogy, he is inclined to consider the birth of a work in folklore to be the first expression of that work by some person. In fact, however, the work belongs to folklore only from the moment it is adopted by the community. Just as individual neologisms cannot be considered changes in the given language (*la langue*, in the Sausurrian sense) until they have entered into general usage, and thereby have become socialized, likewise a folklore work is only that which has been sanctioned and adopted by a given community. Preliminary censorship by the community is a prerequisite for the existence of a folklore work. All those products of individual creativity which are denied socialization by the community do not become facts of folklore: they are condemned to obliteration. On the other hand, literary works not adopted by the community continue to exist and may be sanctioned by succeeding generations (for example, the works of the so-called *poètes maudits* as Lautréamont, Norwid, etc.).

b. There is a difference in content between the concept of "the existence of a literary work" and the concept of "the existence of a folklore work" (and correspondingly a difference between literary and folklore continuity). A folklore work is extra-individual and exists only potentially; it is only a complex of established norms and stimuli; it is a skeleton of actual traditions which the implementers embellish with the tracery of individual creation, in much the same way as the producers of a verbal message (*la parole*, in the Sausurrian sense) act with respect to the verbal code (*la langue*). A literary work is objectivized, it exists concretely apart from the reciter. Each subsequent reader or reciter returns directly to the work. Although the interpretation of previous reciters can be taken into account, this is only one of the components in the reception of the work; whereas for a folklore work the only path leads from implementer to imple-

*"K probleme razmeževanija fol'kloristiki i literaturovedenija," (1929); first published in *Lud Słowiański*, II 1931, pp. 230-233. Translated by Herbert Eagle.

menter. If all bearers of a given folklore tradition die, then a resurrection of that tradition is no longer possible; whereas, on the contrary, the reactualization of the literary works of a distant past is not uncommon, even when such works may have temporarily lost their vitality.

c. The orientations of the creative personality in literary as compared with folklore life are different. A lack of correspondence between the demands of the social milieu and a literary work may be the result of an author's blunder, or it may be the premeditated intention of an author who has in mind a transformation of the demands of the milieu, that is, the literary reeducation of the environment. In the realm of folklore, the unconditional rule of preliminary censorship, condemning any conflict of a work to fruitlessness if censored, results in the formation of a special class of participants in poetic art; it imposes on the creative personality a prohibition against any attempt to overcome censorship.

2. A revision of the fundamental concepts in folklore studies leads to a partial rehabilitation of the Romantic conception of folklore.

a. The Romantics were correct in emphasizing the collective nature of oral-poetic creativity and in comparing it with linguistic creativity.

b. The Romantic thesis concerning the originality of folklore is erroneous in its genetic aspect (since folklore is rich in borrowings from literature) but is correct from the functional point of view. From this standpoint, what is essential is not the extrafolklore source but rather the selection, the transformation, and the new interpretation of the borrowed material against its new background. The transformation of a work of so-called "monumental art" into so-called "primitive art" is not passive reproduction—it is a creative act.

c. A typical assertion of the Romantics and the so-called idealistic school (Naumann and others) is the thesis that collective creativity can only be fulfilled by a community lacking individualistic tendencies. This thesis is incorrect, as is any straightforward projection of the social act on the mind of the community (for example the transition from linguistic forms to forms of thought). Collective and individual creativity may coexist in one and the same society as functionally different forms of activity.

3. The demarcation of folklore studies and literary scholarship leads to a set of specific problems to be investigated:

a. In analyzing the forms of folklore, one must beware of the mechanical application of methods and concepts obtained in the elaboration of literary history. For example, the essential functional difference between literary and folklore verse, or the difference between a literary text and a recording of a folklore work must be taken into account.

b. The typology of folklore forms must be built independently of the typology of literary forms. For example, compare the limited set of fairy tale plots typical of folklore with the diversity of plot characteristic of literature. Like structural linguistic laws, the general laws of poetic composition which result in a spontaneous likeness of plots are much more uniform and strict in their application to collective creativity than in regard to individual creativity.

c. The immediate problem facing synchronic studies of folklore is the characterization of the system of poetic forms which make up the actual repertoire of a given community (geographic, ethnic, professional, coeval, or other similar unions). The relationship of the forms within the system, their hierarchy, and the degree of productivity of each are to be investigated.

1

The study of the fairy tale may be compared in many respects to that of organic formation in nature. Both the naturalist and the folklorist deal with species and varieties which are essentially the same. The Darwinian problem of the origin of species arises in folklore as well. The similarity of phenomena both in nature and in our field resists any direct explanation which would be both objective and convincing. It is a problem in its own right. Both fields allow two possible points of view: either the internal similarity of two externally dissimilar phenomena does not derive from a common genetic root—the theory of spontaneous generation—or else this morphological similarity does indeed result from a known genetic tie—the theory of differentiation owing to subsequent metamorphoses or transformations of varying cause and occurrence.

In order to resolve this problem, we need a clear understanding of what is meant by similarity in fairy tales. Similarity has so far been invariably defined in terms of a plot and its variants. We find such an approach acceptable only if based upon the idea of the spontaneous generation of species. Adherents to this method do not compare plots; they feel such comparison to be impossible or, at the very least, erroneous.[1] Without our denying the value of studying individual plots and comparing them solely from the standpoint of their similarity, another method, another basis for comparison may be proposed. Fairy tales can be compared from the standpoint of their composition or structure; their similarity then appears in a new light.[2]

We observe that the actors in the fairy tale perform essentially the same actions as the tale progresses, no matter how different from one another in shape, size, sex, and occupation, in nomenclature and other static attributes. This determines the relationship of the constant factors to the variables. The functions of the actors are constant; everything else is a variable. For example:

1. The king sends Ivan after the princess; Ivan departs.
2. The king sends Ivan after some marvel; Ivan departs.
3. The sister sends her brother for medicine; he departs.
4. The stepmother sends her stepdaughter for fire; she departs.
5. The smith sends his apprentice for a cow; he departs.

The dispatch and the departure on a quest are constants. The dispatching and departing actors, the motivations behind the

*"Transformacii volšebnyx skazok," *Poètika*, 4 (Leningrad, 1928), pp. 70-89. Translated by C. H. Severens.

dispatch, and so forth, are variables. In later stages of the quest, obstacles impede the hero's progress; they, too, are essentially the same, but differ in the form of imagery.

The functions of the actors may be singled out. Fairy tales exhibit thirty-one functions, not all of which may be found in any one fairy tale; however, the absence of certain functions does not interfere with the order of appearance of the others. Their aggregate constitutes one system, one composition. This system has proved to be extremely stable and widespread. The investigator, for example, can determine very accurately that both the ancient Egyptian fairy tale of the two brothers and the tale of the firebird, the tale of *Morozka,* the tale of the fisherman and the fish, as well as a number of myths follow the same general pattern. An analysis of the details bears this out. Thirty-one functions do not exhaust the system. Such a motif as "Baba-Jaga gives Ivan a horse" contains four elements, of which only one represents a function, while the other three are of a static nature.

In all, the fairy tale knows about one hundred and fifty elements or constituents. Each of these elements can be labeled according to its bearing on the sequence of action. Thus, in the above example, Baba-Jaga is a donor, the word "gives" signals the moment of transmittal, Ivan is a recipient, and the horse is the gift. If the labels for all one hundred and fifty fairy tale elements are written down in the order dictated by the tales themselves, then, by definition, all fairy tales will fit such a table. Conversely, any tale which fits such a table is a fairy tale, and any tale which does not fit it belongs in another category. Every rubric is a constituent of the fairy tale, and reading the table vertically yields a series of basic forms and a series of derived forms.

It is precisely these constituents which are subject to comparison. This would correspond in zoology to a comparison of vertebra with vertebra, of tooth with tooth, etc. But there is a significant difference between organic formations and the fairy tale which makes our task easier. In the first instance, a change in a part or feature brings about a change in another feature, whereas each element of the fairy tale can change independently of the other elements. This has been noted by many investigators, although there have been so far no attempts to infer from it all the conclusions, methodological and otherwise.[3] Thus, Kaarle Krohn, in agreeing with Spiess on the question of constituent interchangeability, still considers it necessary to study the fairy tale in terms of entire structures rather than in terms of constituents. In so doing, Krohn does not (in keeping with the Finnish school) supply much in the way of evidence to support his stand. We conclude from this that the elements of the fairy tale may be studied independently of the plot they constitute. Studying the rubrics vertically reveals norms and types of transformations. What holds true for an isolated element also holds true for entire structures. This is owing to the mechanical manner in which the constituents are joined.

2

The present work does not claim to exhaust the problem. We will only indicate here certain basic guideposts which might subsequently form the basis of a broader theoretical investigation.

Even in a brief presentation, however, it is necessary before examining the transformations themselves to establish the criteria which allow us to distinguish between basic and derived forms. The criteria may be expressed in two ways: in terms of general principles and in terms of special rules.

First, the general principles. In order to establish these principles, the fairy tale has to be approached from a standpoint of its environment, that is, the conditions under which it was created and exists. Life and, in the broad sense of the word, religion are the most important for us here. The causes of transformations frequently lie outside the fairy tale, and we will not grasp the evolution of the tale unless we consider the environmental circumstances of the fairy tale.

The basic forms are those connected with the genesis of the fairy tale. Obviously, the tale is born out of life; however, the fairy tale reflects reality only weakly. Everything which derives from reality is of secondary formation. In order to determine the origins of the fairy tale, we must draw upon the broad cultural material of the past.

It turns out that the forms which, for one reason or another, are defined as basic are linked with religious concepts of the remote past. We can formulate the following premise: if the same form occurs both in a religious monument and in a fairy tale, the religious form is primary and the fairy tale form is secondary. This is particularly true of archaic religions. Any archaic religious phenomenon, dead today, is older than its artistic use in a current fairy tale. It is, of course, impossible to prove that here. Indeed, such a dependency in general cannot be *proved;* it can only be *shown* on the basis of a large range of material. Such is the first general principle, which is subject to further development. The second principle may be stated thus: if the same element has two variants, of which one derives from religious forms and the other from daily life, the religious formation is primary and the one drawn from life is secondary.

However, in applying these principles, we must observe reasonable caution. It would be an error to try to trace all basic forms back to religion and all derived ones to reality. To protect ourselves against such errors, we need to shed more light on the methods to be used in comparative studies of the fairy tale and religion and the fairy tale and life.

We can establish several types of relationships between the fairy tale and religion. The first is a direct genetic dependency, which in some cases is patently obvious, but which in other cases requires special historical research. Thus, if a serpent is encountered both in the fairy tale and in religion, it entered the fairy tale by way of religion, not the other way around.

However, the presence of such a link is not obligatory even in the case of very great similarity. Its presence is probable only when we have access to direct cult and *ritual* material. Such ritual material must be distinguished from a combination of religious and *epic* material. In the first case, we can raise the question of a direct kinship along descending lines, analogous to the kinship line of fathers and children; in the second case we can speak only of parallel kinship or, to continue the analogy, the kinship of brothers. Thus the story of Samson and Delilah cannot be considered the prototype of the fairy tale resembling their story: both the fairy tale and the Biblical text may well go back to a common source.

The primacy of cult material should likewise be asserted with a certain degree of caution. Nonetheless, there are instances when this primacy may be asserted with absolute confidence. True, evidence is frequently not found in the document itself but in the concepts which are reflected there and which underlie the fairy tale. But we are often able to form our judgment about the concepts only by means of the documents. For example, the Rig-Veda, little studied by folklorists, belongs to such sources of the fairy tale. If it is true that the fairy tale knows approximately one hundred and fifty constituents, it is noteworthy that the Rig-Veda contains no fewer than sixty. True, their use is lyrical rather than epic, but it should not be forgotten that these are hymns of high priests, not of commoners. It is doubtless true that in the hands of the people (shepherds and peasants) this lyric took on features of the epic. If the hymn praises Indra as the serpent-slayer (in which case the details sometimes coincide perfectly with those of the fairy tale), the people were able in one form or another to *narrate* precisely how Indra killed the serpent.

Let us check this assertion with a more concrete example. We readily recognize Baba-Jaga and her hut in the following hymn:

Mistress of the wood, mistress of the wood, whither do you vanish? Why do you not ask of the village? Are you afraid then?

When the hue and cry of birds bursts forth, the mistress of the wood imagines herself a prince riding forth to the sound of cymbals.

Cattle seem to be grazing on the edge of the woods. Or is it a hut which stands darkly visible there? In the night is heard a squeaking and creaking as of a heavy cart. It is the mistress of the wood.

An unseen voice calls to the cattle. An ax rings out in the woods. A voice cries out sharply. So fancies the nocturnal guest of the mistress of the wood.

The mistress of the wood will do no harm unless alarmed. Feed on sweet fruits and peacefully sleep to full contentment.

Smelling of spices, fragrant, unsowing but ever having plenty, mother of the wild beasts, I praise the mistress of the wood.

We have certain fairy tale elements here: the hut in the woods, the reproach linked with inquiry (in the fairy tale it is normally couched in the form of direct address), a hospitable night's rest (she provides food, drink, and shelter), a suggestion of the mistress of the wood's potential hostility, an indication that she is the mother of the wild beasts (in the fairy tale she calls them together); missing are the chicken legs of her hut as well as any indication of her external appearance, etc. One small detail presents a remarkable coincidence: wood is apparently being chopped for the person spending the night in the forest hut. In Afanas'ev (No. 99)* the father, after leaving his daughter in the hut, straps a boot last to the wheel of his cart. The last clacks loudly, and the girl says: *Se mij baten'ka drovcja rubae* [Me pa be a-choppin' wood].

Furthermore, all of these coincidences are not accidental, for they are not the only ones. These are only a few out of a great many precise parallels between the fairy tale and the Rig-Veda.

The parallel mentioned cannot, of course, be viewed as proof that our Baba-Jaga goes back to the Rig-Veda. One can only stress that on the whole the line proceeds from religion to the fairy tale,

*All references to Afanas'ev have been adjusted to the 1957 edition of *Narodnye russkie skazki A. N. Afanas'eva* (Moscow, 1957).

not conversely, and that it is essential here to initiate accurate comparative studies.

However, everything said here is true only if religion and the fairy tale lie at a great chronological distance from each other, if, for example, the religion under consideration has already died out, and its origin is obscured by the prehistoric past. It is quite a different matter when we compare a living religion and a living fairy tale belonging to one and the same people. The reverse situation may occur, a dependency which is impossible in the case of a dead religion and a modern fairy tale. Christian elements in the fairy tale (the apostles as helpers, the devil as spoiler) are *younger* than the fairy tale, not older, as in the preceding example. In point of fact, we really ought not to call this relationship the reverse of the one in the preceding case. The fairy tale derives from ancient religions, but modern religions do not derive from the fairy tale. Modern religion does not create the fairy tale but merely *changes* its material. Yet there are probably isolated examples of a truly reversed dependency, that is, instances in which the elements of religion are derived from the fairy tale. A very interesting example is in the Western Church's canonization of the miracle of St. George the Dragon Slayer. This miracle was canonized much later than was St. George himself, and it occurred despite the stubborn resistance of the Church.[4] Because the battle with the serpent is a part of many pagan religions, we have to assume that it derives precisely from them. In the thirteenth century, however, there was no longer a living trace of these religions, only the epic tradition of the people could play the role of transmitter. The popularity of St. George on the one hand and his fight with the dragon on the other caused his image to merge with that of the dragon fight; the Church was forced to acknowledge the completed fusion and to canonize it.

Finally, we may find not only direct genetic dependency of the fairy tale on religion, not only parallelism and reversed dependency, but also the complete absence of any link despite outward similarity. Identical concepts may arise independently of one another. Thus the magic steed is comparable with the holy steeds of the Teutons and with the fiery horse Agni in the Rig-Veda. The former have nothing in common with Sivka-Burka, while the latter coincides with him in all respects. The analogy may be applied only if it is more or less complete. Heteronymous phenomena, however similar, must be excluded from such comparisons.

Thus the study of *basic* forms necessitates a comparison of the fairy tale with various religions.

Conversely, the study of *derived* forms in the fairy tale shows how it is linked with reality. A number of transformations may be explained as the intrusions of reality into the fairy tale. This forces us to clarify the problem concerning the methods to be used in studying the fairy tale's relationship to life.

In contrast to other types of tales (the anecdote, the novella, the fable, and so on), the fairy tale shows a comparatively sparse sprinkling of elements from real life. The role of daily existence in creating the fairy tale is often overrated. We can resolve the problem of the fairy tale's relationship to life only if we remember that artistic realism and the presence of elements from real life are two different concepts which do not always overlap. Scholars often make the mistake of searching for facts from real life to support a realistic narrative.

Nikolaj Lerner, for example, takes the following lines from Puškin's "Bova":

This is really a golden Council,
No idle chatter here, but deep thought:
A long while the noble lords all thought.
Arzamor, old and experienced,
All but opened his mouth (to give counsel,
Perhaps, was the old greybeard's desire),
His throat he loudly cleared, but thought better
And in silence his tongue did bite
[All the council members keep silent and begin to drowse.]

and comments:

> In depicting the council of bearded senility we may presume the poem to be a satire on the governmental forms of old Muscovite Russia. . . . We note that the satire might have been directed not only against Old Russia but against Puškin's Russia as well. The entire assembly of snoring 'thinkers' could easily have been uncovered by the young genius in the society of his own day.

In actual fact, however, this is strictly a *fairy tale* motif. In Afanas′ev (for example, in No. 140) we find: "He asked once—the boyars were silent; a second time—they did not respond; a third time—not so much as half a word." We have here the customary scene in which the supplicant entreats aid, the entreaty usually occurring three times. It is first directed to the servants, then to the boyars (clerks, ministers), and third to the hero of the story. Each party in this triad may likewise be trebled in its own right. Thus we are not dealing with real life but with the amplification and specification (added names, etc.) of a folklore element. We would be making the same mistake if we were to consider the Homeric image of Penelope and the conduct of her suitors as corresponding to the facts of life in ancient Greece and to Greek connubial customs. Penelope's suitors are *false suitors*, a well-known device in epic poetry throughout the world. We should first isolate whatever is folkloric and only afterward raise the question as to the correspondence between specifically Homeric moments and factual life in ancient Greece.

Thus we see that the problem which deals with the fairy tale's relationship to real life is not a simple one. To draw conclusions about life directly from the fairy tale is inadmissible.

But, as we will see below, the role of real life in the *transformtion* of the fairy tale is enormous. Life cannot destroy the overall structure of the fairy tale, but it does produce a wealth of younger material which replaces the old in a wide variety of ways.

3

The following are the principal and more precise criteria for distinguishing the basic form of a fairy tale element from a derived form:

1. A fantastical treatment of a constituent in the fairy tale is older than its rational treatment. Such a case is rather simple and does not require special development. If in one fairy tale Ivan receives a magical gift from Baba-Jaga and in another from an old woman passing by, the former is older than the latter. This viewpoint is theoretically based on the link between the fairy tale and religion. Such a viewpoint, however, may turn out to be invalid with respect to other types of tales (fables, etc.) which on the whole may be older than the fairy tale. The realism of such tales dates from time immemorial and cannot be traced back to religious concepts.
2. Heroic treatment is older than humorous treatment. This is essentially a frequent variant of the preceding case. Thus the idea of entering into mortal combat with a dragon precedes that of beating it in a card game.
3. A form used logically is older than a form used nonsensically.[5]
4. An international form is older than national form.

Thus, if the dragon is encountered virtually the world over but is replaced in some fairy tales of the North by a bear or, in the South, by a lion, then the basic form is the dragon, while the lion and bear are derived forms.

Here we ought to say a few words concerning the methods of studying the fairy tale on an international scale. The material is so expansive that a single investigator cannot possibly study all the one hundred elements in the fairy tales of the entire world. He must first work through the fairy tales of one people, distinguishing between their basic and their derived forms. He must then repeat the same procedure for a second people, after which he may proceed to a comparative study.

In this connection, the thesis on international forms may be narrowed and stated thus: a broadly national form is older than a regional or provincial form. But, if we once start along this path, we cannot refute the following statement: a widespread form predates an isolated form. However, it is theoretically possible that a truly ancient form has survived only in isolated instances and that all other occurrences of it are younger. Therefore great caution must be exercised when applying the quantitative principle (the use of statistics); moreover, *qualitative* considerations of the material under study must be brought into play. An example: in the fairy tale "Pretty Vasilisa" (No. 104 in Afanas'ev) the figure of Baba-Jaga is accompanied by the appearance of three mounted riders who symbolize morning, day, and night. The question spontaneously arises: is this not a fundamental feature peculiar to Baba-Jaga, one which has been lost in the other fairy tales? Yet, after a rigorous examination of special considerations (which do not warrant mention at this point), this opinion must be rejected.

4

By way of example we will go through all the possible changes of a single element—Baba-Jaga's hut. Morphologically, the hut represents the abode of the donor (that is, the actor who furnishes the hero with the magical tool). Consequently, we will direct attention not only to the hut but to the appearance of all the donor's abodes. We consider the basic Russian form of the abode to be the hut on chicken legs; it is in the forest, and it rotates. But since *one* element does not yield all the changes possible in a fairy tale, we will consider other examples as well.

1. *Reduction.* Instead of the full form, we may find the following types of changes:

i. The hut on chicken legs in the forest.
ii. The hut on chicken legs.
iii. The hut in the forest.

iv. The hut.
v. The pine forest (Afanas′ev No. 95).
vi. No mention of the abode.

Here the basic form is truncated. The chicken legs, the rotation, and the forest are omitted, and finally the very hut is dispensed with. Reduction may be termed an incomplete basic form. It is to be explained by a lapse of memory which in turn has more complex causes. Reduction points to the lack of agreement between the fairy tale and the whole tenor of the life surrounding it; reduction points to the low degree of relevance of the fairy tale to a given environment, to a given epoch, or to the reciter of the fairy tale.

2. *Expansion.* We turn now to the opposite phenomenon, by which the basic form is extended and broadened by the addition of extra detail. Here is an expanded form: The hut on chicken legs in the forest rests on pancakes and is shingled with cookies.

More often than not, expansion is accompanied by reduction. Certain features are omitted, others are added. Expansion may be divided into categories according to origin (as is done below for substitutions). Some expanded forms derive from daily life, others represent an embellished detail from the fairy tale canon. This is illustrated by the preceding example. Examination reveals the donor to be a blend of hostile and hospitable qualities. Ivan is usually welcomed at the donor's abode. The forms this welcome may take are extremely varied. (She gave him food and drink. Ivan addresses the hut with the words: "We'd like to climb up and have a bite to eat." The hero sees in the hut a table laid, he samples all the food or eats his fill; he goes outside and slaughters some of the donor's cattle and chickens, etc.) This quality on the part of the donor is expressed by his very abode. In the German fairy tale *Hansel and Gretel*, this form is used somewhat differently, in conformance with the childlike nature of the story.

3. *Contamination.* In general, the fairy tale is in a state of decline today, and contamination is relatively frequent. Sometimes contaminated forms spread and take root. The idea that Baba-Jaga's hut turns continuously on its axis is an example of contamination. In the course of the action, the hut has a very specific purpose: it is a watchtower; the hero is tested to see whether or not he is worthy of receiving the magical tool. The hut greets Ivan with its closed side, and consequently it is sometimes called the "windowless, doorless hut." Its open side, that is, the side with the door, faces away from Ivan. It would appear

that Ivan could very easily go around to the other side of the hut and enter through the door. But this Ivan cannot and in the fairy tale never does do. Instead, he utters the incantation: "Stand with your back to the forest and your front to me," or "Stand, as your mother stood you," and so on. The result was usually: "The hut turned." This "turned" became "spins", and the expression, "When it has to, it turns this way and that" became simply, "It turns this way and that." The expression thus lost its sense but was not deprived of a certain characteristic vividness.

4. *Inversion.* Often the basic form is reversed. Female members of the cast are replaced by males, and vice versa. This procedure may involve the hut as well. Instead of a closed and inaccessible hut, we sometimes get a hut with a wide-open door.

5-6. *Intensification and Attenuation.* These types of transformation only apply to the *actions* of the cast. Identical actions may occur at various degrees of intensity. One example of intensification: the hero is exiled instead of merely being sent on a quest. Dispatch is one of the constant elements of the fairy tale; this element occurs in such a variety of forms that all degrees of dispatch intensity are demonstrable. The dispatch may be initiated in various ways. The hero is often asked to go and fetch some unusual thing. Sometimes the hero is given a task. ("Do me the service.") Often it is an order accompanied by threats, should he fail, and promises, should he succeed. Dispatch may also be a veiled form of exile: an evil sister sends her brother for the milk of a fierce animal in order to get rid of him; the master sends his helper to bring back a cow supposedly lost in the forest; a stepmother sends her stepdaughter to Baba-Jaga for fire. Finally, we have literal exile. These are the basic stages of dispatch, each of which allows a number of variations and transitional forms; they are especially important in examining fairy tales dealing with exiled characters. The order, accompanied by threats and promises, may be regarded as the basic form of dispatch. If the element of promise is omitted, such a reduction may be simultaneously considered an intensification—we are left with a dispatch *and* a threat. Omission of the threat will soften and weaken this form. Further attenuation consists in completely omitting the dispatch. As he prepares to leave, the son asks his parents for their blessing.

The six types of transformations discussed so far may be interpreted as very familiar *changes* in the basic form. There are, however, two other large groups of transformations: substitutions and assimilations. Both of them may be analyzed according to their origin.

7. *Internally Motivated Substitution.* Looking again at the donor's dwelling, we find the following forms:

i. A palace.

ii. A mountain alongside a fiery river.

These are not cases of either reduction or expansion, etc. They are not changes but substitutions. The indicated forms, however, are not drawn from without; they are drawn from the fairy tale's own reserves. A dislocation, a rearrangement of forms and material, has taken place. The palace (often of gold) is normally inhabited by a princess. Subsequently this dwelling is ascribed to the donor. Such dislocations in the fairy tale play a very important role. Each element has its own peculiar form. However, this form is not always exclusively bound to the given element. (The princess, for example, usually a sought member of the cast, may play the role of the donor, or that of the helper, etc.) One fairy tale image suppresses another; Baba-Jaga's daughter may appear as the princess. In the latter case, appropriately enough, Baba-Jaga does not live in her hut but in a palace, that is, the abode normally associated with a princess. Linked to this one are the palaces of copper, silver, and gold. The maidens living in such palaces are simultaneously donor and princess. The palaces possibly came about as the result of trebling the golden palace. Possibly they arose in complete independence, having, for example, no connection whatsoever with the idea of the Ages of Gold, Silver, and Iron, etc.

Similarly, the mountain alongside the fiery river is no other than the abode of the dragon, an abode which has been attributed to the donor.

These dislocations play an enormous role in creating transformations. The majority of all transformations are substitutions or dislocations generated from within the fairy tale.

8. *Externally Motivated Substitutions.* If we have the forms:

i. An inn.

ii. A two-storied house,

it is apparent that the fantastic hut has been replaced by forms of dwelling normal to real life. The majority of such substitutions may be explained very easily, but there are substitutions which require a special ethnographic exegesis. Elements from life are always immediately obvious, and, more often than not, scholars center their attention upon them.

9. *Confessional Substitutions.* Current religion is also capable of suppressing old forms, replacing them with new ones. Here we are involved with instances in which the devil functions as a winged messenger, or an angel is the donor of the magical tool, or an act of penance replaces the performance of a difficult task (the donor tests the hero). Certain legends are basically fairy tales in which all elements have undergone supporting substitutions. Every people has its own confessional substitutions. Christianity, Islam, and Buddhism are reflected in the fairy tales of the corresponding peoples.

10. *Substitution by Superstition.* Obviously, superstition and local beliefs may likewise suppress the original material of a fairy tale. However, we encounter this type of substitution much more rarely than we might expect at first glance (the errors of the mythological school). Puškin was mistaken in saying that in the fairy tale:

Wonders abound, a wood-demon lurks,
Rusalka sits in the boughs.

If we encounter a wood-demon in the fairy tale, he almost always replaces Baba-Jaga. Water nymphs are met with but a single time in the entire Afanas′ev collection, and then only in an introductory flourish of dubious authenticity. In the collections by Ončukov, Zelinin, the Sokolovs, and others, there is not a single mention of Rusalka. The wood-demon only finds its way into the fairy tale because, as a creature of the forest, it resembles Baba-Jaga. The fairy tale accepts only those elements which can be readily accommodated in its construction.

11. *Archaic Substitutions.* We have already mentioned that the basic forms of the fairy tale go back to extinct religious concepts. Based on this fact, we can sometimes separate the basic forms from the derived ones. In certain unique instances, however, the basic form (more or less normal in the fairy tale epic) has been replaced by a form no less ancient which can likewise be traced back to a religious source, but whose occurrence is unique. For example, rather than the battle with the dragon in the fairy tale "The Witch and the Sun's Sister" (No. 93 in Afanas′ev), we have the following: the dragon's mate suggests to the prince, "Let Prince Ivan come with me to the scales and we'll see who outweights whom." The scales toss Ivan sky-high. Here we have traces of psychostasia (the weighing of souls). Where this form—well known in ancient Egypt—came from and how it came to be preserved in the fairy tale are questions which need study.

It is not always easy to distinguish between an archaic substitution and a substitution imposed by superstition. Both have their roots (sometimes) in deep antiquity. But if some item in the fairy tale is also found in a living faith, the substitution may be considered as a relatively new one (the wood-demon). A pagan religion may have two offshoots: one in the fairy tale and the other in a faith or custom. They may well have confronted each other in the course of centuries, and the one may have suppressed the other. Conversely, if a fairy tale element is not attested to in a living faith (the scales), the substitution has its origin in deep antiquity and may be considered archaic.

12. *Literary Substitutions.* Literary material shows the same low degree of likelihood of being accepted by the fairy tale that current superstition does. The fairy tale possesses such resistance that other genres shatter against it; they do not readily blend. If clash takes place, the fairy tale wins. Of all the various literary genres, that of the fairy tale is the most likely to absorb elements from legend and epic. On rare occasions the novel provides a substitution; but even in such a case, it is only the chivalric romance which plays a certain role. The chivalric romance itself, however, is frequently a product of the fairy tale. The process occurs in stages: fairy tale → romance → fairy tale. Therefore, works such as "Eruslan Lazarevič" are among the "purest" of fairy tales in terms of construction, despite the bookish nature of individual elements. The *Schwank*, the novella, and other forms of popular prose are more flexible and more receptive to elements from other genres.

13. *Modification.* There are substitutions whose origin is not readily ascertainable. More often than not, these are imaginative substitutions which came into being through the teller's own resourcefulness. Such forms defy ethnographic or historical specification. We should note, however, that these substitutions play a greater role in animal tales and other types of tales than in fairy tales. (The bear is replaced by the wolf, one bird by another, etc.) Of course, they may occur in the fairy tale, too. Thus, as the winged messenger, we find an eagle, a falcon, a raven, geese, and others. As the sought-after marvel, we find a stag with antlers of gold, a steed with a mane of gold, a duck with feathers of gold, a pig with bristles of gold, and so on. Derived, secondary forms are generally those most likely to undergo modification. This may be shown by comparing a number of forms in which the sought wonder is simply a transformation of the sought princess with

golden locks. If a comparison of the basic and the derived forms exhibits a certain descending line, a comparison of two derived forms reveals a certain parallelism. There are elements in the fairy tale having a particular variety of forms. One example is the "difficult task." If the task does not have a basic form, it makes little difference to the fairy tale, in terms of the unity of its construction, what kind of task is assigned. This phenomenon is even more apparent when we compare elements which have never belonged to a basic type of fairy tale. Motivation is one such element. But transformations sometimes create the need to motivate a certain act. As a result, we see a wide variety of motivations for one and the same act. Thus the hero's exile (exile is a secondary formation) is motivated by widely varied circumstances. On the other hand, the dragon's abduction of the maiden (a primary form) is hardly ever motivated externally but is motivated from within.

Certain features of the hut are also subject to modification. Instead of a hut on chicken legs, we encounter a hut on goat horns or on sheep legs.

14. *Substitutions of Unknown Origin.* We have been discussing substitutions from the point of view of their origin, but their origin is not always ascertainable; it does not always appear as a simple modification. Therefore we require a category for substitutions of unknown origin. For example, the little sister of the sun from the fairy tale "Little Sister" (Afanas′ev No. 93) plays the donor's role and may be considered a rudimentary form of the princess. She lives in the "solar rooms." We cannot know whether this reflects a sun cult, or the creative imagination of the narrator, or some suggestion by the collector asking the storyteller whether he knows any fairy tales dealing with a particular subject, or whether thus and so can be found; in such a case, the teller sometimes fabricates something to please the collector.

This places a limitation on substitutions. We could, of course, set up several more varieties which might be applied to a given isolated case. However, there is no need for that now. The substitutions specified here are meaningful throughout the entire breadth of fairy tale material; their application to isolated cases may be easily inferred and demonstrated by employing the transformational types cited.

Let us turn to another class of changes, that of assimilations. By assimilation we understand an incomplete suppression of one form by another, the two forms merging into a single form.

Because assimilations follow the same classification scheme as the substitutions, they will be enumerated in brief.

15. *Internally Motivated Assimilations.* An example occurs in the forms:

i. A hut under a golden roof.

ii. A hut by a fiery river.

In a fairy tale we often meet with a palace under a golden roof. A hut plus a palace under a golden roof equals a hut under a golden roof. The same is true in the case of the hut by the fiery river.

The fairy tale "Fedor Vodovič and Ivan Vodovič" (Ončukov No. 4) provides a very interesting example. Two such very heterogeneous elements as the miraculous birth of the hero and his pursuit by the dragon's wives (sisters) have been drawn together by assimilation. The wives of the dragon, in pursuing the hero, usually turn into a well, a cloud, or a bed and situate themselves in Ivan's path. If he samples some fruit or takes a drink of water, etc., he is torn to pieces. For the miraculous birth, this motif is used in the following manner: the princess strolls about her father's courtyard, sees a well with a small cup, and by it a bed (the apple tree has been forgotten). She drinks a cupful and lies down on the bed to rest. From this she conceives and gives birth to two sons.

16. *Externally Motivated Assimilations.* Take the form:

i. A hut on the edge of the village.

ii. A cave in the woods.

Here we find that the imaginary hut has become a real hut and a real cave, but the solitude of its inhabitant has been preserved. Indeed, in the second instance, the forest element is also preserved. Fairy tale plus reality produces an assimilation which favors real life.

17. *Confessional Assimilations.* This process may be exemplified by the replacement of the dragon by the devil; however, the devil, like the dragon, dwells in a lake. The concept of evil beings of the deep does not necessarily have anything in common with the so-called lower mythology of the peasants; it is often explained as simply one type of transformation.

18. *Assimilation via Superstition.* This is a relatively rare phenomenon. The wood-demon living in a hut on chicken legs is an example.

19-20. *Literary and Archaic Assimilations.* These are encountered even more rarely. Assimilations with the folk epic and legend are of some importance in the Russian fairy tale. Here, however, we are more likely to find suppression rather than the assimilation of one form by another, while the components of the fairy tale are preserved as such. Archaic assimilations require a detailed examination of each occurrence. They do occur, but identifying them is possible only after highly specialized research.

Our survey of the transformation of types can end at this point. It is impossible to assert that absolutely all fairy tale forms will be accommodated by our classificatory scheme, but at any rate a significant number clearly are. It would have been possible to bring in still other types of transformations, such as specification and generalization. In the first case, general phenomena become particularized (instead of the thrice-tenth kingdom, we find the city Xvalynsk); in the latter case, the opposite occurs (the thrice-tenth kingdom becomes simply a "different, other" kingdom, etc.). But almost all types of specification may also be regarded as substitutions, and generalizations, as reductions. This is true, too, for rationalization (a winged steed becomes an earthbound horse) as well as for the conversion of the fairy tale into an anecdote, etc. A correct and consistent application of the types of transformation indicated will give a firmer foundation to the study of the fairy tale in the process of its development.

What is true for the individual elements of the fairy tale is also true for the fairy tale as a whole. If an extra element is added, we have amplification; in the reverse case, we have reduction, etc. Applying these methods to entire fairy tales is important for comparative studies on fairy tale plots.

One very important problem remains. If we write out all the occurrences (or at least a great many of them) of one element, not all the forms of one element can be traced back to some single basis. Let us suppose that we accept Baba-Jaga as the basic form of the donor. Such forms are a witch, Grannie-Behind-the-Door, Grandma-Widow, an old lady, an old man, a shepherd, a wood-demon, an angel, the devil, three maids, the king's daughter, etc.—all may be satisfactorily explained as substitutions and other transformations of Baba-Jaga. But then we encounter a "fingernail-sized peasant with an elbow-length beard." Such a form for the donor does not come from Baba-Jaga. If such a form does occur in a religion, we have a form which has been coordinated with Baba-Jaga; if not, we have a substitution of unknown origin. Each element may have several basic forms, although the number of such parallel, coordinated forms is usually insignificant.

5

Our outline would be incomplete if we did not show a model for applying our observations. We will use more palpable material to exhibit a series of transformations; let us take the forms:

The dragon abducts the king's daughter—
the dragon tortures the king's daughter—
the dragon demands the king's daughter.

From the point of view of the morphology of the fairy tale, we are dealing here with an element which we will call *basic harm.* Such harm usually serves as the start of the plot. In accordance with the principles proposed in this paper, we should compare not only abduction with abduction, etc., but also with all the various types of basic harm as one of the components of the fairy tale.

Caution demands that all three forms be regarded as coordinated forms, but it is possible to suggest that the first is still the basic form. In Egypt we find death conceived of as the abduction of the soul by a dragon. But this concept has been forgotten, whereas the idea that illness is a demon settled within the body lives on today. Finally, the dragon's demand for the princess as tribute reflects a shadowy archaism from real life. It is accompanied by the appearance of an army, which surrounds the city and threatens war. However, we cannot be certain. Be that as it may, all three forms are very old, and each allows a number of transformations.

Let us take the first form:

The dragon abducts the king's daughter.

The dragon is viewed as the embodiment of evil. Confessional influence turns the dragon into a devil:

Devils abduct the king's daughter.

The same influence affects the object of abduction:

The devil abducts the priest's daughter.

The dragon figure has already become foreign to the village. It has been replaced by a dangerous animal that is better known (externally motivated substitution), the animal acquiring fantastic attributes (modification):

A bear with fur of iron carries off the king's children.

The villain merges with Baba-Jaga. One part of the fairy tale influences another part (internally motivated substitution). Baba-

Jaga is the essence of the female sex, and, correspondingly, the person abducted is a male (inversion):

A witch abducts the son of an old couple.

In one of the forms constantly complicating the fairy tale, the hero's brothers carry out a secondary abduction of their brother's prize. The intent to do harm has now been transferred to the hero's kin. This is a canonical form of complicating the action:

His brothers abduct Ivan's bride.

The wicked brothers are replaced by other villainous relatives from reserve members of the fairy tale's cast (internally motivated substitution):

The king (Ivan's father-in-law) abducts Ivan's wife.

The princess herself may take over the same function, and the fairy tale may assume more amusing forms. Here the figure of the villain has been reduced:

The princess flees from her husband.

In all these cases, a human being was abducted, but, by way of example, the light of day may be abducted (an archaic substitution):

The dragon abducts the light of the kingdom.

The dragon is replaced by other monstrous animals (modification); the object of abduction merges with the imagined life of the court:

The mink-beast pilfers animals from the king's menagerie.

Talismans play a significant role in the fairy tale. They are often the only means by which Ivan can attain his goal. Hence it is understandable that they are often the object of abduction. If the action is thus complicated in the middle of the fairy tale, such an abduction is even obligatory as far as fairy tale canon is concerned. This middle moment in the fairy tale may be transferred to the beginning (internally motivated substitution). The abductor of the talisman is often a cheat, or a landowner, and so on (externally motivated substitution):

A shrewd lad abducts Ivan's talisman.
A landowner abducts the peasant's talisman.

The firebird fairy tale represents a transitional stage leading to other forms; here the stolen apples of gold are not talismans (cf. orpine apples). We should add that the theft of the talisman is not possible as a complication at the fairy tale's midpoint unless the talisman has already been acquired. The talisman can be made off with at the beginning only if its possession is properly motivated, however briefly. It is for this reason that the stolen items which appear at the beginning of the tale are not often talismans. The firebird found its way from the middle section of the tale back to the beginning. The bird is one of the basic forms of transporting Ivan to the thrice-tenth kingdom. Golden feathers and similar features are usually attributed to the animal life of the fairy tale:

The firebird steals the king's apples.

In every case the abduction is preserved. The disappearance of a bride, a daughter, a wife, etc., is ascribed to a mythic substratum in the fairy tale. However, this explanation of such a disappearance is alien to modern peasant life, therefore an alien, imported mythology is replaced by sorcery. Disappearance is ascribed to magic spells cast by evil sorcerers and sorceresses. The nature of the villainous deed changes, but its result is still the same: a disappearance entailing a quest (substitution via superstition):

A sorcerer abducts the king's daughter,
Nursie bewitches Ivan's bride and forces her to flee.

Again we see the activity transferred to wicked relatives:

Sisters force the girl's groom to flee.

Turning to the transformations of our second base form (a dragon tortures the king's daughter), we encounter transformations on the same patterns:

The devil tortures the king's daughter, etc.

Here the torture assumes the nature of seizure and vampirism, which can be fully explained ethnographically. Instead of the dragon and the devil, we see again another of the fairy tale's evil beings:

Baba-Jaga tortures the mistress of the knights.

A third variation of the basic form poses the threat of forced marriage:

The dragon demands the king's daughter.

This reveals a number of transformations:

A water sprite demands the king's son, etc.

This same form, morphologically speaking, may lead to a declaration of war without any of the king's offspring being demanded (reduction); a transfer of similar forms to relatives produces:

The sister, a witch, seeks to devour the king's son (her brother).

This case (Afanas′ev No. 93) is of special interest. Here the prince's sister is called a dragoness. Thus we have a classical example of internal assimilation. It points up the need for caution in studying kinship ties in the fairy tale. The marriage of brother and sister and other forms are not necessarily remnants of an old custom; rather, they may be the results of certain transformations, as the above case clearly shows.

The objection may be raised against all of the preceding that anything at all could be fitted into a single phrase having but two components. This is far from true. How would the start of the plot of the fairy tale "Frost, Sun and Wind" and many others fit into such a form? Second, the observed phenomena represent the same constructional element with respect to the over-all composition. Although differently stated, they result in identical patterns in the progress of the plot's: a plea for help may be masked as a departure from home, as a meeting with a donor, etc. Not every fairy tale containing a theft produces this construction. If this construction does not follow, subsequent patterns, however similar, cannot be compared, for they are heteronymous. Otherwise, we have to admit that an element from the fairy tale has entered a construction foreign to the tale. Thus we return to the necessity of making juxtapositions on the basis of identical components and not external similarity.

Notes

1. Antti A. Aarne warns against such an "error" in his *Leitfaden der vergleichenden Märchenforschung* (Hamina, 1913).

2. See Propp's *Morphology of the Folktale* (Austin, 1968).

3. See F. Panzer, *Märchen, Sage und Dichtung* (Munich, 1905). "Seine Komposition ist eine Mosaikarbeit, die das schildernde Bild aus deutlich abgegrenzten Steinchen gefügt hat. Und diese Steinchen bleiben umso leichter *auswechselbar,* die einzelnen Motive können umso leichter variieren, als auch nirgends für eine Verbindung in die Tiefe gesorgt ist." (His composition is a mosaic that has fashioned the descriptive image out of clearly delienated pieces. And these pieces are more readily *interchangeable,* the individual *motifs* can vary more easily, since at no time is there any provision made for an interconnection in depth.) This is clearly a denial of the theory of stable combinations or permanent ties. The same thought is expressed even more dramatically and in greater detail by K. Spiess in *Das deutsche Volksmärchen* (Leipzig, 1917). See also K. L. Krohn, *Die folkloristische Arbeitsmethode* (Oslo, 1926).

4. J. B. Aufhauser *Das Drachenwunder des heiligen Georg* (Leipzig, 1911).

5. For other examples, see I. V. Karnauxova in *Krest'janskoe iskusstvo SSSR* [Peasant Art in the USSR] (Leningrad, 1927).

Part III

Contributions to the Study of Verse Language
Osip M. Brik

Rhythm as the Constructive Factor of Verse
Jurij Tynjanov

The Meaning of the Word in Verse
Jurij Tynjanov

The syllabo-tonic system of versification, as stabilized in Russian poetry since Lomonosov and Tred'jakovskij, is characterized by two basic features: the first is a rhythmic curve which is implemented in the syllabic structure of speech, and the second is a rhythmic series of intensives which coincide with the intensives of ordinary speech. Therefore, in investigating our syllabo-tonic system, we are not dealing with purely rhythmic speech, but with a certain substratum of it which finds expression in a syllabic series.

This should not obscure the basic position that a syllable is only an arbitrary replacement of the rhythmic impulse and is not an entirely adequate expression of it. Recent investigators vaguely felt this lack of correlation between the syllabic series and the rhythmic series, and therefore they developed theories distinguishing meter from rhythm. By meter, they understood various systems of syllable combination, and by rhythm, an element which violated the smooth flow of syllables and created the very essence of verse. Quite simply, rhythm was conceived as any deviation from the laws of meter.

There a peculiar scientific conception arose asserting that verse observed definite laws of meter and yet violated these same laws again and again, and that the real essence of poetry was embodied precisely in these violations.

Understandably, such an approach was weak and incapable of explaining anything. However, the very awareness that the metric system did not explain verse language was well founded; such an awareness proceeded from a sophisticated rhythmic sensitivity which understood the arbitrariness of the metric system; i.e., the syllabic system.

With these essential conditions in mind, we may proceed to the study of our syllabo-tonic verse, operating not with the initial rhythmic series, but with its substratum—the syllabic system.

The Curve of Intensives

Every movement may show an increase and a decrease. The various combinations of amplification and attenuation all demonstrate that amplification occurs at defined intervals, with the result that the over-all curve of intensives displays an increasing or a decreasing character, depending on whether the initial moment of movement is weak or strong.

*A section of Brik's "Ritm i sintaksis." First published in *Novyj Lef,* 1927; republished in *Michigan Slavic Materials,* 5 (Ann Arbor, 1964). Translated by C. H. Severens.

All possible varieties of syllabic verse can be reduced to several elementary forms: either we have a curve which increases across one syllable, or across two; either we have a series of syllables beginning with a weak syllable, or with a strong one. The result is that the curve of syllabic poetry displays any one of five patterns; it is customary to apply to these patterns the traditional terminology of Greek versification: the iamb, the trochee, the dactyl, the anapest, and the amphibrach.

If poetic language were to deal with "transrational" material, that is, if the words constituting the poetic line did not designate anything and did not possess inherent intensives, these fundamental curves would not undergo any further change whatsoever.

Indeed, if by way of experiment we take a random sequence of meaningless syllables and try to read them as iambs, trochees, dactyls, anapest, or amphibrachs, the result will be completely even, uniform systems of syllables, the systems differing from one another only by virtue of the basic distribution of stressed and unstressed elements. But as soon as we begin to read—using one of the five possible patterns—a series of meaningful words, we quickly discover that the initially regular curve of intensives becomes increasingly complex; what results is an entire system of intensives from weak to very strong.

This circumstance was vaguely perceived in works on Russian verse, but all attempts to find the causes of this phenomenon were in vain. Investigators tried to show that this intricate system had evolved from the nature of the syllables themselves; they tried to prove that between the extremes of unstressed and stressed syllables there was a range of intermediate syllables, more or less stressed. However, all these efforts failed to produce anything, since the basic law, according to which there is no such thing as stressed or unstressed syllables but only stressable and unstressable ones, had been ignored.

The entire complex system of stressed and unstressed syllables has disintegrated owing to changes in intonation and manner of declamation. This is understandable, for strength is not an inherent property of a given syllable; rather, it is the effect gained by reshaping the the syllable in accordance with one rhythmic impulse or another.

The complex system of rhythmic intensives in the poetic line cannot be understood without reference to the semantics and the syntax of poetic language. Precisely such semantics and syntax complicate the so-called metric system of intensives.

The Semantics of Rhythm

There are those who suggest that the correct way to read poetry is to read it as we do prose, that is, with the intonation appropriate to ordinary speech. They suggest that the rhythmic system underlying verse is a secondary matter serving only to heighten somewhat the emotive nature of poetic language; for them, the primary element in the structure of verse is the system of normal conversational intensives.

Such an attitude arises whenever rhythmic requirements press ahead too urgently and threaten to turn verse into transrational language. The reaction to such a break in the rhythmic and semantic system results in the demand to strengthen the intonation of ordinary speech.

Hence the two attitudes toward verse which have existed in all times and in all epochs: the one emphasizes the rhythmic aspect of verse; the other, the semantic. This contraction has been especially strong during the transitional moments in the development of poetry.

At various times in poetic culture, various factors have dominated, first one thing, then another, first the rhythmic aspect, then the semantic aspect. The development of poetry may be characterized as a struggle against the prevailing norms of the moment.

Thus, the Puškin school waged a semantically based struggle against the transrational, rhythmic basis of Deržavin. Nekrasov's verse in turn participated in the struggle against the Puškin transrational, while the poetry of the Symbolists was a reaction against the overloaded semantics in the civic poetry of Nekrasov's followers.

Futurist poetry championed transrational verse as exemplified in works by Xlebnikov and Kručenyx and simultaneously reasserted the importance of semantics as exemplified in Majakovskij's poetry.

Normally, the requirement of heightened semantics arises whenever life imposes new thematics and whenever the old verse forms are no longer capable of carrying the new thematics—a situation which develops because the old forms are inseparably linked to a set of semantics which has become irrelevant.

In studying the link between the rhythmic and semantic series, it is best to begin with those epochs when the break had not yet been perceived and poetry still satisfied the requirement of the does so-called unity of content and form. In this sense, the classical period in the history of Russian verse is the Puškin era, with Puškin himself as the central figure.

It is noteworthy that Puškin in the beginning of his literary activity was thought of as a violator of aesthetic tradition, who lowered the high style of poetic language by interjecting coarse semantic material, whereas by the end of his life he was already considered the epitome of pure aesthetics, in which the prominence of semantics had disappeared. Only in the full bloom of his literary career was he acknowledged as a master able in his verse to unite both the requirements of poetic aesthetics and the requirements of semantic relevance.

That period of literary flowering has provided the most suitable basis for analyzing the semantics of rhythm in Russian verse. This explains that involuntary attraction which Puškin exerts on all scholars when they proceed to a study of Russian verse.

The inseparable link between rhythm and semantics is what people usually have in mind when they refer to the classical harmony of Puškin.

Rhythm and Syntax

If we take the two strophes:

1. *I nedoverčivo i žadno* *Smotrju ja na tvoi cvety.*	[Mistrustfully and greedily I gaze upon your flowers.]
2. *I celomudrenno i smelo* *Do čresl sijaju nagotoj.*	[Virtuously and boldly I radiate nakedness to my loins.]

it is immediately clear that they both begin with the same syntactic structure. Moreover, it is evident that the lines

I nedoverčivo i žadno

and

I celomudrenno i smelo

have the same rhythmic pattern and that this rhythmic pattern depends no less on the arrangement of stress and pause than on the syntactic structure. Here we have what I propose to call a rhythmico-syntactic figure.

The rhythmico-syntactic figures should be considered in order to understand the immediate link between rhythm and semantics. If in a given line we can easily replace one particular word by another having the same syntactic pattern, we are changing the semantics without altering the rhythmico-syntactic whole; such a rhythmico-syntactic figure, then, constitutes the basis of verse language.

This does not mean that semantics do not influence rhythm.

The so-called logical stress strengthens the systems of intensives and pauses, but this influence can be easily separated from the original rhythmico-syntactic configuration.

The Neutral Epithet

In the line, *Rusalka plyla po reke goluboj* [Rusalka floated down the river blue], the word *goluboj* has little or no semantic value; its semantics have been deadened, and another adjective might easily have been substituted. This phenomenon I call the neutral epithet.

At various stages in the development of poetry, attitudes toward the epithet may be at variance. One period demands of the epithet a semantic sharpness; it is then that we find verses like those of Benediktov, which were perceived as mad and affected. Conversely, another period demands a semantically modest epithet; it is not to protrude semantically nor is it to do anything more than occupy the necessary rhythmico-syntactic place. Such lines are felt to be smooth, polished, and harmonious.

Such was the general attitude toward Puškin at the height of his creative power. The lightness of line, so often discussed in connection with Puškin and his school, is explained by precisely the semantic modesty of his epithets.

Neutrality may characterize other parts of speech as well: the noun, the verb, the adverb. In the example cited we do not have in each instance a neutral adverb, but when we contrast the two lines, semantic neutrality is the net result. Semantics, so to speak, are in parenthesis.

The Line as a Rhythmico-Syntactic Unit

Syntax is the system of word combination in ordinary speech. Inasmuch as verse language is still subject to the basic laws of prose syntax, the laws of word combination are laws of rhythm. And these rhythmic laws complicate the syntactic nature of verse.

Externally similar syntactic structures of prose and poetry may be semantically very dissimilar. The line *Ty xočeš znat', čto delal ja na vole* [You want to know what I was doing at liberty] will produce a different prose reading than when read as poetry. The language of prose reaches an intonational peak on the phrase *na vole;* poetic language distributes the intonation regularly over the words *znat'*, *delal ja*, and *na vole.*

In the above example, the prose word order requires a certain intonation, one that the rhythmic arrangement of verse language does not permit. This is why the so-called meaningful, prose-reading style applied to poetry destroys its rhythmic arrangement. When reading poetry, people see the usual syntactic forms of prose and, without considering poetry's rhythmic nature, try to phrase them as they do prose language. The result is a prosaically meaningful but a poetically meaningless reading.

Verse is not regulated simply by the laws of syntax, but by the laws of rhythmic syntax, that is, a syntax in which the usual syntactic laws are complicated by rhythmic requirements.

The primary word combination in poetry is the line. The words in a line have combined according to a definite rhythmic law and, simultaneously, according to the laws of prose syntax. The very fact that a certain number of words coexist with the two sets of laws constitutes the peculiarity of poetry. In the line, we have the results of a rhythmico-syntactic word combination. That combination differs from the purely syntactical one in that the words are included in a defined rhythmic unit (the line); it differs from the purely rhythmic combination in that the words are connected semantically as well as phonetically.

The line is the primary rhythmico-syntactic unit; therefore, a study of the rhythmico-syntactic configuration of verse should begin with the line.*

The Rhythmico-Syntactic Cliché

According to a naive conception, the poet at work first writes down his thought in prose, and then rearranges his words to obtain meter. If certain words will not slip into the meter, he continues to manipulate them until they do, or else replaces them with other, more suitable ones. Thus any unexpected words in a poem or any unexpected turn of speech is understood by the naive mind as poetic license, the unavoidable deviation from the rules of ordinary speech, a deviation carried out in the name of poetry. Some poetry lovers forgive the poet this license, considering that he has a right to it. Others take a sterner attitude toward such distortion and are sceptical of the poet's right to mutilate the language in the name of an ill-defined lyrical motivation. The critics are fond of saying that the accomplishment of poetry is precisely its ability to squeeze words into a meter without distorting the normal structure of language.

*We have here omitted the sections entitled "Rhythmico-Syntactic Patterns in Iambic Tetrameter," "Three-Word Combinations," "Normal Word-Combination," and "Rhythmico-Syntactic Parallelism"; pp. 62-70 of M.S.M., No. 5. [Ed.]

Among those who are more mindful of poetry, an opposite notion has lately developed, according to which the creation of poetry, based on the most recent data and observations, proceeds in reverse. The poet first evolves an undefined idea concerning a given lyrical complex having a certain structure of rhythm and sound; this indeterminate structure is then fitted out with meaningful words. Andrej Belyj wrote about it; Blok and the Futurists spoke about it.

In their opinion, the final result of the creative process should possess some kind of meaning, but this meaning does not have to agree with the meaning usually encountered in ordinary speech. What is involved is not the right of the poet to distort the normal usage of language, but the fact that he condescends to the semantic demands of the reader and drapes his rhythmic inspirations with words that are generally understood.

The naive mind awards priority to the normal structure of ordinary speech and views poetic meter as some sort of decorative supplement to it. Belinskij wrote that in order to understand whether a poem is good or bad, the poem has to be recast in prose, and its "specific gravity" will then become clear. For Belinskij, poetic form was only wrapping paper placed around an ordinary speech complex. It is natural that his prime concern was with the meaning of this speech complex, not with its decorative wrap.

Poets and recent investigators begin with the reverse assumption. They take as the basis of verse language what naive persons see only as a decorative supplement. Conversely, they view the semantic potential of a rhythmic complex either as a decorative supplement outright or as an unavoidable concession to nonpoetic thinking. If everyone were to think in transrational images, the semantic reworking of verse language would not be required.

The first concept deprives verse language of all sense and turns the labors of poetry into an unnecessary exercise, into some sort of verbal legerdemain. For Tolstoj, poets were people who could find a rhyme for any word and who could manipulate words readily. On the same theme, Saltykov-Ščedrin said: "I don't see the point in walking a tightrope, and, what's more, curtsying every three steps." A natural conclusion of such an attitude toward poetry is the proposal to discard this decorative legerdemain and write in the language of normal conversation.

The champions of transrational poetic language separate the language of poetry from ordinary speech and transfer it to the realm of arbitrary sounds and rhythmic images. If the semantic structure of verse is not important, if it is not important that the words of a poem mean something, then it is not important that there should be words at all; sounds would be sufficient. Moreover, sounds are not needed either. The whole business could be reduced to certain signs which would evoke appropriate rhythmic impressions. The poet Čičerin went thus far and recently announced that the principal evil of poetry is the word, and that the poet should not use words but a set of arbitrary poetic signs.

Both viewpoints err in considering the unique rhythmico-semantic complex to consist of two distinct elements, one subordinate to the other. In point of fact, these two elements do not exist separately; they originate simultaneously, creating a specific rhythmico-semantic structure different both from that of ordinary speech and from that of a trans-sense sequence of sounds.

The verse line does not result from the struggle between the transrational state and the semantics of ordinary language; rather, the line has its own rhythmic semantics existing independently and developing by its own laws. We can turn any line of poetry into a transrational one, if, instead of meaningful words, we insert sounds which express the rhythmico-phonic arrangement of these words. But, in depriving the line of its semantics, we go beyond the limits of poetic language; further variations of this line will be conditioned not by its verbal composition, but by its tonality. In particular, the systems of stress and intonation will be independent of the stress and intonation of ordinary speech and will imitate the stress and intonation of a musical phrase. In other words, by depriving the line of its semantic meaning, we transfer it from the domain of language to a new domain—that of music. The poetic line thus ceases to be verbal fact.

Conversely, by rearranging words we can deprive any line of poetry of its poetic shape and convert it into a phrase from the sphere of ordinary speech. This is not hard to do, if for certain words we substitute equivalent ones, introduce ordinary conversational intonation, and smooth out the syntactic structure. In performing such an operation, however, we destroy the poetic line as a specific, verbal structure based on those facets of the word which retreat into the background in ordinary speech.

More accurately, the secondary features (sound and rhythm) have a different function in conversational language than in poetic language, and, by introducing the stress and intonation of everyday speech into verse language, we return the line to the domain of ordinary speech. Constructed according to a definite law, the word complex collapses, and its material reverts to the common warehouse.

If the champions of transrational language isolate poetry from language, the supporters of decorative poetry fail to separate it from the common word mass.

The correct point of view sees in poetry a specifically verbal complex created on the basis of special laws which are not identical to those of ordinary speech. Therefore, it is equally incorrect to approach poetry with generalizations about rhythm which do not account for the fact that we are not dealing with neutral material but with elements of human speech. It is also erroneous to approach poetry thinking that we are dealing with the same language as is used in conversation which has simply been externally draped with frills and trim.

Verse language has to be simultaneously understood in terms of its similarities to everyday language as well as in terms of its dissimilarities; its specifically verbal nature has to be understood.

Rhythm as the Constructive Factor of Verse*

Jurij Tynjanov

1

The study of verbal art is beset by two difficulties: The first arises from the material being used, most simply and conventionally labeled speech or the word; the second, from the constructive principle of this art.

In the first case the object of our study is something closely connected to our everyday awareness, and sometimes it even relies on the closeness of this connection. We willingly overlook the nature of this connection, and, arbitrarily bringing to the subject under consideration all the relationships which have become customary in our everyday existence, we make them the starting points in our study of literature.[1] In so doing we lose sight of the heterogeneous, nonidentical nature of the material, which is determined by its role and purpose. We overlook the fact that words have unequal properties which depend on their functions. One property may be stressed at the expense of all the rest, whereupon they become deformed and are sometimes demoted to the rank of neutral props. The grandiose attempt made by Potebnja to construct a theory of literature ranging from the word as ἕν to a complex literary work as πᾶν was doomed to failure, for the essence of the relationship of ἕν to πᾶν lies in the heterogeneity and varied functional significance of this "ἕν." The concept of "material" does not exceed the boundaries of form, being itself formal. It is a mistake to confuse this concept with extraconstructive properties.

The second difficulty is the usual treatment of the nature of the constructive, forming principle as a *static* one. An example will make this clear. Only recently have we outgrown the type of criticism which considers (and judges) the heroes found in novels as living people. Furthermore, we cannot guarantee the eventual disappearance of those heroes' biographies or of attempts to establish historical reality on the basis of them. They are all based on the premise of a *static hero.*

It is fitting at this point to recall Goethe's remarks concerning artistic fiction: the two sources of light in landscapes by Rubens, and the use of contradictory facts by Shakespeare.

> When the artist wishes to make a picture an actual picture, he is free and may resort to a fiction. The artist speaks with the aid of the whole. This is why the light entering from two sides, although it is a distortion and contrary to nature, is superior to nature. Lady Macbeth, who says at one point: "I nursed my children

*"Ritm, kak konstruktivnyj faktor stixa," *Problema stixotvornogo jazyka* (1924), pp. 7-17. Translated by M. E. Suino.

with my breast," and about whom it is subsequently said: "She has no children," is justified, for Shakespeare "was concerned with the impact of every given speech." In general we should not take the word of the poet or the stroke of the painter in too narrow a sense . . . the poet makes his characters say at a given point just what is necessary, just what best produces an impression at that point, and he does not especially worry about or take into account the fact that the results may completely contradict statements made in a different place.

And Goethe explains this from the point of view of the constructive principle of Shakespearian *drama:*

In general it is doubtful that Shakespeare, while he was writing, thought that his plays would be printed, that people would begin counting lines, comparing and contrasting them. It is more likely that he was visualizing a stage. He saw the way his plays moved and lived, how rapidly they passed before the eyes and by the ears of the audience. He saw that there was no time to stop and criticize details, but rather that he must be concerned only with creating the greatest impression at any given moment.[2]

Thus the static unity of the hero (as, in general, every static unity in a literary work) turns out to be exceedingly unstable. It depends entirely on the principle of construction and may fluctuate in the course of a work in whichever manner the over-all dynamics of the work determine, in every individual circumstance, that it should fluctuate. It is enough that there exists a sign of unity which legitimizes the most extreme cases of its actual violation and compels us to consider such cases as *equivalents of unity.*[3]

It is already completely obvious, however, that such unity is not some naively conceived static unity of the hero; it is marked, not by the sign of a static whole, but by the sign of dynamic integration, of completeness. There is no static hero, there is only a dynamic hero. And it is sufficient to have the sign of the hero or his name so that in every given instance we may not observe the hero himself.[4]

This example of the hero reveals the strength and stability of static habits of perception. The same is true in questions about the "form" of a literary work. We have only recently outgrown the well-known analogy: form is to content as a glass is to wine. But all spatial analogies which are applied to the concept of form are important because they only pretend to be analogies. Actually, a static quality closely connected with spatiality invariably creeps into the concept of form (instead of our perceiving spatial forms as dynamically unique). The same is true for terminology. I would venture to say that in nine out of ten instances the word "composition" covertly implies a treatment of form as a static item. The concept of "poetic line" or "stanza" is imperceptibly removed from the dynamic category. Repetition ceases to be considered as a fact of varying strength in various situations of frequency and quantity. The dangerous concept of the "symmetry of compositional facts" arises, dangerous because we cannot speak of symmetry where we find intensification.

The unity of a work is not a closed symmetrical whole, but an unfolding dynamic integrity; between its elements stands, not the static sign of equation and addition, but always the dynamic sign of correlation and integration.

The form of a literary work must be perceived as a dynamic entity.

This dynamism is revealed, first of all, in the concept of the constructive principle. Not all aspects of a word are of equal value; dynamic form is not the result of uniting or merging such aspects (cf. the often-used term "correspondence"), but rather the result of their interaction which enhances one group of factors at the expense of another. In this process the enhanced factor deforms those subordinated to it. Second, the sensation of form in such a situation is always the sensation of flow (and therefore of change) of interrelation between the subordinating, constructive factor and the subordinated factors. There is absolutely no need to introduce a *temporal* connotation into this concept of progress or "unfolding." Flow dynamics may be taken in isolation, outside of time, as pure motion. Art exists by means of this interaction or struggle. Without the sensation of subordination and the deformation of all factors by the factor which plays the constructive role, the fact of art does not exist. ("The *agreement* of factors is a kind of negative description of the constructive principle."—V. Šklovskij.) The sensation of *interacting* factors assumes the necessary presence of *two* features: the subordinating and the subordinated; if the sensation disappears, the fact of art disappears; it becomes automatized.

This process introduces a historical nuance into the concept of "constructive principle" and "material." However, the history of literature convinces us of the stability of the basic principles of construction and material. The Lomonosov system of metrico-tonic verse was a constructive factor. At about the time when Kostrov was writing, this system merged with a specific system of syntax and vocabulary. Its subordinating, deforming role became weaker, the poetic line became automatic, and it required the revolution of Deržavin to break this union and to change it once again into interaction, struggle, and form. The most important point here is that of the new interaction and not simply the introduction of some factor per se. Introducing, for example, a meter which is no longer perceivable (which has been effaced precisely because of a firm, habitual merging of the meter with the accentual system of the sentence and with certain lexical elements), we cause it to interact with new factors; we renovate the meter itself and refresh the new constructive factors contained in it. (Such is the historical role of poetic parody.) This same renewal of the constructive principle in meter results from the introduction of *new* meters.

The basic categories of poetic form remain constant: historical development does not shuffle the cards, nor does it destroy the difference between the constructive principle and the material. On the contrary, it emphasizes the difference. Of course this does not eliminate the challenge of each given situation with its individual correlation of constructive principle and material and with its own problems of individual dynamic form.

Let me introduce an example of the automatization of a certain verse system and the preservation of the constructive importance of the meter by means of breaking down the system. It is interesting that the destructive role in this case was played by the very same octave which, in the works of Apollon Majkov, is a model of the "harmony of the poetic line."[5]

Professor Ševyrev and ex-student Belinskij have long since interred not only our old men but, and do not get angry, you and Batjuškov and even Puškin. The professor stated that our stiff (a fashionable word) meter and our stiff poetic language are good for nothing and *monotonous* (also a fashionable word). As a model he published in the *Moskovskij nabljudatel'* a translation of the seventh canto of *Jerusalem Liberated* in his octaves.[6] I would like you to compare it with the translation by Raič and then tell me whether you find in the meters and poetic language of Ševyrev the musicality, strength, and expressiveness which, in his words, is lacking in the Russian poetry of our times. . . . But it is difficult to outlive the language of our fathers and to begin studying our ABC's all over again.[7]

Everything in this struggle is typical: the attitude of the old poet to "musicality" and in general to verse as a fixed *system*, the assertion that Ševyrev's revolution reverts to the ABC's (elementary fundamentals), and Ševyrev's attempt to establish a dynamic interaction of verse factors at the expense of overshadowed "musicality."

Ševyrev himself printed a provocative epigram on his own octaves:[8]

The rhymester, dissatisfied with Russian verse,
Created in it a daring revolution.
He broke up verses with heretical insolence,
Highhandedly divorced all rhymes.
Iambs and trochees were left to wander freely
And what was the fruit of all these sins?
A torrent of outcries, wind, and thunder,
And the fervent world of harmony was deafened.

Puškin in turn called the automatized poetic line a *canapé* and compared the new, dynamic verse form to a jolting cart speeding over bumpy roads. The "new verse" was good, not because it was more musical or more perfect, but because it reestablished the dynamics in the interrelation of factors. Thus the dialectical development of form, in altering the relationship of the constructive principle with subordinate ones, saves its constructive role.

2

Everything in the preceding section forces us to take stock of the material used in literary study. This is not an indifferent question for the investigator. The choice of material unavoidably gives a certain direction to our investigations, and in so doing it partially predetermines the results, or else limits their significance. It is also clear that the object under investigation (this investigation purports to be examining art) must be the particular specific which distinguishes it from other areas of intellectual activity, and which makes of them its material or tools. Every work of art is a complex interaction of many factors; consequently, the goal of an investigation is to define the specific nature of this interaction. At the same time, if the material is limited and if it is impossible to apply experimental study methods, one can easily assume that the secondary attributes of factors—resulting from their occurring in a given case—are their basic properties. Hence the widespread erroneous conclusions which are subsequently applied to situations in which the factors play an obviously subordinating role.

From this standpoint the most complex and frustrating material for study turns out to be superficially the easiest and simplest: the area of motivated art. Motivation in art is the justification of some single factor vis-à-vis all the others, the agreement of this factor with all the others (Šklovskij, Èjxenbaum). Each factor is motivated by means of its connections with the remaining factors.[9]

The deformation of factors is applied evenly. The inner motivation which takes place on the constructive level of the work tones down, as it were, the *specifica* of the factors, making the art work "light" and acceptable. Motivated art is deceptive; Karamzin suggested "giving a new meaning to old words, presenting them in a new form, but so skillfully as to mislead the reader and conceal the novelty of expression from him."[10]

It is just this fact, however, that makes the study of the functions of any given factor the most difficult one to accomplish on such "light" art. Investigation of these functions considers not what is quantitatively typical, but what is qualitatively characteristic; and in those elements shared by other areas of intellectual activity it sees the specific "plus" of art. Therefore, in motivated works of art, the characteristic element is the motivation itself (the obscuring of the plus sign), as a sui generis, negative characteristic (Šklovskij), and not the reverse. In other words, the obscured functions of factors cannot be the criteria of a broad study of literature.

This is justified by the course of literary history. The motivated, "exact," and "light" art of the Karamzin school was the dialectical opposite of Lomonosov's principles, according to which he cultivated the self-sufficient word in his "meaningless," "sonorous" odes. It caused a literary storm, since the smooth and motivated aspects were clearly taken as negative features.[11] Thus was born the concept of "difficult lightness." Batjuškov, opposed to the deliberately "difficult" verse of the ode the verse of *poésie fugitive*, asserted that "light verses are the most difficult." (Cf. his *later* statement: "Who does not write light verse these days?")

In order to appreciate equilibrium, it is necessary to know the functions of the factors which balance out one another. Therefore it would be most fruitful in this connection to examine those phenomena in which a given factor is emphasized (not motivated).

Into the same category belong cases that are combinations or conjugations of factors of one (internally motivated) order with the factors of another alien (but also internally motivated) order–i.e., instances of a mixed order. The simplest example of such a combination is a poetic parody, in which, for example, the meter and syntax of one (particular) order are caused to interact with the vocabulary and semantics of another. If we are familiar with one of these orders, if it has previously been given in some literary work, then, when studying this work, it is as if we were participating in an experiment in which some conditions have been altered while others remain unchanged. In separating the conditions and observing the altered factors, we may draw some conclusions concerning the connection and dependency existing between the two factors (their combinatory functions).

The course of the history of poetry, it seems, also justifies such a choice. When revolutions in poetry are closely scrutinized, they usually turn out to be instances of the conjugation or combination of one order with another (cf. the turning to "younger offshoots," in part to comic forms, as cited by Šklovskij). For example, the Romantics took the so-called *trimètre*, which was used in comic verse in eighteenth-century French poetry, and gave it the vocabulary, semantics, etc., of the elevated style so that it became the "heroic verse form" (Grammont). A less remote example: Nekrasov blended a meter usually used in elevated lyrics (the ballad meter) with the lexical and semantic (in a broad sense) elements of a different order.[12] In our day Majakovskij blended the form of the comic verse with a system of grandiose images (compare his verse forms with those of P. Potemkin and other members of the *Satirikon* group).

Thus, in order to avoid making incorrect theoretical conclusions, we must work on material with a perceptible form. The task of literary history, by the way, is precisely to reveal form. From this point of view, literary history which explains the nature of a literary work and its factors is in a sense dynamic archeology.

Of course, the investigation of a feature, not with the aim of explaining its function, but for its own sake (that is, isolated research in which the constructive property is not explained), may be performed on the most diverse material. Even here, however, there are limits which eventually must be considered as tacitly assumed boundaries of an order with one vast constructive feature. The study of meter as such, for example, cannot on an equal basis be applied to verse material and to the material of newspaper articles.

It is easiest to elucidate the constructive function of some factor by using literary material of an emphasized or displaced (unmotivated) order. Motivated varieties, having a negative characteristic, are less suitable, just as it is harder to observe the functions of the formal elements of a *word* when the word has a negative formal characteristic.[13]

Yet another preliminary observation. The constructive principle may be connected through firm associations with the typical system of its application. But the concept of the constructive principle does not coincide with the concept of the systems in which it is applied. Before us lies the infinite variety of literary phenomena—the multiplicity of systems of interacting factors. There are generalizing lines and divisions embracing a vast quantity of phenomena.

That factor, that condition which is observed in the most extreme examples of one order and without which an item passes into another order, is the necessary and sufficient condition for the constructive principle of the given order.

And if we do not take into account these extreme cases which are on the borderlines of the order, we may easily equate the constructive principle with the system of its application.

However, in this system not everything is equally necessary or equally sufficient for assigning a particular phenomenon to one order or another of the construction.

The constructive principle is recognized, not in the maxium of conditions which comprise it, but in their minimum, for evidently these minimal conditions are more closely connected with a given construction, and therefore we must search in them for answers relating to the specific character of construction.

Notes

1. In stating the problem in this way, of course, I am not objecting to the "connection of literature and life." I simply doubt that the question has been properly posed. Can we say "life and art" when art is also "life"? Do we need to look for some special utilitarianism of "art" if we do not look for a utilitarianism of "life"? The unique nature and inner logic of art as compared to everyday existence, science, etc.—that is another matter. How many misunderstandings have arisen among cultural historians because they took an "object of art" as an "object of everyday life"! How many historical "facts" were established which, when examined closely, turned out to be traditional literary facts into which legend had merely inserted historical names! Whenever everyday life enters literature, it becomes itself literature and should be evaluated as a literary fact. It is interesting to trace the importance of everyday artistic existence in periods of literary crisis and revolution, when the leading literary tendency, acclaimed by all, falls to pieces or is exhausted—and a new direction has not yet been recognized. In such periods everyday artistic existence itself becomes temporarily literature and takes its place. When the lofty traditions of Lomonosov collapsed (in the Karamzin period), petty items of domestic literary life—correspondence with friends and ephemeral jokes—became literary facts. And this is just the point; the fact of everyday life was promoted to the rank of literary fact. In an era when lofty genres dominated, this same domestic correspondence was only an element of daily existence having no direct relation to literature.

2. J. P. Eckermann, *Gespräche mit Goethe,* 3 (Leipzig, 1885), pp. 108-111. Also in J. W. von Goethe, *Conversations with Eckermann,* Everyman's Library.

3. In Gogol′'s "The Nose," its entire essence lies in the play with *equivalents for the hero*. Major Kovalev's nose from time to time becomes "the Nose," strolling along the Nevskij Prospekt, etc. "Nose" decides to dash off to Riga but is captured by a policeman while entering a mail coach. Then *he*(!) is returned, wrapped in a rag, to his owner. The remarkable aspect of this grotesque situation is the equivalence of the hero, the equality between the nose and the "Nose," which is never interrupted even for a moment. It is only the play on this double plane that is grotesque. The principle of unity is itself not violated, and herein lies the effect. Thus the reference to the grotesque nature of the work does not deprive the example of its typicality. In any case, Goethe's illustrations do not refer to the province of the grotesque.

4. Often the sign or the names themselves are the most concrete aspects of the hero. Consider the onomatopoetic names in Gogol′. The concreteness which is a result of the unusual articulatory expressiveness of a name is very effective, but the specificity of the concreteness is instantly revealed when we attempt to translate it into another specific concreteness. Illustrations of Gogol′'s works or reliefs on monuments to Gogol′ destroy the Gogolian concreteness. This does not mean that they cannot of themselves be concrete.

5. Using the history of the Russian octave as an example, we can trace the way in which, in various periods, one and the same literary phenomenon fulfilled different functions. In the 1820s the archaist Katenin advocated the octave. It was for him a necessary stanza for long epic genres. In the 1830s the octave played, not a generic, but rather a purely stylistic role.

6. *Moskovskij nabljudatel′*, M. 1835, part III, p. 6.

7. *Pis′ma I. I. Dmitrieva k kn. Vjazemskomu* [Letters of I. I. Dmitriev to Prince Vjazemskij], *Starina i Novizna* (St. Petersburg, 1898), II, p. 182.

8. Barsukov, *Žizn′ i trudy M. P. Pogodina* (St. Petersburg, 1890), III, pp. 304-306.

9. Thus V. Šklovskij properly employs the concept of motivation according to which some motive which is in accord with other motives is initially introduced into the plot.

10. Karamzin, *Polnoe sobranie sočinenij,* III (St. Petersburg, 1848), III, p. 528.

11. See S. Marin on Karamzin: "Let him call a military record a poem" (Reading in *Beseda Ljubitelej Russkogo Slova* (St. Petersburg, 1811), III, p. 121. The exact word of the Karamzinists was a service record for their time and was perceived by its exactness. The very smoothness of the word was a formal element, albeit a negative one. Even more characteristic is the remark on I. I. Dmitriev by one of the leading Karamzinists, P. Makarov: "In order to appreciate this gracious Poet on his own merits we must be aware of the difficulties which he has overcome. We must notice how he strove to conceal them beneath the coloration of lightness. We must discern places which would have turned out worse had another written them." (*Sočinenija i perevody I. Dmitrieva,* P. Makarov, t. I, č, II, 2nd ed., 1817, p. 74.) Only with the disappearance of these conditions, when art had become automatized, could this smoothness appear to be something self-evident, and only then could there arise the idea of seeing in this negative feature of the poetic word its positive feature.

12. See my article: "Stixovaja forma Nekrasova," in *Letopis Doma Literatorov,* 1921, No. 4.

13. We can see the importance of the latter requirement in the classic study by Grammont: *Le vers français, ses moyens d'expression, son harmonie.* Here he strives to explain the expressive function of verse. Starting exclu-

sively from motivated material, he arrived at conclusions whose very essence is arguable.

The conclusions concern mainly the illustrative role of rhythm and harmony. Rhythm and harmony are expressive means when, and only when, they emphasize the sense of the poetic text, that is, when they are motivated. Yet is is clear that here the expressiveness of rhythm completely coincides with the expressiveness of the text, so that it is incapable of being observed. So, essentially, what is being studied is not the question of rhythmic expressiveness, but the extent to which rhythm is semantically justified (and even, if you please, the extent to which a certain kind of semantics requires a certain rhythm: cf. the analysis of Hugo's ode: "Napoleon I"). Taking a motivated instance as a *typical* one, Grammont considers it to be the *norm;* therefore he explains all cases of unmotivated rhythm as being incorrect and erroneous. For this reason he considers all modern free verse, for example, a mistake, since here the changes in rhythmic groups do not coincide with the semantic changes. It is natural, when the question is posed in such a way, that poetic rhythm is given, beforehand, functions which it has in general speech activity (emotionality and communicativeness).

The Meaning of the Word in Verse*

Jurij Tynjanov

1

A word does not have just one definite meaning. It is a chameleon, and every time it occurs there appear not only various shadings but even various colors.

"Word" as an abstraction resembles a vessel that is filled anew with each appearance, depending on the lexical structure in which it occurs and on the functions borne by each aspect of speech. It is a sort of cross section of these various lexical and functional structures.

It is common to find a dualism in any definition of the several areas of word usage. The terms "usual" and "occasional" in Paul, or "meaning" and "representation" in Potebnja—in both cases result from this dualism which is: the word outside a verbal context vs. the word within a verbal context. B. Erdmann contrasts *Sachvorstellung* and *Bedeutungsvorstellung*. This is another example of the same dualism, where the first element corresponds to the word meaning in a sentence, and the second to the meaning of the word in isolation.[1]

The word does not exist outside of a sentence. An isolated word is not found in a nonphrasal environment. Rather it is found in a *different* environment from the word in a sentence. If we pronounce an isolated "dictionary" word, we do not obtain the "basic word," a pure, lexical word, but simply a word in new circumstances as contrasted to contextual circumstances. This is why semantic "word" experiments, in which isolated words are uttered in order to elicit associations from an audience, are only experiments with unsuitable materials, and their results cannot be extended to other areas.

The terminological dualism noted above ought to be used in a different manner. In analyzing a series of word usages, we encounter the *unity of the lexical category*.

Take the Russian "word" *zemlja* [earth, soil, land, ground]. †

1. *Zemlja* and Mars; heaven and *zemlja* (*tellus*).
2. Bury an object in the *zemlja;* black *zemlja* (*humus*).
3. It fell to the *zemlja* (*Boden*).
4. Native *zemlja* (Land).

In this instance there is no doubt that we have different meanings of one "word" in different kinds of usage. And yet, if we say of a

*"Značenie slova v stixe," *Problema stixotvornogo jazyka* (1924). Translated by M. E. Suino.

† Material in brackets [ ] is provided for those readers who do not know Russian.

Martian that he fell onto the ground of Mars—"he fell to the *zemlja*"—it is awkward, even though it is obvious that *zemlja* in the phrase "he fell to the *zemlja*" is far from the meaning of *zemlja* in the other examples. It would also be awkward to say of the soil on Mars "gray *zemlja.*"*

What is happening here? What permits us to say that the word in these very different contexts is *one* word? How can we treat it each time as identical? Because the category of lexical unity is present. We call the presence of this category the basic semantic feature.[2]

Why, in the given context, were we unable to say that the Martian had fallen to the *zemlja*? Why was this usage unsuccessful? Because, in speaking of the Martian, we were always operating on a certain *lexical* level:

Zemlja:
zemlja and Mars
black *zemlja*
fell to the *zemlja*
native *zemlja.*

Speaking of the Martian in various contexts, we always start from the initial meaning. Even when the meaning is different, we have brought in the initial meaning—we are operating on a given lexical level.

This level is possible because the word *zemlja* is always felt to be the same word. Despite the fact that each time it was composed of complex semantic overtones, *secondary features* determined by the nature of the given context and lexical level, the *basic feature* existed in it at all times.

The unity of the lexical category (that is, the presence of the basic semantic feature) is strongly felt in the realization of any context.

Turgenev once wrote to Prince Vjazemskij: "Instead of *protivnikov* [adversaries] you always write *pobornikov,* but this means just the opposite, for *poborat'* means: enable, assist, expedite (cf. all the prayers to our intercessors and to the *pobornikam sil nebesnyx* [minions of the heavenly powers]."[3] Vjazemskij replied: "You are correct, of course. I used *pobornik* incorrectly; *but*

*Note the similarity of this problem to that of the English "earth:"
1. "He affirmed . . . the Moon (to be) an earth" (Cudworth).
2. "Frighted hare fled to cover, or fox to earth" (Defoe).
3. "They kneele, they kisse the earth" (*A Winter's Tale*).
4. "This blessed plot, this earth, this Realme" (*Richard II*).
(*The Shorter Oxford English Dictionary,* 3rd ed. [Oxford, 1966], p. 578.)

in the sense of the language it means what I wish to express . . . . See the *Academy Dictionary:* there you will find *poborat′ kogo* and *poborat′ po kom: Poboroxom vragi Izrailevy* (Maccabees).* So you are right, but I am not completely wrong. I confess *protivnik* is a distasteful (*protivnoe*) word to me, but it can't be helped, and I won't resist (*protivlus′*)."[4]

Thus Vjazemskij used the word *pobornik* instead of *protivnik* and used it in an exactly opposite sense. At the same time, he acknowledged that "in the sense of the language" this word "meant what he wished it to express," while the word *protivnik* was distasteful (*protivno*) to him. How was this possible?

There are two reasons. For Vjazemskij the word *protivnik* was associated with the word *protivnyj* in two meanings simultaneously:

protivnyj: *adversaire*
rebutant.

This was possible since he felt in the word *protivnyj* the category of lexical unity (the basic feature): the word *protivnyj* was felt to be a single lexical word. (If the category of lexical unity had not been present, if it had dissolved into two basic features, then it would have been easy for Vjazemskij to connect *protivnik* with a single meaning of the word *protivnyj*.)

But why did Vjazemskij use the word *pobornik* instead of *protivnik*? He himself admited that *pobornik* was associated with two meanings of *poborat′*. The fact is that the lexical level on which Vjazemskij was operating did not tolerate any connections with the word *protivnyj* in its second sense but easily accommodated any meaning of the word *poborat′*. The lexical level is formed by many conditions, including certain emotional colorations. One such coloration, attached to the second meaning of *protivnyj*, destroyed the coloration of the level in which Vjazemskij was interested (the lofty, oratorical nuances in this instance), while the coloration of *poborat′* exactly matched the desired

*The problem here involves two words, each of which can have two meanings. The Russian *pobornik* is derived from the verb *poborat′* which, when used with the accusative case means "to defeat," or "overcome." When used with the dative case (not the accusative, as Turgenev notes), or with the preposition "*po*" and the prepositional case, it means "to assist," "to fight with someone against a common enemy." Thus *pobornik* potentially can mean either "antagonist" or "ally." *Protivnik* is related to the adjective *protivnyj*, which means either "opposite," "antagonistic," or "repulsive," "distasteful." Vjazemskij was trying to avoid any association with the "distasteful" meaning of *protivnyj*, and hence he selected *pobornik*, although he risked being misunderstood in so doing (Trans.).

coloration. We have assigned this coloration to the category of secondary features.

The awkwardness, then, of using *protivnik*, was attributed to the presence of a primary or basic feature, while the choice of the word depended on secondary features. The basic feature may divide and multiply, and lexical unity may be broken.

Let us examine the following example:

Priroda i Oxota [Nature and Hunting] (title of a journal) "Although he has a noble nature (*priroda*), he has no inclination (*oxota*) for studies."

No one is forcing us to consider the words *priroda* and *oxota* in both phrases as identical or interrelated. Lexical unity is absent, and the words in the two phrases are on two completely different levels.

Thus there is a generalizing line of *unity*, thanks to which a word is recognized as a unit despite its occasional alterations. Dualism may be seen as the fundamental division of the features of meaning into two basic classes: the *basic* semantic feature and *secondary* ones.

One preliminary remark: the concept of basic feature is not in the same relation to the concept of essential word part as the concept of secondary features is to that of the formal part. The basic feature of the word *letaet* [it flies] contains both its essential and its formal attributes. In the phrases "*Čelovek* [Man]—that has a proud sound," and "*Čelovek* [waiter], a glass of tea"—the formal and essential aspects of the word are the same, but the basic features are different.[5]

Here are some examples of secondary features. Let us take the word *čelovek* [man] in some of its uses:

1. "*Čelovek*, that sounds proud. *Čelovek* is you, I, he, *čelovek* is not you, not I, not he" (Gorkij).
2. "In his high position may he not forget the holiest of callings: a man" (Žukovskij).
3. "Yes, he was a man, on all the earth I'll never find such a man."
4. "It is not the job which enhances the man, but the man the job."
5. "A young man stopped by a store window."
6. "Young man" (form of address).
7. "When this same Peter grew up and often, to the advantage of his upbringing and education, had to listen to remarks from members of the troupe in which the word 'man' occurred most frequently, he acquired the nickname of *čelovek*. Half the troupe

was made up of Germans, among whom, just as in some other nationalities, the term 'man' in quotation marks is used as a derogatory term, or at least as an insult" (Oge Madelung, "The Man from the Circus").

8. "The Man from the Restaurant" (a title).
9. *Čelovek–čelo veka* [Man is the forehead of the age].

Let us analyze these examples.

In the word *čelovek* [man] in all the examples (except the sixth and seventh) there is a common *basic* feature of meaning, but in all the examples it varies considerably in *its* (secondary) semantic features.

In the first example, at the beginning of the statement we have a syntactical setting-apart of the word *čelovek*. This setting-apart makes it possible for the object connections of the concept to disappear, as do those features which are determined in the meaning by connections with other members of a statement. The concept of meaning remains. Moreover, the quality of particularizing intonation—the emotional elements which accompany it—acquire great importance. These secondary (in this case, emotional) elements enter into the composition of "meaning."

What follows in the first example supports this coloration and varies it. "Man—is you, I, he." This statement stresses the coloration of "you, I, he" as objects, as a secondary feature. Again the special intonation of "open word-grouping" (Wundt's term) is important, as it considerably weakens the objectness. But this objectness is immediately denied: "Man is not you, not I, not he." This sentence erases the object coloration.

There is another example of semantic coloration in syntactical setting apart (but it is found, not at the beginning, but rather at the end of the grammatical whole), with analogous intonation:

"In his high position may he not forget the holiest of callings: *man.*"

While in the example

"Yes, he was a man, on all the earth I'll never find such a *man. . . .*"

the force of the first complex of secondary features—the intensity of colorations—is transmitted at a distance. If we take the phrase, "on all the earth I'll never find such a man . . ." separately, we will not have the secondary features which were present in the preceding examples of "elevated" word usage (the phrase is close to such phrases as "such a man as he" or "it is impossible to find such a man as he"). Here we have secondary features which are not at all like those found in such phrases as: "Man—that has a proud sound," or "The holiest of callings is—man."

But the phrase we have chosen is preceded by "Yes, he was a man," where the word "man" resembles in its secondary attributes the usage in the phrases: "Man—that has a proud sound," and "The holiest of callings is—man." Here and in the preceding phrase the coloration is so strong and the syntactical bond between the two statements is so strong, that it is preserved in the phrase which follows (which we have just considered separately): "Yes, he was a man, on all the earth I'll never find such a man."

Now let us take the proverb: "It is not the job which enhances the man, but the man the job."

We seem to have a completely different word—and this is because, although the basic feature is preserved, the secondary features which were typical of the preceding examples are absent.[6]

In the group, "A young man stood by a store window," we have an interesting oscillation of the basic feature. It is also partially obscured. It is still possible in this situation to preserve completely the basic feature by establishing the levels of "young man—old man," but the usage of "young man" as a form of address is a much closer approximation. Here both words are closely joined, and the meaning of the attribute has been considerably effaced by the basic feature of the word being defined.[7]

This allows us to use the phrase in addressing any *young* man. (This close bond is also expressed in a facultative sound deformation of the second member: *Čeek* [a conversational realization of *čelovek*].)

This meaning of the particularized group, "young man," may strongly color the undifferentiated group, "A young man was standing by a store window," so that in the word "man," while it retains its autonomy and hence its basic semantic feature, a *group coloration* may arise in the capacity of a secondary feature and somewhat overshadow the basic feature. In the present instance, the secondary feature is no longer emotional.

The effaced basic feature of "man" in the group "young man" plays a group role and is a negative secondary feature (since it affects the entire group). But this process of effacing sometimes allows other, positive, secondary features to emerge. Such is the case with the typical form of address to a waiter in the prerevolutionary era: *Čelovek!* [Waiter!][8] Here the secondary features have completely excluded and replaced the basic feature and in turn have acquired other, emotional, secondary features. (Cf. the excerpt from Oge Madelung.)

Thus, owing to the focus provided by the title, "The Man from the Restaurant," the word "man" may be a play on meanings. "Man" is connected with two opposing orders: "man" equals "Man" (*Čelovek*), where the specific secondary features stand out, and "man" equals *Čeek* where the place of the basic feature is occupied by secondary features of a different, opposite sort than in *čelovek*. So in the title, "The Man from the Restaurant," we have a case of usage in which the place of the basic feature is simultaneously filled by features of two orders, and this mutual crowding makes the meaning extraordinarily complicated.

Now let us examine the pun (by Andrej Belyj): *Čelovek–čelo veka* [Man is the forehead of the age].

What nuances appear in the meaning of *čelovek*? As a result of the pun, there occurs a redistribution of the aspects of substance and form.[9] They also become semasiological, which clearly colors the word *čelovek*. The coloration is not accomplished through the destruction of the basic feature (which would also destroy the pun, which consists primarily in the juxtaposition of two levels), but at the cost of its stability. We have, as it were, a dual semantics with two levels. Each level has a basic feature, and each crowds the other. The oscillation of two semantic levels may cause a partial obscuring of the basic feature and augment the oscillating semantic features, which, in this case, lie mainly in the lexical colorations of the words *čelo* and *vek* (the fact that they, especially *čelo*, belong to the "lofty" level of lexical style). This example shows, therefore, that particulars of usage evoke secondary features which, owing to their instability, we may call oscillating.

It may also happen, however, that the oscillating features completely crowd out the basic semantic feature. It happens that expressivity of speech need not be rendered only through word meanings. Words may have an importance beyond their meanings. They may act as speech elements which bear some other expressive function. In strong, emphatic situations, for example, a number of words may be used without regard to their meanings. But they will have the auxiliary function of "filling up" the intonational pattern with verbal material (cf. swearing or cursing intonations using arbitrary words). Among the frequent manifestations of this type is the strong emphatic-intonational coloration of auxiliary and secondary words which entirely overshadows their basic semantic feature. In place of this basic feature, *oscillating* semantic features may appear.

When this occurs, an unusual importance is imparted to the very *lexical* coloration of the word, and it acts as a constant secondary semantic feature. The more outstanding the lexical aspect of the word, the greater the chance that, when the basic meaning is eclipsed, the lexical coloration of the word and not its basic feature will come to the fore. A typical case is the use of curse words as terms of endearment. These words have the function of filling in the emphatic intonation with verbal material. The basic semantic feature of the words is erased, and the lexical coloration, that is the membership of a given word in a certain category, remains as a connecting link. The sense and effect of using a word whose lexical coloration is the opposite of the intonational coloration lies primarily in the awareness of this opposition. Karl Schmidt notes that, just as one does not pour expensive perfume into an already fragrant vessel in order to smell the odor of the perfume and not the vessel—in the same way curse words are chosen as endearments. A lexical element which contradicts the emotional-intonational coloration makes the endearment that much the more emphatic.

2

Thus the lexical coloration of a word acquires special importance when we investigate the problems of oscillating features which arise in the word. When meaning (and the basic semantic feature) is obscured, its over-all coloration is strengthened. The coloration is owed to the location of the word in a particular verbal context.

Every word is colored by the verbal context in which it is most frequently used. The difference between one context and another depends on the differences in conditions and functions of linguistic activity. Every state and activity has its own special conditions and aims, and, depending on what they are, a word acquires a certain significance for these conditions and aims and is drawn into the verbal context.

Word coloration is strengthened in the direction of the activity or context which originally altered and created it. Additionally, lexical coloration is perceived only outside of the activity and state for which it is typical. Strictly speaking, every word has its own lexical characteristics (created by the epoch, nationality, and environment) but only outside of this epoch and this nationality is its lexically typical nature recognized. In this sense lexical coloration is a clue. In a Berlin court one word of *Gaunersprache*, or in Russia one word of *blatnaja muzyka* [underworld argot] from the accused is enough to establish such a word as being a clue—over and above its basic semantic feature, and in spite of it. (Similarly, foreign and dialect words—shibboleths—function as clues.)

Every speech context has an assimilative power which forces a word to have only certain functions and colors them with the tone of the activity in which they participate. The unique and specific nature of language functions in literature determines the lexical selection. Every word which is found in literature is assimilated by it, but in order for a word to turn up in a poem, its lexical attributes must be constructively recognized on the literary level.

"The traditional nature of literature," writes Paul, "colors the verbal material. The medieval folk epic, the courtly romances of the knights, the *Minnesinger* tradition, etc., leave an enormous number of words completely untouched. A word enters literature only under specific conditions."[10]

The appeal to tradition is important, but it does not exhaust the problem. The poetic vocabulary is not created exclusively by the continuation of a certain lexical tradition but also by contrasting it to itself (the vocabulary of Nekrasov and Majakovskij). "Literary language" evolves, and its development cannot be understood as a planned development of tradition, but rather as colossal displacements of traditions (a considerable role is played in this respect by partial reestablishment of older strata).

The following statement by Paul is even more important: "A highly developed style, one of whose laws is: Do not repeat the same expression too frequently—naturally requires as many means of expression as possible for one and the same idea."

The necessity of using words with a definite sound structure—meter, rhyme, alliteration—requires to an even greater degree the possibility of a choice from among several words with identical meanings (for, if the reverse were true, their coercion [*Zwang*] might become unpleasant). The result is that poetic language uses an equal-valued multiplicity of expressions which is created as needed. It uses this multiplicity interchangeably in situations in which the conversational language fixes the use of every word to particular contexts; it preserves variety, whereas the conversational language tends toward unity. Using the poetic language of any people and any era, we can easily demonstrate that its wealth resides in its close ties with existing poetic techniques.

Notes

1. The Russian language also reflects this dualism: *značenie* [meaning, significance] vs. *smysl* [meaning, sense]. If we say: "use a word in some meaning" (*značenie*)—this involves the usual meaning, but "use a word in some sense" (*smysl*), involves some occasional meaning.

2. Thus the concept of the basic feature in semantics is analogous to the phoneme concept in phonetics.

3. *Ostaf. Arx.*, I, p. 213, 1819.

4. *Ibid.*, p. 219.

5. Therefore the "law of two-memberedness" (*Zweigliedrigkeit*), of Rozwadowski based on the fact that both the "essential" and formal aspects of a word are meaningful, in no way vitiates the general outlines of the scheme for basic and secondary features. It merely intensifies the problem, making both the basic and the secondary features dependent on any changes in either the essential or the formal aspects of words.

6. Owing also to an alteration in the language structure, of course, which colors everything contained in it. But here I am deliberately isolating the question of structure, thus focusing attention on the lexical coloration.

7. Cf. such groups as *železnaja doroga* [railroad; literally: iron road], *belaja noč* [white night], etc.

8. It is probable that the "restaurant" usage was influenced by the term *čelovek* used in the period of Russian serfdom. It was first used only with an effaced basic feature ("100 *čelovek,*" in the sense of 100 serfs). Then it was joined by secondary features which completely replaced the basic one: *čelovek*—serf, servant (his man [*čelovek*]). Thus we have a change in meaning because of a concrete social fact.

9. Irradiation is a term of Michel Bréal. See his *Essai de sémantique* (Paris, 1897), pp. 43-47.

10. Hermann Paul, "Über die Aufgaben der wissenschaftlichen Lexikologie," § 58, *Sitzungsberichte der philosophisch-philologischen Klasse der Bayrischen Akademie der Wissenschaften*, 1894.

Part IV

Reported Speech
V. N. Vološinov

Discourse Typology in Prose
Mixail Baxtin

The Exposition of the Problem

Reported speech is speech within speech, message within message, and at the same time also speech about speech, message about message.

Whatever we talk about is only the content of speech, the themes of our words. Such a theme—and it is only a theme—might be, for instance, "nature," "man," or "subordinate clause" (one of the themes of syntax). A reported message, however, is not just a theme of speech: it has the capacity of entering on its own, so to speak, into speech, into its syntactic makeup, as an integral unit of the construction. In so doing, it retains its own constructional and semantic autonomy while leaving the speech texture of the context incorporating it perfectly intact.

What is more, a reported message treated solely as a theme of speech may be characterized only superficially, at best. If its content is to be had to the full, it must be made a part of a speech construction. When limited to the treatment of reported speech in thematic terms, one can answer questions as to "how" and "about what" so-and-so spoke, but "what" he said could be disclosed only by way of reporting his words, if only in the form of indirect discourse.

However, once it becomes a constructional unit in the author's speech,[1] into which it has entered on its own, the reported message concurrently becomes a theme of that speech. It enters into the latter's thematic design precisely as reported, a message with its own autonomous theme: the autonomous theme thus becomes a theme of a theme.

Reported speech is regarded by the speaker as a message belonging to *someone else*, a message that was originally totally independent, complete in its construction, and lying outside the given context. Now, it is from this independent existence that reported speech is transposed into an auctorial context while retaining its own referential content and at least the rudiments of its own linguistic integrity, its original constructional independence. The author's message, in incorporating the other message, brings into play syntactic, stylistic, and compositional norms for its partial assimilation—that is, its adaptation to the syntactic, compositional, and stylistic design of the author's message, while preserving (if only in rudimentary form) the initial autonomy (in

*"Èkspozicija problemy čužoj reči" and "Kosvennaja reč', prjamaja reč' i ix modifikacii," *Marksizm i filosofija jazyka* (Leningrad, 1930), pp. 113-138. Translated by Ladislav Matejka and I. R. Titunik.

syntactic, compositional, and stylistic terms) of the reported message, which otherwise could not be grasped in full.

Certain modifications of indirect discourse and in particular of quasi-direct discourse in modern languages evince a disposition to transpose the reported message from the sphere of speech construction to the thematic level—the sphere of content. However, even in these instances, the dissolution of the reported utterance in the auctorial context is not—nor can it be—carried out to the end. Here, too, aside from indications of a semantic nature, the reported message perseveres as a construction—the body of the reported speech remains detectable as a self-sufficient unit.

Thus, what is expressed in the forms employed for reporting speech is an *active relation* of one message to another, and it is expressed, moreover, not on the level of theme but in the stabilized constructional patterns of the language itself.

We are dealing here with words reacting on words. However, this phenomenon is distinctly and fundamentally different from dialogue. In dialogue the lines of the individual participants are grammatically disconnected; they are not integrated into one unified context. Indeed, how could they be? *There are no syntactic forms with which to build a unity of dialogue.* If, on the other hand, a dialogue is presented as embedded in an auctorial context, then we have a case of direct discourse, one of the variants of the phenomenon we are dealing with in this inquiry.

The attention of linguists nowadays is drawn more and more to the problem of dialogue; indeed, it sometimes becomes their central concern. This makes perfectly good sense, for, as we now know, the real unit of language that is implemented in speech (*Sprache als Rede*) is not the individual, isolated monologic utterance but the interaction of at least two utterances—in a word, dialogue. The productive study of dialogue presupposes, however, a more profound investigation of the forms used in reported speech, since these forms reflect basic and constant tendencies in the active reception of other speakers' speech, and it is this reception, after all, that is fundamental also for dialogue.

How, in fact, is another speaker's speech received? What is the mode of existence of another's utterance in the actual, inner speech-consciousness of the recipient? How is it manipulated there, and what process of orientation will the subsequent speech of the recipient himself have undergone in regard to it?

What we have in the forms of reported speech is precisely an objective document of this reception. Once we have learned to decipher it, this document provides us with information, not about accidental and mercurial subjective-psychological processes in the "soul" of the recipient, but about steadfast social tendencies in an active reception of other speakers' speech, tendencies that have crystallized into language forms. The mechanism of this process is located, not in the individual soul, but in society. It is the function of society to select and make grammatical (adapt to the grammatical structure of its language) just those factors in the active and evaluative reception of messages that are socially vital and constant and, hence, that are grounded in the economic being of the particular community of speakers.

There are, of course, essential differences between an active reception of another's speech and its transmission in a bound context. These differences should not be overlooked. Any type of transmission—the codified variety in particular—pursues special aims, whether it is a story, legal proceedings, a scholarly polemic, or the like. Furthermore, transmission takes into account a third person—the person to whom the reported utterances are being transmitted. This provision for a third person is especially important in that it strengthens the impact of organized social forces on speech reception. When we engage in a live dialogue with someone, in the very act of dealing with the speech received from our partner, we usually omit those words to which we are answering. We repeat them only in special and exceptional circumstances, when we want to check the correctness of our understanding, or trip our partner up with his words or the like. All these specific factors which may affect transmission must be taken into account. But the essence of the matter is not changed thereby. The circumstances under which transmission occurs and the aims it pursues merely contribute to the implementation of what is already lodged in the tendencies of active reception by one's inner-speech consciousness. And these tendencies for their part can only develop within the framework of the forms used to report speech in a given language.

We are far from claiming that syntactic forms—for instance, those of indirect or direct discourse—directly and unequivocally express the tendencies and forms of an active, evaluative reception of another's utterance. Our speech reception does not, of course, operate directly in the forms of indirect and direct discourse. These forms are only standardized patterns for reporting speech. But, on the one hand, these patterns and their modifications could have arisen and taken shape only in accordance with the governing tendencies of speech reception, and on the other, once these patterns have assumed shape and function in the language, they in turn exert an influence, regulating or inhibiting in their development, on the tendencies of an evaluative reception that operate within the channel prescribed by the existing forms.

Language reflects, not subjective, psychological vacillations, but stable social interrelationships among speakers. Various linguistic forms of these interrelationships, and various modifications of these forms, prevail in different languages at different periods of time within different social groups and under the effect of different contextual aims. What this attests to is the relative strength or weakness of those tendencies in the social interorientation of a community of speakers, of which the given linguistic forms themselves are the stabilized and age-old crystallizations. Should it happen that circumstances conspire to disparage some particular form (for example, certain modifications of indirect discourse, such as the "dogmatic-rationalistic" type in the modern Russian novel), then this may be taken as evidence that the dominant tendencies in understanding and evaluating the messages to be reported are not properly manifested by that particular form—it is too unaccommodating, too hampering.

Everything vital in the evaluative reception of another's utterance, everything of any ideological value, is expressed in the material of inner speech. After all, it is not a mute, wordless creature that receives such an utterance but a human being full of inner words. All his experiences—his so-called apperceptive background—exist encoded in his inner speech, and only to that extent do they come into contact with speech received from outside. Word comes into contact with word. The context of this inner speech is the locale in which another's utterance is received, comprehended, and evaluated, where, that is, the speaker's active orientation takes place. This active inner speech reception proceeds in two directions: first, the received utterance is framed within a context of factual commentary (coinciding in part with what is called the apperceptive background of the words), taking into account the situation (both internal and external), the visual signs of expression, and so on; second, a reply (*Gegenrede*) is prepared. Both the preparation of the reply (*internal retort*) and the *factual commentary* are organically fused in the unity of active reception, and these can be isolated only in abstract terms.

Both lines of reception find their expression, are objectified, in the "auctorial" context surrounding the reported speech. Regardless of the functional orientation of the given context—whether a work of fiction, a polemical article, a defense attorney's summation, or the like—we clearly discern these two tendencies in it, that of commenting and that of retorting. Usually one of them is dominant. Between the reported speech and the reporting context, dynamic relations of high complexity and tension are in force. A failure to take these into account makes it impossible to understand any form of reported speech.

Earlier investigators of the forms of reported speech committed the fundamental error of virtually divorcing the reported speech from the reporting context. That explains why their treatment of these forms is so static and inert (a characterization applicable to the whole field of syntactic study in general). Meanwhile, the true object of inquiry ought to be precisely the dynamic interrelationship of these two factors, the speech being reported (the other person's speech) and the speech doing the reporting (the author's speech). After all, the two do in actual fact exist, function, and take shape only in their interrelation, not on their own, the one apart from the other. The reported speech and the reporting context are but the terms of a dynamic interrelationship. This dynamism reflects the dynamism of social interorientation in verbal-ideological communication between people (within, of course, the vital and steadfast tendencies of that communication).

In what direction may the dynamism of the interrelationship between the auctorial and the reported speech move?

We see it moving in two basic directions.

In the first place, the basic tendency in reacting to reported speech may be to maintain its integrity and authenticity: a language may strive to forge hard and fast boundaries for reported speech. In such a case, the patterns and their modifications serve to demarcate the reported speech as clearly as possible, to screen it from penetration by the author's intonations, to condense and enhance its individual linguistic characteristics.

Such is the first direction. Within its scope we must rigorously define to what extent a given language community differentiates the social reception of the speech to be reported and to what extent the expressiveness, the stylistic qualities of speech, its lexical coloration, and so forth, are felt as distinct and socially important values. It may be that another's speech is received as one whole block of social behavior, as the speaker's indivisible, conceptual position—in which case only the "what" of speech is taken in and the "how" is left outside reception. This content-conceptualizing and (in a linguistic sense) depersonalizing type of receiving and reporting speech predominates in Old and Middle French (in the latter with a considerable development of the depersonalizing modifications of indirect discourse). The same type is found in the literary monuments of Old Russian—though here the pattern of indirect discourse is almost completely lacking. The dominant type in this case was that of the depersonalized (in the linguistic sense) direct discourse.

Within the scope covered by the first direction, we must also define the degree of authoritarian reception of an utterance and the degree of its ideological assurance—its dogmatism. The more dogmatic an utterance, the less the leeway between truth and falsehood or good and bad permitted by its reception by those who comprehend and evaluate, the greater will be the depersonalization which the forms of reported speech undergo. In point of fact, given the situation in which all social value judgments are divided into wholesale, clear-cut alternatives, we have simply no room for a positive and observant attitude toward all those factors which give to another speaker's utterance its individual character. Authoritarian dogmatism of that type characterizes Middle French and Old Russian writings. The seventeenth century in France and the eighteenth century in Russia are characterized by a rationalistic type of dogmatism that likewise tended to curb the individualization of reported speech, though in different ways. In the sphere of rationalistic dogmatism, the dominant forms were the content-analyzing modifications of indirect discourse and the rhetorical modifications of direct discourse. Here the explicitness and inviolability of the boundaries between auctorial and reported speech reach the utmost limits.

This first direction in which the dynamism of the interorientation between reporting and reported speech moves, we may call (borrowing the term from Wölfflin's study of art) the linear style (*der lineare Stil*) of speech reporting. The basic tendency of the linear style is to construct clear-cut, external contours for reported speech, whose own internal individuality is minimized. Wherever the entire context displays a complete stylistic homogeneity (in which the author and his characters all speak exactly the same language), the grammatical and compositional manipulation of reported speech achieves a maximal compactness and plastic relief.

The processes we observe in the second direction in which the dynamism of the interorientation between reporting and reported speech moves are of exactly the opposite nature. Language devises means for infiltrating reported speech with auctorial retort and commentary in deft and subtle ways. The reporting context strives to break down the self-contained compactness of the reported speech, to resolve it, to obliterate its boundaries. We may call this style of speech reporting "pictorial." Its tendency is to obliterate the precise, external contours of reported speech; at the same time, the reported speech is individualized to a much greater degree—the tangibility of the various facets of an utterance may be subtly differentiated. This time the reception includes not only the referential meaning of the utterance, the statement it makes, but also all the linguistic peculiarities of its verbal implementation.

A number of diverse types may be placed within the scope of this second direction. The impetus for weakening the peripheries of the utterance may originate in the author's context, in which case that context permeates the reported speech with its own intonation—humor, irony, love or hate, enthusiasm or scorn. This type characterizes the Renaissance (especially in French letters), the end of the eighteenth century, and virtually the entire nineteenth century. It involves a severe debilitation of both the authoritarian and the rationalistic dogmatism of utterance. Social value judgments were then ruled by a relativism supplying extremely favorable grounds for a positive and sensitive reception of all individualized verbal nuances of thought, belief, feeling. These grounds even encouraged the growth of a "decorative" trend in treating reported speech, leading sometimes to a neglect of the meaning of an utterance in favor of its "color"—for example, in the Russian "Natural School"; indeed, in Gogol′'s case, his characters' speech sometimes loses almost all its referential meaning and becomes instead décor, on a par with clothing, appearance, furnishings, etc.

A rather different type is also possible: the verbal dominant may shift to the reported speech, which in that case becomes more forceful and more active than the auctorial context framing it. This time the reported speech begins to resolve, as it were, the reporting context, instead of the other way round. The auctorial context loses the greater objectivity it normally commands in comparison with reported speech. It begins to be perceived and even recognizes itself as if it were subjective, "other person's" speech. In works of fiction, this is often expressed compositionally by the appearance of a narrator who replaces the author (in the usual sense of the word). The narrator's speech is just as individualized, colorful, and nonauthoritative as is the speech of the characters. The narrator's position is fluid, and in the majority of cases he uses the language of the personages depicted in the work. He cannot bring to bear against their subjective position a more authoritative and objective world. Such is the nature of narration in Dostoevskij, Andrej Belyj, Remizov, Sologub, and more recent Russian writers of prose.

While the incursion of an auctorial context into reported speech is typical of speech reception in the moderate variety of both idealism and collectivism, the dissolution of the auctorial context testifies to a relativistic individualism in speech reception. In the latter, the subjective reported message stands in opposition to a commenting and retorting auctorial context that recognizes itself to be equally subjective.

The entire second trend is characterized by an exceptional development of mixed forms of speech reporting, including quasi-indirect discourse and, in particular, quasi-direct discourse, in which the boundaries of the message reported are maximally weakened. Also, among modifications of indirect and direct discourse, the ones predominating are those which show the greatest flexibility and are the most susceptible to permeation by auctorial tendencies (for example, disseminated direct discourse, texture-analyzing forms of indirect discourse, and others).

Inquiry into all these tendencies shown in the actively responsive reception of speech must take into account every peculiarity of the linguistic phenomena under scrutiny. The teleology of the auctorial context is especially important. In this respect, it is verbal art that most keenly implements all the permutations in sociolingual interorientation. In distinction from verbal art, rhetoric, owing simply to its teleology, is less free in its handling of other speakers' utterances. Rhetoric requires a distinct cognizance of the boundaries of reported speech. It is marked by an acute awareness of property rights to words and by a fastidiousness in matters of authenticity.

Judicial language intrinsically assumes a clear-cut discrepancy between the verbal subjectivism of the parties to a case and the objectivity of the court—between a ruling from the bench and the entire apparatus of judicial-interpretative and investigative commentary. Political rhetoric presents an analogous case. It is important to determine the specific gravity of rhetorical speech, judicial or political, in the linguistic consciousness of the given social group at a given time. Moreover, the position that a specimen of speech to be reported occupies on the social hierarchy of values must also be taken into account. The stronger the feeling of hierarchical eminence in another's utterance, the more sharply defined will its boundaries be, and the less accessible will it be to penetration by retorting and commenting tendencies from outside. So, for instance, it was possible within the neoclassical sphere for the low genres to display striking deviations from the rationalistic-dogmatic, linear style of speech reporting. It is symptomatic that quasi-direct discourse achieved its first powerful development precisely there—in the fables and tales of La Fontaine.

In summarizing all we have said of the various possible tendencies in the dynamic interrelationship of reported and reporting speech, we may mark out the following chronological sequence:
1. *authoritarian dogmatism,* characterized by the linear, impersonal, monumental style of reported speech transmission in the Middle Ages;
2. *rationalistic dogmatism* with its even more pronounced linear style in the seventeenth and eighteenth centuries;
3. *realistic and critical individualism* with its pictorial style and its tendency to permeate reported speech with auctorial retort and commentary (end of the eighteenth century, early nineteenth century); and finally
4. *relativistic individualism* with its decomposition of the auctorial context (the present period).

Language exists not in and of itself but only in conjunction with the individual structure of a concrete utterance. It is solely through the utterance that language makes a contact with communication, is imbued with its vital power, and becomes a reality. The conditions of verbal communication, its forms, and its methods of differentiation are dictated by the social and economic prerequisites of a given period. These changing sociolingual conditions are what in fact determine those changes in the forms of reported speech brought out in our analysis. We would even venture to say that in these forms by which language registers the impressions of received speech and of the speaker, the history of the changing types of socioideological communication stands out in particularly bold relief.

Indirect and Direct Discourse and Their Variants

We have now outlined the basic directions of the dynamism characterizing the interorientation of the reporting and the reported speech. This dynamism finds its concrete linguistic expression in the patterns of reported speech and in the variants of those patterns—which may be said to be the indices of the balance between reporting and reported messages achieved at any given time in the development of a language.

Let us now turn to a brief characterization of these patterns and their principal variants from the standpoint of the tendencies already pointed out.

First, a few words must be said about the relation of variants to pattern. This relation is analogous to the relation of the actuality of rhythm to the abstraction of meter. A pattern may be implemented only in the form of its specific variant. Changes within variants build up over periods of time, whether centuries or decades, and new habits of active orientation toward the speech to be reported take hold, later to crystallize as regular linguistic formations in syntactic patterns. The position of the variants is on the borderline between grammar and stylistics. From time to time, disputes arise as to whether a given form of speech transmission is a pattern or a variant, a matter of grammar or a matter of style. An example of such a dispute was waged over the question of quasi-direct discourse in French and German, with Bally taking one side and Kalepky and Lorck the other. Bally refused to recognize in quasi-direct discourse a legitimate syntactic pattern and regarded it as nothing more than a stylistic variant. The same argument might be applied to quasi-indirect discourse in French. From our point of view, the demarcation of a strict borderline between grammar and style, between a grammatical pattern and its stylistic variant is methodologically unproductive and in fact impossible. This borderline is fluid because of the very mode of existence of language, in which, simultaneously, some forms are undergoing grammatization while others are undergoing degrammatization. It is precisely these ambiguous, borderline forms that are of the greatest interest to the linguist: this is precisely where the developmental tendencies of a language may be discerned.

We shall keep our brief characterization of the patterns of direct and indirect discourse confined to the standard Russian literary language, and even so, with no intention of covering all their possible variants. We are here concerned exclusively with the methodological aspect of the problem.

In Russian, as is well known, the syntactic patterns for reporting speech are very poorly developed. Aside from quasi-direct discourse (which in Russian lacks clear-cut syntactic markers, as is also true of German), we have two patterns: direct and indirect discourse. But these two patterns are not so strictly delimited from one another as in other languages. The hallmarks of indirect discourse are weak, and in colloquial language they easily combine with those of direct discourse.

A lack of *consecutio temporum* and the subjunctive mood deprives indirect discourse in Russian of any distinctive character of its own. Thus there is no favorable ground for the wide development of certain modifications that are particularly important and interesting from our point of view. On the whole, one must acknowledge the unqualified primacy of direct discourse in Russian. The history of the Russian language knows no Cartesian, rationalistic period, in which an objective "auctorial context," self-confident in its power of reason, has analyzed and dissected the referential structure of the speech to be reported and created complex and remarkable devices for the indirect transmission of speech.

All these peculiarities of the Russian language create an extremely favorable situation for the pictorial style of speech reporting—though, granted, of a somewhat loose and flaccid kind, that is, without that sense of boundaries forced and resistance overcome that one feels in other languages. An extraordinary ease of interaction and interpenetration between reporting and reported speech is the rule. This is a circumstance connected with the negligible role (in the history of the Russian literary language) played by rhetoric with its clear-cut linear style of handling utterances to be reported and its wholesale, but distinct and single-minded, intonation.

Let us first of all describe the characteristics of indirect discourse, the pattern least elaborated in Russian. And let us begin with a brief criticism of the claims made by the grammarian, A. M. Peškovskij. Having noted that forms of indirect discourse in Russian are underdeveloped, he makes the following exceedingly peculiar declaration:[2]

To convince oneself that the Russian language is naturally uncongenial to indirect speech reporting, one need only try rendering any piece of direct discourse, even just slightly exceeding a simple statement, into indirect discourse. For example: The Ass, bowing his head to the ground, says to the Nightingale *that not bad, that no kidding, it's nice listening to him sing, but that what a shame he doesn't know their Rooster, that he could sharpen up his singing quite a bit, if he'd take some lessons from him.*

If Peškovskij had performed the same experiment of mechanically transposing direct discourse into indirect discourse, using the French language and observing only the grammatical rules, he would have had to come to exactly the same conclusions. If, for instance, he had attempted translating into forms of indirect discourse La Fontaine's use of direct discourse or even of quasi-direct discourse in his fables (in which instances of the latter form are very common), the results obtained would have been just as grammatically correct and stylistically inadmissible as in the example given. And this would have happened despite the fact that quasi-direct discourse in French is extremely close to indirect discourse (the same shift of tenses and persons occurs in both). There are whole sets of words, idioms, and turns of speech appropriate in direct and quasi-direct discourse that would sound weird if transposed into a construction in indirect discourse.

Peškovskij makes a typical grammarian's error. His mechanical, purely grammatical mode of translating reported speech from one pattern into another, without the appropriate stylistic reshaping, is nothing but a bogus and highly objectionable way of manufacturing classroom exercises in grammar. This sort of implementation of the patterns of speech reporting has nothing even remotely to do with their real existence in a language. The patterns express some tendency in one person's active reception of another's speech. Each pattern treats the message to be reported in its own creative fashion, following the specific direction proper to that pattern alone. If, at some given stage in its development, a language habitually perceives another's utterance as a compact, indivisible, fixed, impenetrable whole, then that language will command no other pattern than that of primitive, inert direct discourse (the monumental style). It is exactly this conception of the immutability of a message and the absolute literalness of its transmission that Peškovskij asserts in his experiment; yet at the same time he tries to apply the pattern of indirect discourse. The results of that experiment do not by any means prove that the Russian language is naturally uncongenial to reporting indirect speech. On the contrary, they prove that, however weakly developed its pattern, indirect discourse in Russian has enough character of its own so that not every case of direct discourse lends itself to literal translation.

This singular experiment of Peškovskij's makes evident his complete failure to recognize the linguistic essence of indirect discourse. That essence consists in the analytical transmission of someone's speech. An analysis simultaneous with and inseparable from transmission constitutes the obligatory hallmark of all variants of indirect discourse whatever. They may differ only with respect to the degree and direction of the analysis.

The analytical tendency of indirect discourse is manifested by the fact that all the emotive-affective features of speech, in so far as they are expressed, not in the content but in the form of a message, do not pass intact into indirect discourse. They are translated from form into content, and only in that shape do they enter into the construction of indirect discourse or are shifted to the main clause as a commentary modifying the *verbum dicendi.*

Thus, for example, the direct utterance, "Well done! What an achievement!" cannot be registered in indirect discourse as, "He said that well done and what an achievement." Rather, we expect:

He said that that had been done very well and was a real achievement.

or:

He said delightedly that that had been done well and was a real achievement.

All the various ellipses, omissions, and so on, possible in direct discourse on emotive-affective grounds, are not tolerated by the analyzing tendencies of indirect discourse and can enter indirect discourse only if developed and filled out. The Ass's exclamation, "Not bad!" in Peškovskij's example cannot be mechanically registered in indirect discourse as:

He says that not bad . . .

but only as

He says that it was not bad . . .

or even

He says that the nightingale sang not badly.

Neither can the "no kidding" be mechanically registered in indirect discourse, nor can "What a shame you don't know . . ." be rendered as, "But that what a shame he doesn't know . . ."

It is obvious that the same impossibility of a mechanical transposition from direct into indirect discourse also applies to the original form of any compositional or compositonal-inflectional means which the speaker being reported used in order to convey his intention. Thus the compositional and inflectional peculiarities of interrogative, exclamatory, and imperative sentences are relinquished in indirect discourse, and their identification depends solely on the content.

Indirect discourse "hears" a message differently; it actively receives and brings to bear in transmission different factors, different aspects of the message than do the other patterns. That is what makes a mechanical, literal transposition of messages from other patterns into indirect discourse impossible. It is possible only in instances in which the direct utterance itself was somewhat analytically constructed–in so far, of course, as direct discourse will tolerate such analysis. Analysis is the heart and soul of indirect discourse.

A closer scrutiny of Peškovskij's "experiment" reveals that the lexical tint of expressions such as "not bad" and "sharpen up" does not fully harmonize with the analytical spirit of indirect discourse. Such expressions are too colorful; they not only convey the exact meaning of what was said but they also suggest the manner of speech (whether individual or typological) of the Ass as protagonist. One would like to replace them with a synonym (such as "good" or "well" and "perfect /his singing/") or, if these "catchy" terms are to be retained in indirect discourse, at least to enclose them within quotation marks. If we were to read the resulting case of indirect discourse aloud, we would speak the expressions within quotation marks somewhat differently, as if to give notice through our intonation that they are taken directly from another person's speech and that we want to keep our distance.

Here we come up against the necessity of distinguishing between the two directions which the analyzing tendency of indirect discourse can take and, accordingly, of distinguishing its two basic variants.

The analysis involved in a construction of indirect discourse may indeed go in two directions or, more precisely, it may focus attention on two fundamentally different objects. A message may be received as a certain particular ideational position of the speaker, and, in that case, by the agency of the indirect discourse construction, its exact referential makeup (what the speaker said) is transmitted analytically. Thus in the example we have been using, it is possible to transmit precisely the referential meaning of the Ass's evaluation of the Nightingale's singing. On the other hand, a message may be received and analytically transmitted as an expression characterizing not only the referent but also, or even more so, the speaker himself—his manner of speech, individual, or typological, or both, his state of mind as expressed not in the content but in the forms of his speech (disconnectedness, pauses between words, expressive intonation, and the like), his ability or lack of ability to express himself, and so on.

These two objects of analysis by the transmission of indirect discourse are profoundly and fundamentally different. In the one case, meaning is dissected into its constitutent, ideational, referential units, while in the other the message per se is broken down into the various stylistic strands that compose its verbal texture. The second tendency, carried to its logical extreme, would amount to a technical linguistic analysis of style. However, simultaneously with what would appear to be stylistic analysis, a referential analysis of the speech to be reported also takes place in this type of indirect discourse, with a resulting dissection of the referential meaning and of its implementation by the verbal envelope.

Let us term the first variant of the pattern of indirect discourse as the *referent-analyzing* variant, and the second, the *texture-analyzing* variant. The referent-analyzing variant receives a message on the purely thematic level and simply does not "hear" or take in whatever there is in that message that is without thematic significance. Those aspects of the formal verbal design which do have thematic significance—which are essential to an understanding of the speaker's ideational position—may be transmitted thematically by this variant or may be incorporated into the auctorial context as characterization on the author's part.

The referent-analyzing variant provides a wide opportunity for the retorting and commenting tendencies of auctorial speech, while at the same time maintaining a strict and clear-cut separation between reporting and reported utterance. For that reason it makes an excellent means for the linear style of speech reporting. It has unquestionably a built-in tendency to thematicize another speaker's utterance, and thus it preserves the cohesiveness and autonomy of the utterance, not so much in constructional terms as in terms of meaning (we have seen how an expressive construction in a message to be reported can be rendered thematically). These results are achieved, however, only at the price of a certain depersonalization of the reported speech.

The development of the referent-analyzing variant to any appreciable extent occurs only within an auctorial context that is somewhat rationalistic and dogmatic in nature—one at any rate in which the focus of attention is strongly ideational and in which the author shows through his words that he himself, in his own right, occupies a particular ideational position. Where this does not hold true, where either the author's language is itself colorful and particularized, or where the conduct of speech is directly handed over to some narrator of the appropriate type, this variant will have only a very secondary and occasional significance (as it does, for instance, in Gogol′, Dostoevskij, and others).

On the whole, this variant is but weakly developed in Russian. It is found primarily in discursive or rhetorical contexts (of a scientific, philosophical, political, or similar nature), in which the author must deal with the problem of explaining, comparing, and putting into perspective the opinions of other people on the topic being discussed. Its occurrence in verbal art is rare. It takes on a certain stature only in works by writers who are not loath to have their own say with its special ideational aim and weight, such as Turgenev, for instance, or more especially, Tolstoj. Even in these cases, however, we do not find this variant in that richness and diversity of variation we observe in French and German.

Let us now turn to the texture-analyzing variant. It incorporates into indirect discourse words and locutions that characterize the subjective and stylistic physiognomy of the message viewed as expression. These words and locutions are incorporated in such a way that their specificity, their subjectivity, their typicality are distinctly felt; more often than not they are enclosed in quotation marks. Here are four examples:

1. About the deceased, Grigorij remarked, making the sign of the cross, that he was a good hand at a thing or two, but was thick-headed and *scourged by his sickness*, and a *disbeliever to boot*, and that it was Fedor Pavlovič and the oldest son who had taught him his *disbelief* (Dostoevskij, *The Brothers Karamazov*).

2. The same thing happened with the Poles: they appeared with a show of pride and independence. They loudly testified that, in the first place, they were both "*in the service of the Crown*" and that "*Pan Mitja*" had offered to buy their honor for 3,000, and that they themselves had seen large sums of money in his hands (*ibid.*).

3. Krasotkin proudly parried the accusation, giving to understand that it would indeed have been shameful "*in our day and age*" to play make-believe with his contemporaries, other thirteen-year olds, but—that he did it for the "*chubbies*" because he was fond of them, and no one had any business calling him to account for his feelings (*ibid.*).

4. He found Nastas'ja Filippovna in a state similar to utter derangement: she continually cried out, trembled, shouted that Rogožin was hidden in the garden, in their very house, that she had just seen him, that he would *murder her . . . cut her throat*! (Dostoevskij, *The Idiot.* Here the indirect-discourse construction retains the expressive intonation of the original message.)

The words and expressions incorporated into indirect discourse with their own specificity detectable (especially when they are enclosed in quotation marks) are being "made strange," to use the language of the Formalists, and made strange precisely in the direction that suits the author's needs: they are particularized, their coloration is heightened, but at the same time they are made to accommodate shadings of the author's attitude—his irony, humor, and so on.

It is advisable to keep this variant separate from cases of unbroken transition from indirect to direct discourse, although both types have virtually identical functions. In the latter, when direct discourse continues indirect discourse, the subjectivity of speech acquires a heightened definition and moves in the direction that suits the author's needs. For example:

1. Try as he might to be evasive, nevertheless, Trifon Borisovič, once the peasants had been interrogated about the thousand ruble note, made his confession, adding only that right then and there he had scrupulously returned and remitted everything to Dmitrij Fedorovič "out of the strictest sense of honor," and that "only, you see, the gentleman himself, having been at the time dead drunk, cannot recall it" (Dostoevskij, *The Brothers Karamazov*).
2. Though filled with the profoundest respect for the memory of his ex-master, he nevertheless, among other things, declared that he had been negligent toward Mitja and had "brought the children up wrong. The little child without me would have been eaten alive by lice," he added, recounting episodes from Mitja's earliest years (*ibid.*).

Such an instance, in which direct discourse is prepared for by indirect discourse and emerges as if from inside it—like those sculptures of Rodin's, in which the figure is left only partly emerged from the stone—is one of the innumerable variants of direct discourse treated pictorially.

Such is the nature of the texture-analyzing variant of the indirect-discourse construction. It creates highly original pictorial effects in reported speech transmission. It is a variant that presupposes the presence in the linguistic consciousness of a high degree of individualization of other speakers' utterances and an ability to perceive differentially the verbal envelope of a message and its referential meaning. None of that is congenial either to the authoritarian or the rationalistic type of reception of other speakers' utterances. As a viable stylistic device, it can take root in a language only on the grounds of critical and realistic individualism, whereas the referent-analyzing variant is characteristic of the rationalistic kind of individualism. In the history of the Russian literary language, the latter period hardly existed. And that explains the absolute preeminence of the texture-analyzing variant over the referent-analyzing variant in Russian. Also, the development of the texture-analyzing variant benefited to a high degree from the lack of *consecutio temporum* in Russian.

We see, therefore, that our two variants, despite their liaison through the common analytical tendency of the pattern, express profoundly different linguistic conceptions of the reported addresser's words and the speaker's individuality. For the first variant, the speaker's individuality is a factor only as it occupies some specific ideational position (epistemological, ethical, existential, or behavioral), and beyond that position (which is transmitted in strictly referential terms) it has no existence for the reporter. There is no wherewithal here for the speaker's individuality to congeal into an image.

The opposite is true of the second variant, in which the speaker's individuality is presented as subjective manner (individual or typological), as manner of thinking and speaking, involving the author's evaluation of that manner as well. Here the speaker's individuality congeals to the point of forming an image.

Still a third and a not inconsiderable variant of the indirect discourse construction in Russian may be pointed out. It is used mainly for reporting the internal speech, thoughts, and experiences of a character. It treats the speech to be reported very freely, it abbreviates it, often only highlighting its themes and dominants, and therefore it may be termed the impressionistic variant. Auctorial intonation easily and freely ripples over its fluid structure. Here is a classic example of the impressionistic variant from Puškin's *Bronze Horseman:*

What were the thoughts he pondered then? That he was poor; that he perforce must labor to achieve respect, security; that God just might have granted him more brains and money. That goodness knows, there are those idle lucky dogs with little brains, those loungers, *for whom life is just a lark!* That he had been in service in all two years; his thoughts remarked as well that the weather wasn't calming down; that the river kept on rising; that all the bridges over the Neva were most likely up and that he would be two or three days cut off from his Paraša. Thus went his pondering.

Judging from this example, we note that the impressionistic variant of indirect discourse lies somewhere midway between the referent-analyzing and the texture-analyzing variants. In this or that instance, a referential analysis has quite definitely taken place. Certain words and locutions have clearly originated from the mind of the hero, Evgenij (though no emphasis is put on their specificity). What comes through most is the author's irony, his accentuation, his hand in ordering and abbreviating the material.

Let us now turn to the pattern of direct discourse, which is extremely well worked out in the Russian literary language and commands an immense assortment of distinctively different modifications. From the cumbersome, inert, and indivisible blocks of direct discourse in Old Russian literary monuments to the modern, elastic, and often ambiguous modes of its incorporation into the auctorial context stretches the long and instructive path of its historical development. But here we must refrain from examining that historical development; nor can we inventory the existing variants of direct discourse in the literary language. We shall limit ourselves only to those variants which display a mutual exchange of intonations, a sort of reciprocal infectiousness between the reporting context and the reported speech. Furthermore, within those limits, our concern lies not so much with those instances in which the author's speech advances upon the reported message and penetrates it with its own intonations—as with instances in which, on the contrary, elements of the reported message creep into and are dispersed throughout the entire auctorial context, making it fluid and ambiguous. It is true, however, that a sharp dividing line cannot always be drawn between these two types of instances: often it is indeed a matter of a reciprocity of effect.

The first direction of the dynamic interrelationship, characterized by the author's "imposition," may be termed pre-set direct discourse.

The case of direct discourse emerging out of indirect discourse (with which we are already familiar) belongs in this category. A particularly interesting and widespread instance of this variant is the emergence of direct discourse out of quasi-direct discourse. Since the nature of the latter discourse is half-narration and half-reported speech, it presets the apperception of the direct discourse. The basic themes of the impending direct discourse are anticipated by the context and are colored by the author's intonations. Under this type of treatment, the boundaries of the reported utterance become extremely weak. A classic example of this variant is the portrayal of Prince Myškin's state of mind on the verge of an epileptic fit, which takes up almost the entire fifth chapter of Part II of Dostoevskij's *Idiot* (magnificent specimens of quasi-direct discourse are also to be found there). In this chapter Prince Myškin's directly reported speech resounds within his self-enclosed world, since the author narrates within the confines of his, Prince Myškin's, purview. Half the apperceptive background created for the "other speaker's" utterance here belongs to that other speaker (the hero), and half to the author. However, it is made perfectly clear to us that a deep penetration of auctorial intonations into direct discourse is almost always accompanied by a weakening of objectivity in the auctorial context.

Another variant in the same direction may be termed "particularized direct discourse." The auctorial context here is so constructed that the traits the author used to define a character cast heavy shadows on his directly reported speech. The value judgments and attitudes in which the character's portrayal is steeped carry over into the words he utters. The referential weight of the reported utterances declines in this modification but, in exchange, their characterological significance, their picturesqueness, or their time-and-place typicality grows more intense. Similarly, once we recognize a comic character on stage by his style of makeup, his costume, and his general bearing, we are ready to laugh even before we catch the meaning of his words. Such is the way direct discourse is usually handled by Gogol′ and by representatives of the so-called "Natural School." As a matter of fact, Dostoevskij tried to reanimate this particularized treatment of reported utterances in his first work, *Poor Folk*.

The presetting of the reported speech and the anticipation of its theme in the narrative, its judgments, and accents may so subjectivize and color the author's context in the tints of his hero that that context will begin to sound like "reported speech," though a kind of reported speech with its auctorial intonations still intact. To conduct the narrative exclusively within the purview of the hero himself, not only within its dimensions of time and space but also in its system of values and intonations, creates an extremely original kind of apperceptive background for reported messages. It gives us the right to speak of a special variant: anticipated and disseminated reported speech concealed in the auctorial context and, as it were, breaking into real, direct utterances by the hero.

This variant is very widespread in contemporary prose, especially that of Andrej Belyj and the writers under his influence (for instance, in Erenburg's *Nikolaj Kurbov*). However, the classical specimens must be sought in Dostoevskij's work of his first and second periods (in his last period this variant is encountered less often). Let us look at his *Skvernyj anekdot* [Nasty Story].

One might enclose the whole narrative in quotation marks as narration by a "narrator," though no such narrator is denoted, either thematically or compositionally. However, the situation within the narrative is such that almost every epithet, or definition, or value judgment might also be enclosed in quotation marks as originating in the mind of one or another character.

Let us quote a short passage from the beginning of the story:

Once in winter, on a cold and frosty evening—very late evening, rather, it being already the twelfth hour—three *extremely distinguished* gentlemen were sitting in a *comfortable*, even sumptuously appointed, room inside a *handsome* two-story house on Petersburg Island and were occupied in *weighty* and *superlative* talk on an *extremely remarkable* topic. All three gentlemen were officials of the rank of general. They were seated around a small table, each in a *handsome* upholstered chair, and during pauses in the conversation they *comfortably* sipped champagne. [Italics added.]

If we disregarded the remarkable and complex play of intonations in this passage, it would have to be judged as stylistically wretched and banal. Within the few lines of print the epithets "handsome" and "comfortable" are used twice, and others are "sumptuously," "weighty," "superlative," and "extremely distinguished"!

Such style would not escape our severest verdict if we took it seriously as description emanating from the author (as we would in the case of Turgenev or Tolstoj) or even as a narrator's description, provided the narrator be of the monolithic *Ich-Erzählung* variety.

However, it is impossible to take this passage in that way. Each of these colorless, banal, insipid epithets is an arena in which *two* intonations, *two* points of view, *two* speech acts converge and clash.

Let us look at a few more excerpts from the passage characterizing the master of the house, Privy Councilor Nikiforov:

A few words about him: he had begun his career as a minor official, had contentedly fiddle-faddled his way through the next forty-five years or so. . . . He particularly despised untidiness and excitability, considering the latter moral untidiness, and toward the end of his life he submerged himself completely in a state of *sweet and relaxed comfort* and systematic solitude. . . . His appearance was that of an *extremely respectable and well-shaven* man who seemed younger than his years, was well preserved, showed promise of living for a long time to come, and abided by the *most exalted gentlemanly code.* His position was a quite comfortable one: he was the head of something and put his signature on something from time to time. *In short, he was considered to be a most excellent man.* He had only one passion or, rather, one ardent wish: to own his own house—one, moreover, built along manorial, not tenement, lines. His wish at last came true.

Now we see clearly where the first passage derived its banal and monotonous epithets (but with their banal monotony pointedly *sustained*). They originated not in the author's mind but in the mind of the general savoring his comfort, his very own house, his situation in life, his rank—the mind of Privy Councilor Nikiforov, a man who has "come up in the world." Those words might be enclosed in quotation marks as "another's speech," the reported speech of Nikiforov. But they belong not only to him. After all, the story is being told by a narrator, who would seem to be in solidarity with the "generals," who fawns upon them, adopts their attitude in all things, speaks their language, but nonetheless provocatively overdoes it and thus thoroughly exposes all their real and potential utterances to the author's irony and mockery. By each of these banal epithets, the author, through his narrator, makes his hero ironic and ridiculous. This is what creates the complex play of intonations in the passage cited—a play of intonations virtually unproducible if read aloud.

The remaining portion of the story is constructed entirely within the purview of another main character, Pralinskij. This portion, too, is studded with the epithets and value judgments of the hero (his hidden speech), and against that background, steeped in the author's irony, his actual, properly punctuated, internal and external direct speech arises.

Thus almost every word in the narrative (as concerns its expressivity, its emotional coloring, its accentual position in the phrase) figures simultaneously in two intersecting contexts, two speech acts: in the speech of the author-narrator (ironic and mocking) and the speech of the hero (who is far removed from irony). This simultaneous participation of two speech acts, each differently oriented in its expressivity, also explains the curious sentence structure, the twists and turns of syntax, the highly original style, of the story. If only one of the two speech acts had been used, the sentences would have been structured otherwise, the style would have been different. We have here a classic instance of a linguistic phenomenon almost never studied—the phenomenon of speech interference.

In Russian, this phenomenon of speech interference may to a certain extent take place in the texture-analyzing variant of indirect discourse, in those comparatively rare instances in which the reported clause contains not only some of the original words and expressions but also the expressive structure of the message reported. We have seen an example of this above, one in which indirect discourse incorporated the exclamatory structure—granted, it was somewhat toned down—of the original message. What resulted was a certain counterpoint between the calm, businesslike, narrational intonation of the author's analytical transmission and the emotional, hysterical intonation of his half-crazed heroine. This also accounts for the peculiar disfigurement of the syntactic physiognomy of the clause—a clause serving two masters, participating simultaneously in two speech acts. Indirect discourse, however, does not supply to this phenomenon of speech interference the grounds for anything like a distinctive and durable stylistic expression.

The most important and, in French at least, the most syntactically standardized case of an interreferential merging of two differently oriented speech acts is quasi-direct discourse. Here we have a phenomenon of extraordinary importance, one that deserves an entire chapter of its own, in which, among other things, we could also subject to critical analysis the controversy being waged on the subject of quasi-direct discourse and the various opinions of it (especialy those of the Vossler School), all of this being of considerable methodological interest. Within the scope of the present chapter, we shall be concerned with examining a few other phenomena related to quasi-direct discourse, which probably, in Russian, are to be identified as the basis for its inception and formation.

In our exclusive concern with the duplex variants of direct discourse in its given pictorial treatment, we have left out one of the most important of the *linear* variants of direct discourse: rhetorical direct discourse. This persuasive variant with its several subvariants has great sociological significance. We cannot dwell on these forms but shall focus some attention on certain phenomena associated with rhetoric.

There is in social intercourse what is called the *rhetorical question,* or the *rhetorical exclamation.* Certain instances of this phenomenon are especially interesting because of the problem of their localization in context. They would seem to be situated on the very boundary between auctorial and reported speech (usually, internal speech) and often they slide directly into one or the other. Thus they may be interpreted as a question or exclamation on the part of the author or, equally, as a question or exclamation on the part of the hero, addressed to himself.

Here is an example of such a question:

But who is approaching, stealthy footed, by moonlit path, amid deepest stillness? The Russian suddenly comes to. Before him stands, with tender, wordless greeting, the Circassian maid. He gazes at her silently and thinks: this is some lying dream, the hollow play of flagging feelings. . . . (Puškin, *The Captive of the Caucasus*).

The hero's concluding (internal) words seem to respond to the rhetorical question posed by the author, and that rhetorical question may be interpreted as part of the hero's own internal speech.

Here is an example of rhetorical exclamation:

All, all, the dreadful sound betrayed. The world of nature dimmed before him. He is a slave! (*ibid.*).

A particularly frequent occurrence in prose is the case in which some such question as "What is to be done now?" introduces the hero's inner deliberations or the recounting of his actions—the question being equally the author's and also one the hero poses to himself in a predicament.

It will surely be claimed that in these and similar questions and exclamations the author's initiative takes the upper hand, and that that is why they never appear enclosed in quotation marks. In these particular instances, it is the author who steps forward, but he does so on his hero's behalf, he seems to speak for him.

Here is an interesting example of this type:

The Cossacks, leaning on their pikes, gaze over the rushing water of the river, and unnoticed by them, blurred in fog, a villain and his weapon float past. . . . What are you thinking, Cossack? Are you recalling battles of bygone years?. . . . Farewell, free frontier villages, paternal home, the quiet Don, and war, and pretty girls. The unseen enemy has reached the bank, an arrow leaves the quiver—takes flight—and down the Cossack falls from the bloodied rampart.

Here the author stands in for his hero, says in his stead what the hero might or should have said, says what the given occasion calls for. Puškin bids farewell to the Cossack's homeland for him (naturally, something the Cossack himself could not have done).

This talking in another's stead comes very close to quasi-direct discourse. Let us term this case, substituted direct discourse. Such a substitution presupposes a *parallelism of intonations*, the intonations of the author's speech and the substituted speech of the hero (what he might or should have said), both running in the same direction. Therefore, no interference takes place here.

When a complete solidarity in values and intonations exists between the author and his hero within the framework of a rhetorically constructed context, the author's rhetoric and that of the hero begin to overlap: their voices merge; and we get long passages that belong simultaneously to the author's narrative and to the hero's internal (though sometimes also external) speech. The result obtained is almost indistinguishable from quasi-direct discourse; only interference is missing. It was on the grounds of the young Puškin's Byronic rhetoric that quasi-direct discourse (presumably for the first time) took shape in Russian. In *The Captive of the Caucasus*, the author shares a complete solidarity in values and intonations with his hero. The narrative is forged in the hero's tones, and the hero's utterances in the author's tones. We find the following, for instance:

There, mountain peaks, each one alike, stretch out in line; a lonely track among them winds and fades in gloom. . . . *Oppressive thoughts* beset the captive youth's tormented breast. . . . The distant track leads back to Russia, land where his ardent youth began, so proud, so free of care: where he knew early joy, where found so much to love, where he embraced dire suffering, where he destroyed delight, desire, and hope in stormy life. . . . The world and its ways he fathomed, and he knew the price of a faithless life. In people's hearts he found betrayal, in dreams of love, a mad illusion. . . . Freedom! For *you alone* he kept the quest in this sublunar world. . . . It came to pass. . . . Now he sees nothing in the world on which to set his hopes, and even *you*, his last fond dream, *you*, too, are gone from him. He is a slave.

Here, clearly, it is the captive's own "oppressive thoughts" that are being transmitted. It is *his* speech but is being formally delivered by the author. If the personal pronoun "he" were changed everywhere to "I," and if the verb forms were adjusted accordingly, no dissonance or incongruity, whether in style or otherwise, would result. Symptomatically enough, this speech contains apostrophes in the second person (to "freedom," to "dreams"), which all the more underscore the author's identification with his hero. This instance of the hero's speech does not differ in style or ideas from the rhetorical direct discourse reported as delivered by the hero in the second part of the poem:

Forget me! I am unworthy of your love, your heart's delight. . . . Bereft of rapture, empty of desire, I wither, passion's victim. . . . O why did not my eyes behold you long ago, in days when still I laid my trust in hope and rapturous dreams! But now it is too late! To happiness I am no more alive, the phantom Hope has flown away. . . .

All writers on quasi-direct discourse (perhaps with the single exception of Bally) would acknowledge that this is a perfectly genuine specimen.

We, however, are inclined to regard it as a case of substituted direct discourse. True, only one step is needed to turn it into quasi-direct discourse. And Puškin took that step when he succeeded in standing apart from his heroes and brought to bear the contrast of a more objective auctorial context with its own values and intonations. The example cited above still lacks any interference on the part of the author's speech and the character's speech. Consequently, it also lacks the grammatical and stylistic features which such interference generates and which characterize quasi-direct discourse, differentiating it from the surrounding auctorial context. The fact is that in our example we recognize the speech of the "captive" only by signs having a purely semantic nature. We do not sense here the merging of two differently oriented speech acts; we do not sense the integrity and resistance of the reported message behind the author's transmission.

Finally, to demonstrate what we regard as real quasi-direct discourse, we reproduce below a remarkable specimen from Puškin's *Poltava:*

But his rage for action Kočubej hid deep within his heart. "His thoughts had now, all woebegone, addressed themselves to death. No ill-will did he bear Mazeppa—his daughter was alone to blame. But he forgave his daughter, too: to God let her give answer, now that she had already plunged her family into shame and Heaven and the laws of man forgot. . . ." But meanwhile he with eagle eye his household scanned, seeking for himself companions bold, unswerving, incorruptible.

Translators' Notes

1. Here "author" means any sender or reporter.

2. A. M. Peškovskij, *Russkij sintaksis v naučnom o sveščenii,* 3rd ed. The "piece of direct discourse" Peškovskij uses for his example is from the well-known fable by Ivan Krylov "The Ass and the Nightingale." In the fable the Ass says to the Nightingale, after the latter's demonstration of his art: "Not bad! No kidding, it's nice listening to you sing. But what a shame you don't know our Rooster! You could sharpen up your singing quite a bit if you'd take some lessons from him." Peškovskij makes a purely

mechanical rendition of this statement in indirect discourse. The result is awkward, indeed, impossible. The English translation aims at mirroring this result.

Discourse Typology in Prose*

Mixail Baxtin

A set of certain verbal devices used in literary art has recently attracted the special attention of investigators. This set comprises stylization, parody, *skaz* (in its strict sense, the oral narration of a narrator), and dialogue.

Despite the fundamental differences among them, all these devices have one feature in common: in all of them discourse maintains a double focus, aimed at the referential object of speech, as in ordinary discourse, and simultaneously at a second context of discourse, a second speech act by another addresser. If we remain ignorant of this second context, if we accept stylization or parody as we accept ordinary speech with its single focus on its referential object, then we shall fail to grasp these devices for what they really are; we shall take stylization for straight style and read parody as poor writing.

Skaz and dialogue, restricted to the single "reply" of one participant, are the less obvious cases of this double orientation. *Skaz* may indeed have sometimes only one focus—a focus on its own referential object. Likewise, a single line of dialogue may well refer directly to the object without any mediation. In the majority of cases, however, both are oriented toward another speech act, one which *skaz* stylizes and which the line of dialogue reflects upon, or replies to, or anticipates.

Stylization, parody, *skaz*, and dialogue are phenomena of the most fundamental importance; they call for a thoroughly new approach to the analysis of discourse—an approach unamenable to the usual framework of stylistic and lexicological study. The fact is that the usual approach treats word-usage within the bounds of a single monologic context, defining each lexical item in relation to its referential object (the study of tropes) or in relation to the other words of the same context, of the same speech act (stylistics, in the narrow sense). It is true that lexicology does know a somewhat different approach to word usage. The lexical tint of a word, for instance, an archaism or a provincialism, points to some other context, in which it normally functions (as in ancient literary monuments, or regional speech). In such a case, however, we are dealing with a language system, not a concrete context of speech; the words in question are not utterances from another speech act, but are impersonal language material not implemented in any concrete utterance. If, however, the lexical tint is individualized, even slightly, if it

* "Tipy prozaičeskogo slova," in *Problemy tvorčestva Dostoevskogo* (Leningrad, 1929), pp. 105-135. Translated by Richard Balthazar and I. R. Titunik.

points to some speech act from which it was borrowed or after which it was patterned, then we are already dealing with stylization, or parody, or some analogous phenomenon. Thus lexicology also remains restricted to a single monologic context, recognizing only the direct, unmediated relationship between word and referent, without consideration of any other speech act, any second context.

The very fact that instances do exist of doubly oriented discourse in which a relationship with another speech act is the essential factor makes it incumbent upon us to furnish a complete and thorough-going classification of types of word usage in accordance with the new principle we have suggested, a principle that neither stylistics, nor lexicology, nor semantics has taken into account. There is no trouble in seeing that, besides a word usage carrying out direct referential aims and a word usage focusing on another speech act, there yet must be a third type. But even within this third type of doubly oriented word usage (in which another speech act is a factor), differentiation is necessary, since it embraces such disparate phenomena as stylization, parody, and dialogue. The fundamental variants of these phenomena have to be brought to light from the vantage point of this same new principle. Inevitably there will arise the question as to whether, and how, heterogeneous types of word-usage may be combined within a single context. On these grounds, a whole set of new stylistic problems arises, problems which until now stylistics has failed to take into account. As concerns style in prose, it is precisely these problems that have a paramount significance.[1]

On the one hand, we observe discourse of a direct, unmediated, intentional nature, which names, or communicates, or expresses something, and which involves a comprehension of the same nature (the first type of word usage); and on the other hand, discourse which is represented or objectified (the second type). The most typical and extensive variety of represented or objectified word usage is the direct speech of characters. Such speech has its own immediate referential object, yet it does not occupy a position on the same plane with the direct speech of the author; instead, it stands at a certain remove from the author's speech, as if in perspective. It is meant not only to be understood in terms of its own referential object, but, by virtue of its character-defining capacity, or its typicality, or its colorfulness, it also appears as the object of another (the author's) intention.

Whenever we have the direct speech of a single character within the context of the author's speech, we confront, within that one context, two speech centers and two speech complexes: the complex of the author's message, and the complex of the character's message. The second complex, however, is not independent of the first; it is subordinated to it and figures as one of its components. The stylistic handling of each of the two messages is different. The character's utterance is handled precisely as the words of another addresser—as words belonging to a personage of a certain specific individuality or type, that is, it is handled as an object of the author's intentions, and not at all in terms of its own proper referential aim. The author's speech, on the contrary, is handled stylistically as speech aimed at its direct referential denotation: it must be adequate to its object (of whatever nature, discursive, poetic, or other); it must be expressive, forceful, pithy, elegant, and so on, from the point of view of its direct referential mission—to denote, express, convey or depict something; and its stylistic treatment is concurrently oriented toward the comprehension of the referent. However, should the author's speech be so treated as to display the individual or typical features of a particular person, or of a particular social status, or of a particular literary manner, then what we are dealing with is already stylization, either the usual kind of literary stylization or that of a stylized *skaz*. Such an instance belongs to the third type of discourse. We shall come to this type later.

Discourse that is directly intentional in nature knows only itself and its referential object, and it aims to be maximally adequate to the latter. If in the course of carrying out its mission it shows that it has imitated or learned something from someone, that does not in the least change things—all that is merely the scaffolding, which the builder could hardly do without but which does not become part of the architectural structure. The fact of imitation itself and the evidence of all sorts of influences (easily detectible by the literary historian or by any competent reader) do not enter into the mission the discourse carries out. If this were the case—if the discourse itself clearly marked its reference to another speech act—then once again we would be dealing with discourse of the third (not the first) type.

The stylistic handling of objectified discourse—the discourse of the characters—is subsumed under and becomes part of the stylistic missions of the author's context, which bears the ultimate, the highest, authority. This fact gives rise to a number of stylistic problems having to do with the introduction and the organic incorporation of the directly reported speech of the character into the author's context. The ultimate conceptual authority and consequently the ultimate stylistic authority are lodged in the author's direct speech.

The ultimate conceptual authority, which calls directly for a concurring comprehension of the referent, occurs as a matter of course in any literary work, but it is not always presented in the author's direct speech. The author's direct speech may be altogether absent–the speech of a narrator functioning as its compositional replacement, or, if the instance is a play, without any compositional equivalent in the work. In all these cases, the entire verbal material of the work belongs to either the second or third type of discourse. A play is almost always made up of represented, objectified utterances. But in certain stories, for instance, Puškin's *Tales of Belkin*, the narrative (Belkin's words) is made up of utterances of the third type; the utterances of the other characters belong to the second type. The absence of discourse carrying out the direct auctorial intent is a common phenomenon. The ultimate conceptual authority (the author's intention) is brought out, not in the author's direct speech, but by manipulating the utterances of another addresser, utterances intentionally created and deployed as belonging to someone other than the author.

The degree to which the represented utterance of a character is objectified may vary considerably. One need only point to the contrast between, say, the words of Tolstoj's Prince Andrej and those of any of Gogol′'s characters, Akakij Akakijevič, for instance. As the force of direct referential intentionality in a character's words increases and as, correspondingly, objectification decreases, the relationship between the author's speech and that of the character begins to approach the relationship between the two sides in a dialogue. The perspective between them diminishes, and they may come to occupy the same plane. However, this may be postulated only as a tendency toward an extreme never actually reached.

We have an instance of a dialogic relationship among directly intentional utterances within a single context in the typical scholarly article in which statements by various writers are cited, some for the purpose of refutation, others for the purpose of corroboration or supplementation. These binary relations (agreement vs. disagreement, assertion vs. supplementation, question vs. answer) are purely dialogic in nature. Moreover, these relations are not, of course, between separate words, or sentences, or other segments of a statement, but between whole statements. In dramatic dialogue, or in dramatized dialogue presented within the author's context, these relations coordinate represented, objectified utterances, and therefore they are themselves objectified. What occurs here is not the confrontation of two ultimate conceptual authorities but the objectified (plotted) confrontation of two represented positions—a confrontation wholly subordinated to the supreme, ultimate authority of the author. In this situation, the monologic context does not weaken or disintegrate.

The weakening or destruction of a monologic context comes about only when two directly intentional statements converge. Two directly intentional utterances of equal rank within a single context cannot occur together without interacting as a dialogue; it makes no difference in what specific way (by corroborating, or mutually supplementing each other, or by engaging in some other dialogic form of relationship, as, for instance, the question-answer form of colloquy). Two statements of equal weight on the same subject, once they come together, cannot line up in a row like two objects—they must make an inner contact, that is, they must enter into a conceptual bond.

The unmediated, intentional utterance is focused on its referential object, and it constitutes the ultimate conceptual authority within the given context. The objectified utterance is likewise focused only on its referential object, but at the same time it is itself the object of another, the author's, intention. Still, this other intention does not penetrate the objectified utterance; it takes that utterance as a whole and, without altering its meaning or tone, subordinates it to its own purposes. It does not impose upon the objectified utterance a different referential meaning. An utterance which becomes objectified does so, as it were, without knowing it, like a man who goes about his business unaware that he is being watched. An objectified utterance sounds just as if it were a direct, intentional utterance. Utterances both of the first and the second type of discourse have each one intention, each one voice: they are single-voiced utterances.

Yet an author may utilize the speech act of another in pursuit of his own aims and in such a way as to impose a new intention on the utterance, which nevertheless retains its own proper referential intention. Under these circumstances and in keeping with the author's purpose, such an utterance must be recognized as originating from another addresser. Thus, within a single utterance there may occur two intentions, two voices. Such is the nature of parody, stylization, and stylized *skaz*. We now come to a characterization of the third type of discourse.

Stylization presupposes style; it presupposes that the set of stylistic devices it reproduces had at one time a direct and immediate intentionality and expressed the ultimate conceptual authority. Only discourse of the first type can be the object of stylization. Stylization forces another intention (an artistic-thematic intention) to serve its aims, its own new intentions. The stylizer makes use of another speech act as such and in that way casts a somewhat objectified tint over it. In fact, however, that speech act does not become an objectified utterance. After all, what is uppermost for the stylizer is another person's set of devices precisely as the expression of a special point of view. He operates with this other point of view. Therefore, a certain tint of objectification does fall on that point of view, on that other intention, and, as a consequence, it becomes conventional. The objectified speech of a character is never conventional. A character's speech is always seriously spoken. The author's intention does not penetrate the character's speech but observes it from without.

A conventionalized utterance is always a double-voiced utterance. Only what was once perfectly serious and nonrelative to another point of view can become conventional. What was once a straightforward and nonconventional value now serves new aims, aims which take possession of it from inside and render it conventional. That is what distinguishes stylization from imitation. Imitation does not make a form conventional, owing to the simple fact that it takes the object of imitation seriously, makes it its own, directly appropriates the other speech act, and assimilates it to itself. The voices in this case merge completely. If we hear another voice, then we hear something which did not figure in the imitator's plan.

Though a sharp conceptual dividing line separates stylization and imitation, as has just been established, historically a set of extremely subtle and sometimes subliminal transitions does exist between them. The weaker the original seriousness of a style becomes in the hands of its epigone-imitators, the more nearly its devices become conventionalized–imitation thus becoming semi-stylization. Stylization in turn may become imitation, should the stylizer's fascination with his model destroy the distance between them and undermine the deliberate marking of the reproduced style as the style belonging to another writer. What, after all, creates conventionality is, in fact, distance.

A narrator's narration, which compositionally replaces the

author's discourse, is analogous to stylization. Such narration may take the form of the standard written language (Puškin's Belkin or Dostoevskij's narrator-chroniclers) or the form of oral speech (*skaz*, in the direct sense of the word). Here, too, the verbal manner of another addresser is utilized by the author as a point of view, a position, essential to the way the author wants to conduct the story. But here the tint of objectification in the narrator's speech is much heavier, and the conventionality much weaker, than in stylization. Needless to say, the degrees involved vary substantially. Still, the narrator's discourse can never become purely objectified discourse, even when he himself is one of the cast of characters and assumes only a part of the narration. After all, his importance to the author is not only a matter of his individual or typical manner of thinking, experiencing, and speaking, but is above all a matter of his seeing and depicting, for it is in this area that his direct designation as a narrator replacing the author consists. Thus the author's intentions, just as in stylization, penetrate the narrator's utterances, making them to a greater or lesser degree conventional. The author does not exhibit the narrator's speech to us (as he does exhibit the objectified utterances of the characters) but manipulates it from within for his own purposes, forcing us to be keenly aware of the distance between himself and this other speech act.

The element of *skaz* in the direct sense (an orientation toward oral speech) is a factor necessarily inherent in any storytelling. Even if the narrator is represented as writing his story and giving a certain literary polish to it, all the same he is not a literary professional; what he commands is not a specific style but only a socially or individually defined manner of storytelling, a manner that gravitates toward oral *skaz*. If, on the other hand, he does command a certain specific literary style, a style which the author reproduces in the narrator's name, then we are dealing with stylization, not with narrator's narration—there are, indeed, various ways of introducing and motivating stylization.

Both narrator's narration and even pure *skaz* may drop all their conventionality and become the author's direct speech expressing his intentions without any mediation. Such is almost always the nature of Turgenev's *skaz*: when Turgenev introduces his narrator, he does not in most instances stylize a distinct individual and social manner of storytelling. For instance, in "Andrej Kolosov," the story is told by the intelligent and cultured kind of man of Turgenev's own circle. He himself would have spoken thus about matters of the greatest seriousness in his own life. There is no effort here that is directed toward creating a socially different "*skaz*ified" tone or a socially different manner of observing and reporting observations; nor is there any effort to create an individually characteristic manner. Turgenev's *skaz* is unequivocally referential and contains only one voice, directly expressing the author's intentions. Here *skaz* is a simple compositional device. The nature of the *skaz* in the narration of *First Love* is identical (there presented by the narrator in written form).[2]

It is impossible to say the same thing about Belkin as a narrator. He is important to Puškin as a different, separate voice, above all, as a socially distinct person with a spiritual diapason and an approach to the world appropriate to him, and next in order of importance, he is a figure of certain individual characteristics. Consequently, the author's intentions in this case are refracted in the speech of the narrator; discourse here is double-voiced.

The problem of *skaz* was brought forward for the first time by B. M. Èjxenbaum.[3] He saw *skaz* exclusively as oriented toward the oral form of narration, orientation toward oral speech and its concomitant linguistic features (the special intonation, the syntactic arrangement, the lexicon, etc., of oral speech). He completely failed to consider the fact that in the majority of cases *skaz* consists above all in an orientation toward another speech act, and only in turn, and as a consequence, toward oral speech.

Our conception of *skaz* seems to us far more to the point in treating the problem in its literary historical dimensions. We believe that in the majority of cases *skaz* is brought in precisely for the sake of a different voice, one which is socially distinct and carries with it a set of viewpoints and evaluations which are just what the author needs. In point of fact, it is a storyteller who is brought in, and a storyteller is not a literary man; he usually belongs to the lower social strata, to the common people (precisely the quality the author values in him), and he brings with him oral speech.

Direct auctorial discourse is not possible in every literary period; not every period commands a style, since style presupposes the presence of authoritative points of view and authoritative, durable, social evaluations. Such styleless periods either go the way of stylization or revert to extraliterary forms of narration which command a particular manner of observing and depicting the world. When there is no adequate form for an unmediated expression of an author's intentions, it becomes necessary to refract them through another's speech. Moreover, the tasks facing literature are sometimes such that there is no other way open to implement them than by means of double-voiced discourse. That was exactly the case with Dostoevskij.

We believe that Leskov resorted to a narrator primarily for the sake of socially different speech and world outlook, and only secondarily for the sake of the oral quality in *skaz* (since he was interested in folk speech). Conversely, Turgenev looked to a narrator precisely for the sake of an oral form of narration which would directly express his own intentions. An orientation toward oral speech, not toward another speech act, was indeed characteristic of him. Turgenev could not refract his intentions through another speech act, nor did he like to do so. He managed very poorly with double-voiced discourse (for instance, in the satiric and parodic passages in *Smoke*). For this reason he chose a narrator from his own social circle. Since a narrator inevitably had to speak in the literary language, he could not sustain the oral quality of the narration throughout; for Turgenev it was important only to enliven his literary speech with oral intonations. In contrast, the attraction to *skaz* in contemporary literature is, as we see it, an attraction to another speech act. Direct auctorial speech is at present undergoing a socially conditioned crisis.

This is not the place to go into the proofs of all our assertions concerning literary history. Let them remain simply suppositions. One thing, however, we must insist on: that the strict distinction within *skaz* of an orientation toward another speech act and an orientation toward oral speech is absolutely essential. To see in *skaz* only oral speech is to miss the main point. Moreover, a large number of intonational, syntactic, and other linguistic phenomena are to be explained in *skaz* (given the author's orientation toward another speech act) precisely by its double-voiced quality, the intersecting of two voices and two accents within it. There are no similar phenomena in Turgenev, for instance, though his narrators show a much stronger tendency to oral speech than do those of Dostoevskij.

Ich-Erzählung is analogous to narrator's narration: sometimes it is marked by orientation toward another speech act, and sometimes (as in Turgenev's narration) it will approach and finally merge with the author's direct speech, that is, operate with the single-voiced discourse of the first type.

One must keep in mind that compositional forms do not of themselves decide the question of what type of discourse will be used. Such descriptive terms as *Ich-Erzählung*, "narrator's narration," "author's narration," and so on, are purely compositional terms. These compositional types of narration do gravitate, it is true, toward specific types of discourse, but they are not in obligatory bond with them.

All the instances of the third type of discourse thus far investigated—stylization, narrator's narration, and *Ich-Erzählung*—have a common feature sufficient to class them as a special (first) variety of that type. The common feature is that the author manipulates another speech act in the direction of his own intentions. Stylization stylizes another style in the direction of its own projects. All it does is make those projects conventional. Similarly, the narrator's narration, through which the author's intentions are refracted, does not deviate from its straight path but is sustained in the tones and intonations which really do belong to it. The author's intention, having penetrated the other speech act and having become embedded in it, does not clash with another intention; it follows that intention in the latter's own direction, only making that direction conventional.

The case is different with parody. Here, too, as in stylization, the author employs the speech of another, but, in contradistinction to stylization, he introduces into that other speech an intention which is directly opposed to the original one. The second voice, having lodged in the other speech, clashes antagonistically with the original, host voice and forces it to serve directly opposite aims. Speech becomes a battlefield for opposing intentions. Thus the merger of voices which is possible in stylization or in a narrator's narration (in Turgenev, for instance) is not possible in parody; the voices in parody are not only distinct and set off from one another but are also antagonistically opposed. That is why the other speech act in parody must be so very clearly and sharply marked and why the author's intentions must be individualized to a higher degree and given the fullest substance. It is possible to parody another style from different angles and to bring to bear in it a wide variety of new accents, whereas it can be stylized only, by and large, in one direction—in accordance with the task proper to stylization.

Parody allows considerable variety: one can parody another's style as a style, or parody another's socially typical or individually characteristic manner of observing, thinking, and speaking. Furthermore, the depth of parody may vary: one can limit parody to the forms that make up the verbal surface, but one can also parody even the deepest principles of the other speech act. Moreover, the parodic speech act itself may be variously utilized by the author: parody may be a goal in itself (for example, literary parody as a genre), or it may serve to achieve other, positive goals (as Ariosto's parodic style, or Puškin's). But in all the varieties of parodic discourse possible the relationship between the author's intention and that of the other speech remains the same: the two intentions are at odds, are vari-directional, as against the uni-directional orientation of intentions in stylization, narrator's narration, and analogous forms.

Thus the difference between simple *skaz* and parodic *skaz* is a very fundamental one. The struggle between two intentions in parodic *skaz* gives rise to the extremely distinctive linguistic phenomena mentioned above. If we ignore the orientation toward another speech act in *skaz* and, consequently, its double-voiced nature, we preclude any understanding of those complex relationships into which the voices within *skaz* discourse can enter when their orientation becomes vari-directional. *Skaz* in contemporary literature for the most part has parodic coloring. Zoščenko's *skaz*, for instance, is parodic *skaz*. In Dostoevskij's stories parodic elements of a special type are always present.

Parodic word usage is analogous to an ironic or any other ambivalent use of another addresser's words, since in these cases, too, the other person's words are utilized to convey antagonistic intentions. In our everyday speech such a use of another person's words is extremely common, particularly in dialogue. There one speaker very often repeats literally an assertion made by another speaker, investing it with a new intention and enunciating it in his own way: with an expression of doubt, indignation, irony, mockery, derision, or the like.

Leo Spitzer, in his book on the special features of conversational Italian, makes the following remark:

When we reproduce in our own speech a portion of what our conversational partner said, a change of tone inevitably occurs if for no other reason than that the addressers have been shifted around: the words of the "other" in our mouths always sound like something foreign, very often with a mocking, exaggerated, or derisive intonation. . . . In this connection I should like to make a special point of the funny or sharply ironic repetition of the verb of our partner's question in our subsequent reply. In such a situation it may be seen that we often resort, not only to grammatically incorrect, but even to very daring, sometimes completely impossible constructions for the sole purpose of somehow repeating a part of our partner's speech and giving it an ironic twist.[4]

Someone else's words introduced into our speech inevitably assume a new (our own) intention, that is, they become double-voiced. It is only the relationship between these two voices that may vary. Even the transmission of another's assertion in the form of a question leads to a clash of the two intentions in one utterance: we not only question his assertion, we make a problem out of it. Our everyday speech is full of other people's words: with some of them our voice is completely merged, and we forget whose words they were; we use others that have authority, in our view, to substantiate our own words; and in yet others we implant our different, even antagonistic intentions.

Let us proceed to the final variety of the third type of discourse. In both of the preceding varieties, exemplified by stylization and parody, respectively, the author utilizes what are distinctly another person's words for the expression of his own particular intentions. In the third variety, the other speech act remains outside the bounds of the author's speech, but is implied or alluded to in that speech. The other speech act is not reproduced with a new intention, but shapes the author's speech while remaining outside its boundaries. Such is the nature of discourse in hidden polemic and equally, as a rule, in a single line of dialogue.

In hidden polemic the author's discourse is oriented toward its referential object, as is any other discourse, but at the same time each assertion about that object is constructed in such a way that, besides its referential meaning, the author's discourse brings a polemical attack to bear against another speech act, another assertion, on the same topic. Here one utterance focused on its referential object clashes with another utterance on the grounds of the referent itself. That other utterance is not reproduced; it is understood only in its import; but the whole structure of the author's speech would be completely different, if it were not for this reaction to another's unexpressed speech act. In stylization, the actual model reproduced (the other style) also remains outside the author's context, its existence being merely understood. Likewise, in parody the existence of the actual, particular speech being parodied is only understood. In these instances, however, the author's speech itself either poses as someone else's speech (stylization) or lays claim to someone else's speech as its own (parody). In any case, it operates directly with another speech act, the implied model (the other actual speech act) only supplying the material and functioning as a document proving that the author is really reproducing another particular speech act. In the hidden polemic, on the other hand, the other speech act is reacted to, and this reaction, no less than the topic of discussion, determines the author's speech. This radically changes the semantics of the discourse involved: alongside its referential meaning, a second meaning—the fact of its taking bearings on another speech act—comes into play. One cannot completely and properly understand such speech when only its direct referential denotation is considered. The polemical shading of the discourse also shows up in other purely linguistic features: in intonation and in syntactic construction.

To draw a distinct dividing line between the hidden and the overt, open polemic in a concrete case sometimes proves quite difficult, but the conceptual differences are essential. Overt polemic is simply directed toward the other speech act, the one being refuted, as its own referential object. Hidden polemic is usually focused on some referential object which it denotes, depicts, expresses—and only obliquely does it strike at the other speech act, somehow clashing with it on the grounds of the referent itself. As a result, the latter begins to influence the author's speech from within. It is for that reason we call hidden polemic double-voiced, although the relationship of the two voices here is special. The other intention does not enter explicitly into the discourse but is only reflected in it, determining its tone and meaning. One speech act acutely senses another speech act close by, one addressed to the same topic, and this recognition determines its entire internal structure.

Internally polemical speech—speech that is aware of another and an antagonistic speech act—is especially widespread in everyday as well as literary speech, and it has an enormous significance in the formation of style. In everyday speech, instances of internal polemics are all "barbed" words and words used as "brickbats." This category also includes any speech that is servile or overblown, any speech that has determined beforehand not to be itself, any speech replete with reservations, concessions, loopholes, and so on. Such speech seems to cringe in the presence, or at the presentiment of, some other persons's statement, reply, objection. The individual manner of a person's own speech construction is determined to a considerable degree by his own peculiar feeling for the speech of other people and by his means of reacting to it.

In literary speech the significance of hidden polemic is enormous. In every style, properly speaking, there is an element of internal polemic, the difference being only in its degree and character. Any literary discourse more or less keenly senses its listener, reader or critic, and reflects anticipated objections, evaluations, points of view. Moreover, literary discourse senses other literary discourse, other style, alongside it. An element of the so-called reaction against a previous literary style which is present in every new style is just such an internal polemic; it is a hidden antistylization, so to speak, of another style, which often unites with an outright parody of that other style. The significance of the internal polemic for the formation of style is especially great in autobiographies and in forms of *Ich-Erzählung* of the confessional sort. Rousseau's *Confession* is a sufficient example.

Analogous to the hidden polemic is the single line of dialogue (assuming the dialogue to be of some weight and substance). In such a line every utterance, while focused on its referential object, at the same time displays an intensive reaction to another utterance, either replying to it or anticipating it. This feature of reply and anticipation penetrates deeply into the intensively dialogic utterance. Such an utterance appears to be taking in, sucking into itself, the utterances and intentions of the speaker and intensively reworking them. The semantics of dialogic discourse is of a completely special kind. All those subtle alterations in meaning which occur in the heat of a dialogic exchange unfortunately still remain totally unstudied. Once the counterstatement (*Gegenrede*) is taken into consideration, certain specific changes in the structure of dialogic discourse come into play: dialogue becomes an arena of events within itself and its very topic of discourse is seen in a new light, disclosing new facets inaccessible to monologic discourse.

Especially significant and important for our subsequent aims is hidden dialogue (not to be identified with hidden polemic). Imagine a dialogue between two persons in which the statements of the second speaker are deleted, but in such a way that the general sense is not disrupted. The second speaker's presence is not shown; his actual words are not given, but the deep impression of these words has a determining effect on all the utterances made by the only one who does speak. We feel that this is a conversation of the most intense kind, because each uttered word, in all its fiber, responds and reacts to the invisible partner, referring to something outside itself, beyond its limits, to the unspoken word of the other speaker. In Dostoevskij's works this hidden dialogue occupies a very important place and is extremely subtle and profoundly elaborated.

The third variety of the third type, as we see, differs sharply from the two preceding varieties of this type. We may call this third variety the active one, in distinction from the others, which are more passive. It is indeed a fact that in stylization, narrator's narration, and parody the other speech act is completely passive in the hands of the author who avails himself of it. He, so to speak, takes someone else's speech act, which is defenseless and submissive, and implants his own intentions in it, making it serve his new aims. Contrastingly, in hidden polemic and dialogue, the other speech act actively influences the author's speech and forces it to change shape in whatever ways its influence and initiative dictate.

It is possible, however, for the role of the other speech act to become more active in all occurrences of the second variety of the third type. When parody becomes aware of substantial resistance, a certain forcefulness and profundity in the speech act it parodies, it takes on a new dimension of complexity via the tones of the hidden polemic. Such a parody already "sounds" quite different: the speech act being parodied sounds more active and brings a counteraction to bear on the author's intention. A process of inner dialogization takes place within the parodic speech act. Similar phenomena also occur when hidden dialogue combines with narrator's narration—in general, in all manifestations of the third type wherever the author's intentions and those of the other speech act diverge.

With a decrease in the objectification of the other speech act (objectification being, as we know, an inherent trait, to one or another degree, of the third type) in all the instances of uni-directional discourse (stylization, uni-directional narrator's narration) there occurs a merging together of the author's voice and the other voice. The distance between the two is lost; stylization becomes style; the narrator is transformed into a simple compositonal convention. In the case of vari-directional discourse, a decrease in objectification and a corresponding increase in the active role of the intentions belonging to the other speech act lead inevitably to the internal dialogization of discourse. In such discourse the author's intention no longer retains its dominant hold over the other intention; it loses its composure and assuredness, becomes perturbed, internally indecisive and ambiguous. Such speech is not only double-voiced, but also double-accented. It would be difficult to sound such speech aloud, because any actual enunciation would overmonologize it and fail to do justice to the other intention present in it.

This internal dialogization—connected with a decrease in objectification in vari-directional variants of the third type—does not, of course, constitute a new category of that type. It is only a tendency, one inherent in every occurrence of the given type (provided that it is vari-directionally oriented). At its upper limit this tendency leads to the splitting of double-voiced discourse into two speech acts, into two entirely separate and autonomous voices. Conversely, the tendency with the variants of uni-directional discourse, given a decrease in the objectification of the other speech act, leads at its upper limit to a complete fusion of voices and consequently to single-voiced discourse of the first type. All occurrences of the third type fluctuate between these two limits.

We have by no means exhausted all the possible occurrences of double-voiced discourse or all the possible means of orientation with respect to another speech act which gives the usual referential orientation of normal speech a new complexity. A more profound and refined classification, with a larger collection of varieties, even perhaps of types, might be possible. However, for our aims the given classification appears to be sufficient. The following is its schematic representation.

The classification outlined below naturally bears a purely conceptual, abstract character. A concrete instance of discourse may belong simultaneously to different varieties, and even to different types. Also, relationships with another speech act in a concrete, continuing context do not have a static, but rather a dynamic character. The relationship of voices in discourse may change sharply: uni-directional utterances may turn vari-directional; internal dialogization may become stronger or weaker; a passive type may undergo activization, and so on.

1
Direct unmediated discourse, focused solely on its referential object, as expression of the speaker's ultimate conceptual authority.

2

Objectified discourse (the speech of a person represented).

1. With a predominance of sociotypical determinations. 2. With a predominance of individually characteristic determinations.	Various degrees of objectification.

3.

Discourse with emphasis on another speech act (double-voiced discourse).

1. Uni-directional variants. a. Stylization. b. Narrator's narration. c. Unobjectified speech of a character who carries out the author's intentions (in part). d. *Ich-Erzählung.*	With reduced objectification, these variants approach a fusion of voices, i.e., approach the first type of discourse.
2. Vari-directional variants. a. Parody with all its shadings. b. Parodic narration. c. Parodic *Ich-Erzählung.* d. Speech of a character who is parodically represented. e. Any reportage of someone else's speech with an altered accent.	With reduced objectification of the other intention, these variants become internally dialogized to some degree and approach a division into two speech acts (two voices) of the first type.
3. Active type (another speech act reflected). a. Hidden, internal polemic. b. Polemically colored autobiography and confession. c. Any speech with an awareness of another's speech. d. The single line of dialogue. e. Hidden dialogue.	The other speech act exerts an influence from within; the forms of relationship between the two voices may vary widely, as may the degree of the deforming influence of the other speech act.

The plane of the investigation of discourse we have proposed, with its focal point on the relationship of one speech act with another, has, we believe, exceptionally important meaning for the understanding of artistic prose. The speech of poetry in the narrow sense requires a unified usage of all words, their reduction to a common denominator of intention, that denominator either being discourse of the first type or belonging to certain watered-down varieties of the other types. Of course, poetic works in which not all the speech material is reduced to a common denominator are possible, but these are rare occurrences, such as, for example, the "prosaic" lyrics of Heine, Barbier, Nekrasov, and others. One of the essential peculiarities of prose fiction is the possibility it allows of using different types of discourse, with their distinct expressiveness intact, on the plane of a single work without reduction to a common denominator. Here resides the profound difference between style in prose and style in poetry. Yet even in poetry a whole series of crucial problems cannot be solved without considering the system of investigation here proposed, because different types of discourse require a different stylistic treatment in poetry.

Contemporary stylistics, which ignores this plane of investigation, is in fact stylistics of the first type of discourse alone, that is, the author's direct referent-oriented speech. Contemporary stylistics, with its roots going back to the poetics of Neoclassicism, cannot to the present day give up Neoclassicist norms and schemes. Neoclassicist poetics was oriented on direct intentional discourse somewhat slanted toward conventionalized stylized speech. Semiconventionalized, semistylized discourse sets the tone in classical poetics. And stylistics up to the present day has taken for its orientation just such semiconventionalized direct speech, which in fact it has identified with poetic speech per se. For Classicism discourse belongs to the level of language; words are common property, objects which go to make up the poetic lexicon, and any item taken from the storehouse of poetic language is transferred directly into the monologic context of the given poetic expression. Thus, a stylistics nurtured on Classicism recognizes only the existence and viability of discourse in a single closed context. It ignores those changes which come about in discourse during the process of shifting words from one concrete utterance to another and during the process of the mutual orientation of those utterances. It recognizes only those changes which come about when words are shifted from the language system into a monologic poetic utterance. The viability and function of words in the style of a concrete utterance is assumed to be the face value of their viability and function in the language system. The inner dialogic relationship that may exist between a word in one context and the same word in the context of another speech act, on someone else's lips, is ignored. Stylistics has operated within this framework up to the present time.

Romanticism brought with it direct-intentional words with no deviation toward conventionality. Direct, expressive auctorial speech, untempered by any sort of refraction through the verbal medium of any other speech act, was characteristic of Romanticism to the point of utter distraction. In Romantic poetics considerable significance was attached to variants of the second and, particularly, of the last categories of the third type,[5] but all the same directly intentional discourse, discourse of the first type, extended to its limits, dominated to such a degree that no alterations with any real bearing on the problem under discussion could come about in Romanticism. In this respect the poetics of Classicism was hardly affected. Nevertheless, contemporary stylistics is far from being sufficient even to deal with Romanticism.

Prose fiction, especially the novel, is completely beyond the reach of such stylistics. It treats with some degree of success only minor areas of the art of prose, those areas least characteristic and least crucial for prose. To the prose writer the world is full of other people's speech acts; he orients himself among these, and he must have a keen ear for perceiving and identifying their peculiarities. He has to incorporate them on the plane of his own speech, but in such a way that that plane will not be destroyed.[6] He works with a very rich speech palette, and he works exceptionally well with it. And we, while we are reading prose, must also orient ourselves very sensitively among all the types and varieties of discourse analyzed above. What is more, even in ordinary life, that same sensitivity enables us to hear distinctly all these shades in the speech of people surrounding us; and we ourselves work with all these colors on the speech palette. We are quick to detect the smallest deviation in intention, the faintest counterpoint of voices in whatever of interest is said to us by another person in the ordinary business of life. All those verbal side-glances, reservations, loopholes, insinuations, thrusts do not escape our hearing and are not alien to our own usage. This makes it all the more astonishing that until now this whole situation has not found a clear-cut theoretical cognizance, a due evaluation. In theory, we analyze only the stylistic relationship of elements within a closed message, against a background of abstract linguistic categories. Only such single-voiced phenomena are within the reach of that superficial linguistic stylistics which until now, for all its linguistic worth, has been capable of registering in literary creation only the traces and outcroppings of artistic aims (of which it is ignorant) on the verbal periphery of literary works. The actual living nature of discourse in prose is not amenable to such a framework. That framework is even too narrow for poetry.

The problem of the orientation of speech toward another utterance also has a sociological significance of the highest order. The speech act by its nature is social. The word is not a tangible object, but an always shifting, always changing means of social communication. It never rests with one consciousness, one voice. Its dynamism consists in movement from speaker to speaker, from one context to another, from one social community to another, from one generation to another. Through it all the word does not forget its path of transfer and cannot completely free itself from the power of those concrete contexts into which it had entered. By no means does each member of the community apprehend the word as a neutral element of the language system, free from intentions and untenanted by the voices of its previous users. Instead, he receives the word from another voice, a word full of that other voice. The word enters his context from another context and is permeated with the intentions of other speakers. His own intention finds the word already occupied.

Thus the orientation of the word among words, the various perceptions of other speech acts, and the various means of reacting to them are perhaps the most crucial problems in the sociology of language usage, any kind of language usage, including the artistic. Each social group in each historical period has its own individual perception of the word, its own range of verbal possibilities. By no means can the ultimate conceptual authority of the artist always be expressed in direct, unrefracted, nonconventionalized auctorial speech in every social situation. When one does not have one's own proper "ultimate word," any creative intention, any thought, feeling, or experience must be refracted through the medium of another speech act, another style, another manner, with which it cannot immediately merge without reservation, distance, refraction. If a given social group has at its disposal an authoritative and durable medium of refraction, then conventionalized discourse in one or another of its varieties will hold sway, and to one or another degree of conventionality. If there is no such medium, then vari-directional, double-voiced discourse will hold sway: parodic speech in all its varieties, or a special type of semiconventionalized, semi-ironic speech (that of late Classicism). In such periods, especially when conventionalized discourse is dominant, directly intentional, reservationless, unrefracted speech appears to be a barbaric, coarse, bizarre kind of speech. Cultured speech is speech refracted through the authoritative canonical medium.

Which type of discourse dominates in a given period in a given social setting, which forms of speech refraction exist, and what serves as the medium of refraction—all these are questions of paramount significance for the sociology of artistic speech.

Notes

1. The classification of the types and varieties of discourse offered below is without examples, since in the following chapter [of Baxtin's book] extensive material from the works of Dostoevskij is given for each case discussed.

2. Boris Èjxenbaum quite correctly, but from a different point of view, remarks on this peculiarity of Turgenev's narration: "The form of the author's motivated introduction of a special narrator to whom the narration is entrusted is especially common. However, very often this form has a completely conventional character (as in Maupassant or Turgenev), evincing only the vitality of the tradition of the narrator as a special personage in the story. In such cases the narrator remains the same as the author, and the motivation for his insertion plays the role of a simple introduction." (Boris Èjxenbaum, *Literatura: teorija, kritika, polemika*, Leningrad, 1927), p. 217.

3. First in the article "Kak sdelana 'Šinel′' " in the collection, *Poètika* (1919). Then in particular in the article "Leskov i sovremennaja proza," *ibid.* pp. 210 ff.

4. Leo Spitzer, *Italienische Umgangssprache* (Leipzig, 1922), pp. 175-176.

5. In connection with the interest in folkways (not as an ethnographic category), an enormous significance in Romanticism was attached to different forms of *skaz* as another speech act used as refractor with a weak degree of objectification. For Classicism, "folk speech" (in the sense of another type of speech that was socially typical and individually characteristic) was purely objectified speech (in the low genres). Among the variants of the third type, polemical *Ich-Erzählung* (particularly the confessional type) was especially important.

6. The majority of prose genres, particularly the novel, are constructive in nature: they are structures of elements that are whole utterances, though these utterances are not fully authoritative and are subordinated to the monologic unity.

Part V

Afanasij Nikitin's *Journey Beyond the Three Seas* as a Work of Literature
Nikolaj S. Trubeckoj

The Mystery Novel: Dickens's *Little Dorrit*
Viktor Šklovskij

O. Henry and the Theory of the Short Story
Boris M. Èjxenbaum

Afanasij Nikitin's *Journey Beyond the Three Seas* as a Work of Literature*

Nikolaj S. Trubeckoj

The immediate apprehension of Old Russian literature is very difficult, not only for the foreign reader, but for the contemporary Russian reader as well. We do not understand it and are unable to appraise it as literature. The Old Russian icon now has been "discovered" not only physically—in that all the soot and more recent layers of paint have been removed—but also spiritually; we have learned how to look at it, how to see and understand what it says. But we continue to be deaf and blind toward the works of Old Russian letters.

The specific features of the scholarly study of "the history of Old Russian literature" are grounded in this fact. I write this phrase in quotation marks, for this study, as "history of literature," is very strange, not resembling other such efforts. One can be easily convinced of this by examining any textbook or university course in this field of study. Strictly speaking, little is said in these textbooks and courses about literature as such. They speak about enlightenment (more precisely, about the absence of enlightenment), about the features of contemporary life-style reflected (more precisely, insufficiently reflected) in sermons, chronicles, and the lives of saints; they speak about the emendation of religious texts, and so on—in short, they concern themselves with a great deal. But of literature little is said. There exist several hackneyed appraisals which are applied to extremely diverse works in Old Russian literature: some of these works are said to be written in "an ornamental manner," others, in an "artless" or "ingenuous manner." The attitude of the authors of textbooks and university courses toward all these works is invariably contemptuous and scornful, at best condescendingly contemptuous, but sometimes openly indignant and hostile. An Old Russian literary work is considered "interesting," not in and of itself, but only in so far as it reflects some features of the contemporary life-style (that is, in so far as it exists, not as an entity in the history of literature, but as an artifact in the history of life-style); or it is "interesting" in so far as it contains direct or indirect indications of the author's familiarity with some other literary works (for the most part, translations). For some reason, expressions of the *Weltanschauung* and links with folk poetry are invariably demanded from an Old Russian author. If such elements cannot be found in his work, he is treated with contempt

*"*Xoženie za tri morja Afanasija Nikitina*, kak literaturnyj pamjatnik," *Versty*, I (1926), pp. 164-186. Translated by Kenneth Brostrom.

and a touch of indignation; if such elements can be found in his work, he is praised, but nevertheless with a touch of condescending contempt.

It goes without saying that all these features of scholarship in the history of Old Russian literature (as this scholarship is reflected in textbooks and university courses) are conceivable only on the assumption that Old Russian literature is not literature. This becomes particularly evident if one attempts, as an experiment, to approach modern Russian literature with the same criteria that have been applied to Old Russian literature. Puškin's *Evgenij Onegin* would be interesting only because it reflects the lifestyle of the Russian gentry at the beginning of the nineteenth century and testifies to the author's familiarity with Richardson and Adam Smith. One would have to condemn Turgenev because he did not link his work to folk poetry and was devoid of the *Weltanschauung*, and so forth. Of course, the generally hostile attitude of the Russian intelligentsia toward pre-Petrine Rus as a realm of barbarism, darkness, and squalor in every area of life is to blame for these characteristics of the history of Old Russian literature. But it would seem that this widespread prejudice against the old Rus should have been shaken by the "discovery" of the icon, which demonstrated that in pre-Petrine Russia a high esthetic culture existed along with a deep religiosity, which was mystically and theologically conceived and was by no means barbaric and primitive. If, nevertheless, the history of Old Russian literature continues as at present to treat its object in the same way as it has in the past, this may be explained, of course, by the fact that the works of Old Russian literature up until now have been "discovered" only physically but not spiritually, and that we still are unable to perceive their artistic value.

There is only one remedy which can deliver us from these difficulties. It is necessary to approach the works of Old Russian literature with the same scholarly methods that have been adopted in the approach to modern Russian literature and all literature in general. In this regard, a powerful technique for the scholarly study of literature has recently been developed: the Formal method. To apply this method in studying Old Russian literature opens up completely unexpected horizons to the investigator; works formerly considered by general consent to be artless turn out to be an intricate web of devices, which in the majority of cases are rather artful. And each such device has not only its own meaning, its own purpose, but also its own history.

The entire understanding of the history of Old Russian literature becomes altered; instead of a vision of centuries of helpless floundering in the toils of ignorance, as the history of Old Russian literature is represented in widely used textbooks, one acquires a vision of labor aimed at the resolution of formal problems. In short, the form of Old Russian works of literature comes to life and acquires meaning. When we comprehend this meaning and begin to appraise the purely technical, formal aspects of Old Russian works of literature, we gain as well the possibility of perceiving the real artistic value of these works.

Of course, the Formal method alone—that is, the rational understanding of the meaning and purpose of the Old Russian compositional and stylistic devices alone—is insufficient for such an evaluation. What is necessary is to open up one's soul to these perceptions, to make it receptive to the role of all these devices, and to abolish all resistance to this role. To do this, one must abandon the widespread preconceived hostility and scorn characteristic of the attitude toward Old Russian culture and replace them with an attitude of preconceived good will. This is an indispensable condition for the evaluation of every art form. An acute hatred for any people or culture renders an evaluation of the art of this people impossible; on the contrary, an evaluation of this art becomes possible only when we regard such a people with affection, with a maximum degree of good will (if only in a conditional, methodological sense).

In the following pages I will try to apply such an approach in the case of an Old Russian work of literature belonging to the end of the fifteenth century, Afanasij Nikitin's *Journey Beyond the Three Seas.* This work has been studied by historians of Russian literature primarily from a cultural-historical point of view. Since its content constitutes a description of the journey of the Tver merchant Afanasij Nikitin to India in 1468, they have attempted to extract from it material for the history of India, for the history of Russia's relations with the East, and so forth. Such an approach is of course fully justified, just as it is completely acceptable to view Karamzin's *Letters of a Russian Traveler* as a work describing the life-style in Europe at the end of the eigthteenth century or to extract information from Gončarov's *Frigate Pallada* concerning the enthnography and geography of the various countries Gončarov visited. To limit oneself to such an approach to all such literary works would, of course, be incorrect. However, with regard to Afanasij Nikitin's *Journey*, the literary historians have not limited themselves to such an approach; they have used this work as evidence of the low level of culture in fifteenth- century Russia and of the absence of scholarly concerns and interests in Russian society at that time. For the sake of even greater persuasiveness, they have contrasted Nikitin with Vasco da Gama, who traveled through India at approximately the same time. However, their argument has not concerned itself in any way with a comparison of the literary merits of Nikitin's *Journey* with those of Vasco da Gama's memoirs. Thus Nikitin's *Journey* has not been analyzed from a specifically literary point of view by anyone up to the present time.

In the following paragraphs we will first deal with the composition of the *Journey Beyond the Three Seas*, and then move to its stylistic features; in conclusion, we will attempt to grasp the inner meaning of the work through its form.

Nikitin's manner of exegesis may be described thus: he opens his exposition in a calm tone, then, suddenly remembering how he had been alone among people of another faith, he begins to lament, to complain, to grieve, and to pray; then he resumes his calm exegesis, but soon he falls anew into complaints and prayers; then again he resumes his calm exposition, but soon he passes once again to complaints and prayers, and so on. In a word, the whole work consists of an alternation between rather long segments of calm exposition and shorter segments of religious-lyrical digression.

Thus calm exposition and religious-lyrical digression are the two fundamental compositional elements, the two building materials, utilized by Nikitin. These two elements are distinguishable one from the other not only by their content but also by the forms of their verbal expression. Exclamatory sentences are frequent, and addresses to the reader are also encountered. Neither of these is observed in the segments of calm exposition. The language of the religious-lyrical digressions is more "literary," that is, it contains more Church Slavonic elements and features than does the conversational and commercial language, the almost pure Russian, in the segments of calm exposition. This distinction between two linguistic stylistic types reaffirms the distinction between the two fundamental compositional elements of the book and makes their mutual opposition especially vivid.

The separate segments of calm exposition are quite clearly distinguishable by their content. Two segments are located at the very middle of the *Journey;* one of them is dedicated exclusively to the religion of India, and the other, to information about Indian "refuges" (port cities). Each of these segments is a closed and internally homogeneous entity, a systematic collection of facts concerning one defined subject.

Two other segments adjoin the two at the center, one preceding and the other following. These contain uncoordinated observations about the natural environment and life-style in India, observations that are expounded in chaotic disorder. The first of these two auxiliary segments begins with a discussion of marine commerce and piracy, then discusses the bazaar in the city of Beder, then the Khorasan rulers who govern India and the arms of their soldiers, a marketplace on a day dedicated to the memory of the sheik Alauddin, the wonders of Indian fauna (the *gukuk* bird [a type of heron] and monkeys), the Khorasan nobles and the luxuriousness of their carriages, the magnificence of the Beder sultan's palace, and finally the snakes crawling on the streets of Beder.

The exposition of the second of these two segments is every bit as disconnected as is that of the first. The heterogeneity of the observations grouped together in these two segments distinguishes them sharply from the two internally homogeneous central segments. On the other hand, besides this shared formal characteristic of disordered exposition, there exists a resemblance in the content of these two flanking segments: thus both describe the luxuriousness of the Beder sultan's equipage, and both give information about the climate.

All four of the segments examined above, taken together, constitute a static description of India. This description is (more or less) systematic only in its most central portions, but in the flanking segments it is unsystematic and disordered. Apparently, the distribution of the separate pieces of information depends on their significance: the most essential are placed in the center, while the less essential data are placed on either side. This characteristic is underlined by the arrangement, which is systematic at the center but disordered on either side. As a merchant and at the same time a religious man, Nikitin attributed the greatest significance to whatever he happened to learn about the religion of India and the commercial opportunities to be found in the Indian port cities.

In contrast to the static-descriptive character of the four segments in the central part of the *Journey*, the beginning and the end of the book have a dynamic-narrative character: at the beginning there is a narrative of the events of the trip from Tver to Gurmyz (a city located on an island in the Persian Gulf); and at the end there is a narrative of the return trip from the last Indian "refuge," Dabil, in the Crimea. In these two segments Nikitin speaks exclusively of the events of the trip, without a single pause for describing what he saw during the journey. Conversely, in the middle portion of the *Journey* (dedicated, as was pointed out earlier, to a static description of India), there are no data concerning those experiences and adventures which undoubtedly accompanied the author's journeys, his movements inside India, from one town to another. Thus static description and dynamic narration in the *Journey* are compositionally differentiated: all the "statics" are concentrated at the center, while the "dynamics" are distributed along the boundaries of the work.

Between the static-descriptive center and the dynamic-narrative boundaries of the *Journey* there are segments we may call "transitional." The first of these is essentially a transition from dynamic narration to static description. At the end of the segment describing the events of the journey from Tver to Gurmyz, one finds a number of cryptic bits of information of a descriptive nature which are injected into an enumeration of Persian towns. After the arrival in Gurmyz, the narration of the events of the journey is constantly intermingled with descriptions of the country and its inhabitants. The first impressions of India have already been given a subjective coloration.

> And here was the land of India. All the people walk about naked, their heads uncovered, their breasts bared, and their hair braided into one plait. And they all go about big-bellied; they give birth to children every year, and they have many children. Both men and women are dark, and wherever I go, many people follow me; they are amazed at a white man.

In the remainder of this segment, every piece of information of a descriptive character occurs as if prompted by some episode in the journey. Owing to the stimulus of the arrival in Khunar, the residence of Asad-Khan, data are provided regarding the life-style of the Khorasan nobles in India. The onset of winter, which forces Nikitin to remain for a time in Khunar, has provided a motive for communicating information about the climate, about the fact that "at this time they plow and sow," and in general for providing various pieces of information about agriculture. The approach of winter has also provided a stimulus for discussing the winter dress of the Indians.

In general, we find in this segment the same disorder in communicating uncoordinated observations which is characteristic of the flanking segments of the central, purely static-descriptive part of the *Journey*. In contrast to these flanking segments, in which this disordered exposition is given no motivation, here it is motivated by the fact that these are "travel notes." In the segment being examined, the descriptive and narrative elements are conjoined, and thus the entire segment provides a gradual transition from the purely dynamic narration of the beginning of the *Journey* to the purely static description of the central portion.

The opposite transition (from the static description of the middle of the *Journey* to the dynamic narration at the end) is realized in two "transitional" segments which follow one another. Both these segments are closely connected by their content: in both, the narration concerns wars and military incidents which took place in India during Nikitin's residence. Just before the first of these segments, while lamenting the fact that it had become difficult to leave India as a result of the ubiquitous warfare ("everywhere *budgak* had arisen," that is, sedition, dissension), Nikitin sketches briefly the political situation which had come about in the East:

> Everywhere the princes were driven out; Uzun Osambek killed the Murza Yansha, and Soltamusait was poisoned. Uzun Osambek occupied Shiryaza; his territory wasn't secure, but Edger Makhmet didn't move against him, since he was looking out for his own safety.

The first of these segments then begins with a discussion of the Bederian sultan's general, Meliktukhar, who "seized two Indian towns, which had been 'pillaging' [that is, had been engaged in piracy] on the Indian Ocean. And he caught seven princes and seized their treasury. . . . He camped near one city for two years; there were two hundred thousand troops with him, one hundred elephants, and three hundred camels." Then the arrival of this Meliktukhar in Beder is related, along with his meeting with the sultan, and the departure of the Bederian sultan's troops for a campaign against the prince of Khunedar. Along with the narration of these events, there are incidental descriptions of the luxuriousness of Meliktukhar's mode of life, of the sultan's voluptuous equipage, and a detailed enumeration of the various bodies of troops in the sultan's army, along with brief remarks about their armament. In this way, the dynamic narration of events is linked to description. In this case, description predominates over narration and, in content and form, is strongly reminiscent of the description of the Bederian sultan's luxurious equipage in the foregoing flanking segment of the central, purely static-descriptive part of the *Journey.*

In the opening section of the next segment there is a continuation of the narrative of the campaign of the Bederian sultan, but, inserted into this narrative, there is a short description of one town especially difficult to conquer. Then there follows the story of Afanasij Nikitin's removal from Kelberg to Dabil, which is accompanied by incidental bits of information concerning the sights in several towns.

Thus the element of dynamic narration in this segment is mingled with the element of static description, but, in contrast to the foregoing segment, narration predominates here over description. Thus the way is prepared for the final segment of the book (which follows the one just examined), a purely dynamic-narrative exposition of the return trip from Dabil to the Crimea.

In this way, the gradual transition from the dynamic-narrative beginning to the static-descriptive middle portion is accomplished through a "transitional" segment containing travel notes, while the converse, the gradual transition from the static-descriptive core of the work to the dynamic-narrative conclusion, is accomplished by two transitional segments dedicated to military affairs. This distinction between the contents of the transitional segments depends on the distinctions in content between the purely narrative parts of the book to which the transitional segments are joined. Nikitin's journey from Tver to India took place in peaceful political conditions; but the return trip from India to the Crimea was accomplished against a background of military activity, which is mentioned not only in the transitional segments but also in the purely narrative conclusion. Nevertheless, in spite of these differences, the transitional segments in their formal, compositional function are analogous to one another, since they serve as links between the two fundamental types of calm exposition, dynamic narration and static description. Owing to this fact, they unite the core of the *Journey* with its beginning and also with its conclusion.

To summarize all we have said of the segments of calm exposition, we present the following general schema: the closer one moves toward the center, the purer the static-descriptive type becomes; the further one moves from the center, the purer the dynamic-narrative type becomes. This curve, which passes from dynamic narration to static description and returns to dynamic narration, is not "continuous"; rather, it decomposes into nine segments, each of which represents a deviation in a definite direction. These are as follows:

1. "The Journey from Tver to Gurmyz" (pure dynamic narration).
2. "First Travel Impressions" (a mixture of dynamic narration and static description).
3. "Scattered Information about the Natural Environment and the Inhabitants of India" (static description of a disordered and unsystematic character).
4. "Information about the Religion of India" (systematic static description).
5. "Description of the Port Cities of India" (systematic static description).
6. "Scattered Information about the Natural Environment and the Inhabitants of India" (static description of a disorganized and unsystematic character).
7. "Military Incidents in India" (a mixture of static description and dynamic narration, with the former predominating).
8. "Military Incidents in India. Afanasij Nikitin's Removal to the Seashore" (a mixture of static description and dynamic narration, with the latter predominating).
9. "The Return Trip from Dabil to the Crimea" (pure dynamic narration).

It is impossible to ignore the striking symmetry, the harmony, of this compositional schema.

We turn now to the other compositional element of the *Journey*, to the religious-lyrical digressions. In contrast to the heterogeneity of content in the segments of calm exposition, the religious-lyrical digressions are homogeneous in content. They are all related to one another by some reference to one or another of the twelve major holidays in the Orthodox calendar; they all emphasize the oppressive feeling of loneliness experienced by an Orthodox Christian among people of another faith, as well as the difficulty of preserving his faith for such a Christian (in the sense of customary religious observances and practices). These digressions are distinguished from one another for the most part by the fact that some of them are extensive and developed, while others are shorter and, in a manner of speaking, "undeveloped," that is, they contain only an indication of a psychological state, but not an elaboration of that state. As noted above, each of these religious-lyrical digressions is located in an interval between two segments of calm exposition; that is, it is located at a point of discontinuity on the above-mentioned compositional "curve," thus bringing about the actual segmentation of that curve. If we examine the distribution of the religious-lyrical digressions more closely, we note that the extensive and fully developed digressions appear in all those instances in which at least one of the segments of calm exposition immediately adjoining the given digression is of a purely static-descriptive character. An exception to this rule is found only at the juncture of the third and fourth segments, where, in spite of the purely static-descriptive character of both segments, the religious-lyrical digression is only brief, not developed; that is, there is a laconic reference to a major Orthodox holiday and also an indication of Afanasij Nikitin's religious activities among the non-Orthodox; but lyricism is absent and must be supplied by the imagination of the reader. This is explainable, of course, by the fact that the fourth segment, following this digression, is completely dedicated to the religion of India. An excessively insistent emphasis upon Nikitin's spiritual isolation at this point would have been unwarranted and might have impeded the transition to calm exposition which follows.

Wherever neither of the neighboring segments is of a purely static-descriptive character, the religious-lyrical digressions appear in a foreshortened and undeveloped state. This is explainable by the relatively rapid tempo inherent in a dynamic narration, one which does not allow any delay for digressions. At the junction between the first and second segments, there is, strictly speaking, no religious-lyrical digression at all; there is only a brief reference to the fact that Nikitin was on the island of Gurmyz during Easter ("the Great Day"). It is left to the reader's imagination to amplify the traveler's melancholy mood, his sense of isolation, as he spends the great Christian holiday among people of another faith, far from his homeland, on some island in the Persian Gulf. But there is no time for the author to linger over this; instead, he hurries on in the narration of his travel impressions.

In this way, the extent and the degree of development of the several religious-lyrical digressions depend upon the character and content of those segments of calm exposition surrounding these digressions. What is more, the content of all these religious-lyrical digressions is approximately the same. Owing to this fact, the religious-lyrical element is a feature which runs all through the book; it is a homogeneous mortar which binds together the separate segments and at the same time "frames" each of these segments considered in isolation.

This compositional principle of framing through the use of the religious-lyrical element is carried out with complete consistency. The religious-lyrical element frames not only each separate segment of calm exposition, but the book as a whole. Before the beginning of the *Journey* proper, there is a short prayer in Church Slavonic. At the end of the work, after the story of the arrival in the Crimea (accompanied by prayerful exclamations) and after a concluding remark, there is a long prayer in Arabic, bringing to a close the entire *Journey*. In this way, the whole book is placed within two prayers functioning as a frame.

We pass now from the compositional devices of the *Journey* to the question of its style and diction. First and foremost, one is struck here by the purely acoustical exoticism with which the entire book is adorned. This effect is achieved by the intensive use of names, words, idioms, and phrases from the Indian, Arabic, Persian, and Turkish languages.

Eastern geographical names are scattered throughout the book, but from time to time they are concentrated and gathered together into a larger series. The motivations for such enumerations of exotic geographical names are diverse. Often (in six cases out of thirteen) such an enumeration is motivated by a reference to Nikitin's route of travel, which enables the mention of each geographical name at least twice. But geographical names are frequently enumerated for some other reason. The real purpose of these enumerations, of course, lies in the piling up of exotic words having distinctive combinations of sounds. This aim becomes abundantly clear from the fact that, in such enumerations, Nikitin allots Arabic and Persian names even to those countries for which Slavic languages usually use names of Greek origin; thus, "Egipet" [Egypt] he calls "Misjur," and "Sirija" [Syria] becomes "Sham," while "Aravija" [Arabia] becomes "Oroobstan" or "Rabast."

In general, proper names are encountered less frequently than are geographical names, but the fairly clearly expressed tendency to group such names into a more or less lengthy series may again be observed. In this connection, the motivations for such enumerations once again are rather various.

Besides proper names, a multitude of individual words from the Eastern languages are found in the *Journey*. The majority of these are technical terms, the designations of specifically indigenous objects and concepts. Nikitin provides an explanation for these words, but in only a very few instances. For the most part, to divine the meaning of a given word is left to the reader himself. Sometimes it is possible to guess correctly, since, in a parallel passage, the corresponding Russian word is used; in other cases, it is possible to guess from the context to what category of objects the given object, designated by an obscure Eastern name, belongs.

Very often, though, it is simply impossible to guess the meaning of the word without a knowledge of the appropriate language. Words from Eastern languages are often used to designate concepts which could quite easily be designated by a Russian or Church Slavonic word. The use of these Eastern words lends a special *couleur locale* and, simultaneously, a special audial exoticism to the exposition. The process of divining the meanings of these words places an especially intense emphasis upon verbal expression. Some of Nikitin's phrases produce the impression of a kind of Russo-Asiatic gibberish, through which the meaning may only be glimpsed.

Finally, besides Eastern names and isolated words, Nikitin introduces into the Russian text of his *Journey* a whole series of Arabic, Persian, and Turkish phrases. In the fifteenth century, the Persian and Arabic languages were known only by an insignificant number of Russians. A knowledge of Turkish or the "Tatar" language was somewhat more extensive, especially among the merchants of cities along the middle and lower Volga. Nevertheless, neither Arabic nor Persian nor Turkish was known to the majority of Nikitin's possible readers. He undoubtedly took this into account. Wherever an understanding of some Tatar phrase is essential to an understanding of the general course of the story, Nikitin supplied this phrase with a Russian translation. Hence, in all those numerous and similar instances of which Arabic and Persian phrases are not furnished with a translation, Nikitin quite consciously counted upon the fact that his readers would not understand him. Therefore, the purpose of all these rather numerous untranslated Eastern phrases scattered throughout the book (for the most part in the religious-lyrical digressions or the segments of static-descriptive exposition) is merely to create a particular, exotic effect, achieved by the alien quality of the sound combinations and the unintelligibility of the phrases themselves.

Strictly speaking, this effect could be achieved by the simple selection of words with no connected meaning from various

Eastern languages. But, it must be said, all the Arabic, Persian, and Turkish phrases which Nikitin introduced into the text do make sense. This meaning, intelligible only to the author and to a small minority of his readers, is interesting only in relation to the author's psychology and characteristics, but not in relation to the literary characteristics of the work itself. These phrases, as has been said, are simply a means for the creation and intensification of a general impression of the alien, exotic nature of the described environment. Nevertheless, we must examine these phrases from the point of view of their meaning, since this will aid us in sensing with greater clarity the spirit of the *Journey*.

A significant portion of the Eastern phrases in the *Journey* consists of prayers or prayerful exclamations. Such "Eastern" exclamations exist, along with their Russian counterparts, in all the developed religious-lyrical digressions; but, after the conclusion of the *Journey* proper, a long prayer in Arabic is introduced, as was already noted. The motives that induced Nikitin to resort to Eastern languages in these prayers are of course various. There was a necessity for turning to God, in a language which was not ordinary and not understood by everyone–a necessity noted in the religious psychology of various times and peoples. Here as well, there is an original diction of religious isolation, an exceptionally original diction, because the individual item of diction, so to speak, is diametrically opposed to the condition to which it refers. During his residence in the East, Nikitin acutely felt his religious isolation and, forced to conceal his Christian beliefs from those around him, he prayed secretly (perhaps aloud at times) in Russian, that is, in a manner unintelligible to those around him. Then, as he was describing his wanderings remembering vividly this dominance of spiritual isolation, he symbolized it all by again praying in a language unintelligible to those surrounding him. But since his "audience" was now Russian, it had become necessary to pray, not in Russian, but in Arabic, or in Persian, or in Tatar. In this way, a change in environment elicited a turn-about in the linguistic expression of a psychic state, the linguistic expression itself being opposed to this state. In India, the diction utilized in Nikitin's intimate, personal religious life was Russian; in the *Journey*, however, written in Russian for Russians, such diction was borrowed from Eastern languages. Thus Nikitin later recorded in these languages thoughts which occurred to him in Russian while he was in India, thoughts which remained unuttered or hidden from the people around him. It is significant that the one and only prayer about Russia included in the *Journey*, containing an unrestrained expression of Nikitin's love for his homeland, is in Tatar, as yet without a Russian translation.

Although the use of Eastern languages is associated with the psychological nexus of secrecy in personal religious experiences and memories of spiritual isolation, it is also connected to several other related psychological contexts. Thus we find phrases written in Eastern languages in places in which the author remembers the profane acts he committed as a result of his long residence among people of another faith. In the Tatar tongue, he confesses that, having forgotten the exact dates of the Orthodox fasts, he sometimes fasted together with Moslems in the Moslem manner, and that when this happened he prayed to God that it would not be held against him as a betrayal of the faith. The awareness of his own profane acts appears particularly strong when he had occasion to enter into sexual relations with dark-skinned slave girls and, in general, with unbaptized native women. Consequently, he records in Tatar all his information about prostitution and the remunerated satisfaction of sexual needs in India. It is characteristic that, after an extremely cynical Tatar phrase on this subject, there follows immediately a religious-lyrical digression in which he laments over the temptations surrounding him and the difficulty of preserving religious purity when living among people of another faith. He also records (in Tatar) that during fasts he abstained from sexual relations.

It is in this singular situation, in which Eastern languages play the same symbolic role as in Nikitin's *story* that the role of the Russian language in his intimate *personal* life in India is realized in other instances as well. Nikitin is struck by the indecency of several Brahmin idols, obviously not by the indency in and of itself but by the fact that this indecency was bestowed upon the image of a deity to whom people bowed down. Nikitin obviously thought this in Russian, but of course he did not utter it aloud. However, when he described these idols in his *Journey*, he referred to their indecency in Tatar. Another time, at the sight of the power and military might of the Moslem rulers, who were waging war victoriously against "unbelievers," the thought flashed through his mind that, even from outward appearances alone, Islam seemed to be aiding its adherents, God nevertheless knew which faith was true and which was false. Once again this sudden thought was in Russian and was not uttered aloud;

however, in the exposition of his reminiscences, Nikitin expressed this thought in Persian.

In this way, the phrases in Eastern languages in Nikitin's *Journey* have their own defined sphere of meaning and are bound together by a defined psychological nexus of associations. But the inner meaning of these phrases is accessible, and exposed, only to Nikitin and a very restricted circle of his readers. For most readers, these phrases are devoid of meaning and, as a result of precisely this meaninglessness, combined with the foreign quality of their acoustical properties, they are merely a means of intensifying the impression of the exoticism of the amazing phenomena, the customs and events described.

The formal characteristics of Afanasij Nikitin's *Journey Beyond the Three Seas* constitute intrinsic features that are exclusive to this one work. Yet, in comparing the work with other works of Old Russian literature, we note that its principal characteristics are also found in a defined group of works (true, in a differing, less developed state)—the Old Russian pilgrim literature.

Thus the device of differentiating between dynamic-narrative and static-descriptive elements, with the description of foreign lands being placed in the center of the narrative of the journey, away from Russia and back, at the beginning and at the end of the work—all are to be found in the majority of works in the Russian literature of pilgrimage, beginning at the end of the fourteenth century. But the differentiation between the two types of exposition and the gradual transitions from one type to the other are not carried out in any of these works with such consistency, nor are they elaborated with such mastery as is found in the *Journey*.

The custom of beginning and ending a work with prayers was widespread in Old Russian literature, in particular, in the pilgrimage literature. But Nikitin exploited this device in a completely original manner, by transforming the religious-lyrical element into a tool for dividing his work into segments and for welding these separate segments together—a feature not to be observed in any work of the Old Russian pilgrimage literature.

The device of enumerating geographical names (along with a notation of distance and the number of days of a journey) was widespread in pilgrimage literature, in which it fulfilled the role of an extremely schematic substitute for a dynamic narrative about the journey. Nikitin utilized this device in an original manner for completely different purposes, specifically, for the creation of particular, exotic, sound effects. Therefore, he expanded the applications of this device, introducing various motivations for enumerating geographical names, introducing as well analogous types of Eastern proper names and phrases from Eastern languages (which were senseless from the point of view of most readers, etc.).

Finally, we have already seen that in several parts of his book Nikitin utilized the device of unsystematic, disordered exposition (motivated by the use of the form of travel notes in the second segment, but completely unmotivated in the third and sixth segments). The same device was widely utilized in the pilgrimage literature as well (where it was usually motivated by the form of travel notes). It is now an opportune moment for us to mention the fact that this device most certainly cannot be explained by the notorious "artlessness" or "simplicity" of the pilgrims. The significance of this device lies in the fact that through this method of exposition an illusion of the heterogeneity and multiplicity of impressions is created, while as regards systematic description, the material seems to be more circumscribed and meager simply because it is more easily apperceived.

In this sense, an unquestionable connection exists between Nikitin's *Journey* and the Old Russian pilgrimage literature. It only remains for us to explain the nature of this connection.

We have already stated that, as with many works of the pilgrimage literature, the *Journey* also begins and ends with prayers. However, both the opening and concluding prayers in the pilgrimage literature are in Church Slavonic and are Christian, while in Nikitin's *Journey* the concluding prayer is in Arabic and is Islamic. At first glance this creates the impression of some kind of parody. But in actual fact, of course, this is not the case.

The relationship between Nikitin's *Journey* and the pilgrimage literature is expressed by the following brief formula: while a work of the pilgrimage literature is a description of a journey to a *holy* land, Nikitin's *Journey Beyond the Three Seas* is a description of a journey to a *pagan* land.

This fact creates a profound difference in the religious-psychological situation. The pilgrim journeys about holy places, which are filled to overflowing with sacred objects and which represent at every step the material and tangible vestiges of memories drawn from the Old and New Testaments. He carries within himself, in his own consciousness, a special atmosphere of devout feelings, thoughts, moods, and concepts, while the world about him, the external environment of the holy land, acts upon the pilgrim's inner world like a powerful resonator, increasing the intensity of all his experiences, thoughts, and feelings. Both worlds, the external and internal, flow together into one, and the pilgrim is unable to distinguish where one ends and the other begins. In that environment, he sees and heeds only those things which are in harmony with his inner world; he drinks this all in, and, simultaneously, imposes his own personal religious experiences upon everything he sees and hears.

Conversely, Nikitin journeyed in non-Christian lands, Moslem and heathen, where there were not only no Christian traditions and where non-Christian religions reigned, but where the alien, non-Christian religious forces were present at every step, full of vigorous life. Between Nikitin's inner religious world and the Moslem or heathen environment surrounding him, there was not only no harmony, but even a diametrical opposition, constantly and intensely felt. Consequently, instead of that osmosis between the traveler's inner world and the external world of the reality surrounding him, instead of that confluence of these two worlds, and that dissolving of the inner world in the external world, which can be seen in the case of the pilgrim—precisely the opposite must have obtained with Nikitin.

He experienced an equally intense sense of his separateness, of his alienation from the external world, his religious isolation. Just as it was necessary for him to struggle against the penetration of this external, non-Christian world into his inner world (since such penetration was confessed as a profanation), so he struggled against revealing his inner religious world to others, since such revelation might prove dangerous to his own personal existence.

In other words, he had to shrink into himself, and, in so doing, not to weaken, but to strengthen his spiritual alienation and his religious isolation. This was a lengthy and strenuous religious experience. It is precisely this intense religious coloration to interconnected experiences by a journey which is analogous to pilgrimage literature, in spite of all the differences in the actual courses of these experiences. Just as for the pilgrim, the memory of the journey was for Nikitin above all else the memory of a powerful religious experience. And exactly like the pilgrim, Nikitin considered himself obligated to record these memories for posterity, since in Old Rus, in principle, only what was recorded and clothed in a literary form was religiously valuable, while everything religiously neutral was in principle left as a subject—not for written but for oral literature.

What has been said here defines the real meaning and essence of the contents of Nikitin's *Journey*. It is neither a simple description of curious travel adventures nor one of remarkable sights observed in distant lands. It is rather the tale of an unfortunate Orthodox Christian, the "poor servant of God," Afanasij, who was carried by fate into non-Christian lands, where he suffered from his religious isolation and longed for his native Christian environment. Only with this understanding is it possible to approach the *Journey* as a work of literature.

The entire book is permeated with a genuine sense of Nikitin's religious isolation in the non-Christian religious environment surrounding him. At the same time, he knew the Moslems and the Brahmanists too well simply to despise them. Their religious world was separated from his inner world by an impenetrable wall. But he knew that this world, even if alien, was still a *religious* world, and, therefore, he could neither despise nor condemn those who belonged to this world. Nonetheless, he felt that, with all the internal and material differences between his own Russian Orthodox faith and the alien Moslem and Brahman environment, there was still a certain formal parallelism between them, a formal analogy, which he constantly emphasized. In mentioning Moslem holidays and fasts, he always noted to which Orthodox holiday or fast they corresponded in terms of the time of year or their meaning: "in memory of the Sheik Aladin, at the time of the Russian holiday, the Feast of the Intercession of the Holy Virgin; to be celebrated in Sheik Aladin's honor for two weeks, as during the Feast of the Intercession"; "the Christian Easter comes nine or ten days before the beginning of the *Bessermen* Bhagram"; "on Kurbantbhagram or, in Russian, on St. Peter's Day." Afanasij Nikitin says of the sacred Brahman city, Parvat:

> They came to Pervot [*sic*] on the day before the beginning of Lent; for them this is their Jerusalem, as Myakuka is for the Bessermen, Jerusalem for the Russians, and for the Indians, Parvat.

He mentions the external similarity between several details of the Brahman ritual and the Orthodox: "Their *namaz* [a ritual prayer] to the East is done in the Russian manner; . . . and their *bukhtany* [temples] are placed facing the east, while their *booty* [idols] faces to the east; . . . Some of them bow down like monks, reaching both hands to the ground." The strangeness of the Brahman religious world view, of course, was striking to Afanasij Nikitin. In the description of the principal temple in Parvat, he related, without embellishment, what he saw there, and this description alone is sufficient for one to be convinced of the completely alien qualities of Brahmism:

And their temple is tremendous, half the size of Tver, and of stone, carved with the deeds of Boöt. Around the whole temple there are twelve scenes of how Boöt worked miracles, how he appeared in many forms: in the first, in human form; in the second, as a man with an elephant's trunk; in the third, as a man with the appearance of an ape; in the fourth, as a man with the form of a wild beast; always he appeared to them with a tail, and, carved out of stone, his tail, six feet over him.

It would seem that for every Russian of the fifteenth century all these images would have suggested that the conclusion defined this "Boöt" as simply Satan. It is possible that such a thought occurred to Nikitin, but he repressed the notion and did not express it even in his *Journey*; he only noted the external, formal resemblance of the principal idol of the Parvat temple to a statue of Justinian described by Russian pilgrims:

The Boöt is carved out of stone and is very big, and his tail is up over him; he has his right hand raised high and stretched out, like the emperor Justinian of Constantinople.

Thus, even here, there is again a formal parallelism of the distinct religious worlds. The affirmation of this *formal* parallelism, however, only strengthens the impression of the complete internal, *material* heterogeneity of these worlds. Nikitin describes just as calmly and objectively other details of India's religious life, even the strangest and most repulsive, from the Russian Orthodox point of view (i.e., the religious esteem accorded horned cattle, etc.). Nowhere is there a hint of condemnation, disdain, or mockery: every man, Nikitin says, believes according to his own way; there is no need to judge others, but only to look after oneself, to keep the faith, not to fall away from God.

It must not have been easy for Nikitin to remain constant in his faith, not only because of the fact that, as a Christian, he did not enjoy any rights and was exposed to the oppression of the Moslem nobles, such as that of the ruler of Khunar, Asad-khan. More importantly, this was a result of the fact that he was physically deprived of the possibility of fulfilling the rituals and precepts of his faith while he saw people around him strictly observing their religious obligations and living from day to day according to a devout ritual, one resembling formally his own Russian Orthodox ritualistic observances.

In any case, the temptation was great; it was impossible to keep his own law and his own faith while the *Bessermen* lived so piously; they remained constant in their faith, they kept their law so unwaveringly that envy took hold of him. Why did he not pass over to their faith? After all, God is one, and only the religious laws are diverse. This is the sense of Nikitin's conversation with the Besserman Melik, who tried to coerce Nikitin into "keeping the Besserman faith", reproaching him for the fact that he had fallen away from Christianity, but that he did not adopt Islam.

Nikitin, however, stood firm. In spite of all the respect he felt for every other faith, and in spite of the fact that he never allowed himself to condemn or scorn those around him for their religious views, in the depths of his soul he felt and knew that the true faith was his own Russian belief, and he adhered to it firmly, although he hid this from everyone and even adopted for the benefit of those around him the assumed *Bessermen,* otherwise known as *Khozya Yussuf Khorasani.*

Thus Nikitin lived "between the faiths," hiding his personal religious world from everyone and suppressing its external manifestations. It is this life that he has described in his *Journey.* Only from time to time, during the advent of some great Christian holiday or fast, did this element of the Russian Orthodox faith, hidden in the depths of his soul, rise up and take possession of his being, forcing him to feel acutely his spiritual isolation. Then he began to weep, to grieve, and to long for a Christian environment, and for the good Russian traditional rituals, and he turned in prayer to the true Christian God. But even here, in the *Journey,* his religious diffidence and the reticence caused by the conditions of his life interfered with the full expression of these boiling emotions, and he immediately hid his prayer under the cloak of the Arabic, Persian, or Tatar languages–the symbols of the long period of his spiritual isolation.

These surging waves of intimate religious experience have their own periodicity. The religious life of a man who has grown up in a religious culture and has been nurtured in ritualistic observances is always rhythmical and cyclical. Its intensity and force at times grow stronger and at times weaker, and these intensifications are connected to particular moments in the day, to particular days in the week, and to particular weeks in the year. To the extent that the calendar for such a man is inseparable from the observances of the faith, it becomes a category in religious life. And it was precisely because of the fact that the secret movements of his inner religious world were subjected to a defined rhythm and periodicity that the idea could occur to Afanasij Nikitin, as he wrote *Journey Beyond the Three Seas*, to utilize the revelations of his moments of religious anguish as a device for the internal account of the story of his journey and of all he saw and experienced in distant lands.

Anne Radcliffe, one of the originators of the mystery novel, organized her tales on such a pattern: the heroine finds herself in a castle; she sees a decomposing corpse behind a curtain; spirits wander through the castle; someone invisible interjects his remarks into the conversations of drunken robbers, and so on. The solutions to these mysteries are revealed only at the end of the volume. The corpse is made of wax; it was placed there as a penance by one of the proprietor's ancestors, a count, under the Pope's instructions. The mysterious voice belongs to a prisoner who wanders through the castle through secret passages. As you see, the solutions to these mysteries (as a contemporary remarked) are at best only partially satisfactory.

In the second part, the scenario begins again. A new castle. New mysterious voices are heard. These prove subsequently to belong to smugglers. Music resounds all around the castle: this turns out to be a nun playing, and so forth. . . .

It is noteworthy, however, that these mysteries at first present false solutions (as is also the case with Dickens); we usually suspect something far more terrifying than what we actually find. In the second part, for example, the author quite pointedly suggests the idea of incest in a manner reminiscent of obscene ditties with risqué rhymes, a device that is also canonical for Russian folk riddles, such as: "It hangs dangling. Everybody grabs for it." The solution: "A towel."[1]

In solving these riddles a pause takes place which stands for the "false," obscene solution. Here is an example of how a similar riddle is worked into the plot. The tale cited below was recorded as narrated by an old peasant woman. It is interesting because it displays the device of the false or misleading solution. The play of riddles furnishes the tale's content:

> A young tailor used to live at my place, and he gave me a riddle to figure out: "Two years pass in a crow's life; what comes next?" I answer him, "The third year." The tailor thinks it's funny that I guessed his riddle. I give him another riddle: "If daddy didn't keep busy, mother's. . . . would have overgrown long ago." The young tailor thinks that it has a bad meaning. He can't solve it. I give him the answer: "Bushes grow quickly on the furrows, on the furrows of Mother Earth."

Thus we see that the false or misleading solution is a very common element of either a tale or a mystery novel. The manipulation of false and true solutions is what constitutes the method of

*Excerpts from "Roman tajn," *O teorii prozy* (Moscow, 1925), pp. 117-138. Translated by Guy Carter.

organizing the mystery. The dénouement consists in shifting from one to the other. The interrelation of the parts is the same as that found in plots based on puns.

The mystery type is characterized by its kinship with the device of inversion, that is, the rearrangement of the parts. The most common type of mystery in the novel is the narration of an earlier event after the depiction of the present one. The mystery of the "watch" in Dickens's *Little Dorrit* and the "double" are examples of such riddles.

On the other hand, the mystery of the "house," Dorrit's secret love for Clennam, and Clennam's love for Pet are built up without a plot inversion. In this case, the mystery is achieved by means of the exposition; the metaphorical and factual series form a parallel. In mysteries based on a rearrangement of cause and effect, the parallel is formed from a false solution.

In Dickens's last novel, *Our Mutual Friend*, the organization of the mystery is most interesting. The first mystery is the secret of John Rokesmith: the author seems to conceal the fact that Rokesmith is none other than John Harmon. Boffin's secret is the second mystery. We see how wealth destroys the Golden Dustman, and we do not know that Boffin is playing a hoax on us. Dickens himself says that he did not even consider hiding Rokesmith's true identity from the reader. In this case John Harmon's secret is a false plot line. It does not allow us to solve or even notice Boffin's secret. The novelistic technique is therefore quite complex.

The direct heir to the mystery novel is the detective novel in which the detective is a professional solver of mysteries. First, a mystery is presented, the crime, then a misleading solution appears, and the police investigation follows. Only later is the truth about the murder established. In such a work inversion is obligatory, and it sometimes takes the form of a complex omission of separate details. That is how the mystery in *The Brothers Karamazov* is achieved (but without a detective). For a more detailed analysis of the mystery technique, I have chosen Dickens's *Little Dorrit.*

This novel is built around several simultaneous actions. The link between these parallel actions is achieved: (1) through the participation of characters of one line in the action of another, and (2) through locale. The heroes move next door to each other. Thus Arthur Clennam lives in the Bleeding Hearts Yard. The "patriarch" also lives here, as does Baptist, the Italian. The *fabula*[2] of the work consists of: (1) Dorrit and Clennam's love; (2) the history of the rise to wealth and the subsequent ruin of the Dorrit family; (3) Rigaud's attempted blackmail and his threat to expose Mrs. Clennam.

However, the novel can be related in the above form only after we have finished reading it. While reading we have before us a collection of mysteries. The interrelationships of the characters are also presented as interwoven mysteries. We can distinguish the following mysteries running throughout the novel:

1. The mystery of the watch.
2. The mystery of dreams.

} These are basic mysteries. They frame the plot, but are unresolved.

3. Mr. Pancks' mystery (the inheritance). This is a partial mystery, one which does not run the length of the novel. It creates an imbalance between Dorrit and Clennam through the device of plot inversion.
4. Mr. Merdle's secret (likewise an auxiliary mystery) which plays the same role as Pancks's above.
5. The mysterious noises in the house. They prepare the solution to the first two mysteries.
6. The mystery of Dorrit and Clennam's love. These belong to the central plot, but technically they represent a developed negative parallelism.[3]

The device of using several simultaneous actions whose interrelationship is not immediately specified by the author serves as plot impediment, a special continuation of the mystery technique.

Little Dorrit begins with such a device. In this novel two plot lines are given in the very beginning: Rigaud's line and Clennam's. The beginning of each line is worked up into a chapter. In the first chapter, "Sun and Shadow," Monsieur Rigaud and the Italian, John Baptist, appear. They are both in prison—Rigaud on a murder charge, and Baptist for smuggling. Rigaud is taken away to court. As he leaves, a boisterous crowd gathers round the prison and threatens to tear him to pieces. Neither Rigaud nor his cellmate Baptist is a major character in the novel.

Beginning a novel in such a fashion, with a secondary character, is quite common for Dickens. *Nicholas Nickleby*, *Oliver Twist*, *Our Mutual Friend*, and *Martin Chuzzlewit* all begin in this way. This device may be related to the technique of the riddle. The second group of characters appears in the second chapter,

“Fellow-travelers.” This chapter is linked to the first by the sentence: “No more of yesterday’s howling, over yonder, today, sir; is there?”

Little Dorrit is a multileveled novel. In order to unite these levels, it is necessary to contrive the assemblage of all the characters at the beginning of the novel. Dickens chooses a quarantine for this task. In this context the quarantine corresponds to the tavern or monastery found in collections of tales (e.g., *The Heptameron* of Marguerite d’Angoulême or the tavern in the *Canterbury Tales.*) The Meagles, husband and wife, their daughter Pet, their servant Tattycoram (whose story is told in that chapter), Mr. Clennam, and Miss Wade are all in quarantine at the beginning of *Little Dorrit.* The same situation exists in *Our Mutual Friend.* In the first chapter, “On the Look-Out,” Gaffer is introduced together with his daughter on the boat, which is towing a corpse. This chapter is permeated with mystery: we do not know exactly what the people in the boat are looking for, and the corpse is presented through negation.

Lizzie’s father, composing himself into the easy attitude of one who had asserted the high moralities and taken an unassailable position, slowly lighted a pipe, and smoked, and took a survey of what he had in tow. What he had in tow, lunged itself at him sometimes in an awful manner when the boat was checked, and sometimes seemed to try to wrench itself away, though for the most part it followed submissively. A neophyte might have fancied that the ripples over it were dreadfully like faint changes of expression on a sightless face but Gaffer was no neophyte and had no fancies.

It is interesting to compare this description with the “angling for fish” in *A Tale of Two Cities.*

The second chapter, “A Man from Somewhere,” describes Veneering’s house. The lawyer Mortimer is introduced along with the whole of higher society, which will later function as a “chorus,” as does Anna Pavlovna’s salon in *War and Peace.* At the end of the second chapter we learn, by way of connection with the first, that a certain heir to an enormous estate has drowned; and we link his fate to that of the corpse trailing the boat.

In the third chapter, “Another Man,” a new character, Julius Handford, is introduced; in the fourth chapter, the Wilfer family; and in the fifth, the Boffins, and so forth.

The given plot lines are maintained to the end of the novel, and they tend not so much to intersect as to converge from time to time. The plot lines intersect even less frequently in *A Tale of*

Two Cities. In this novel, the transitions from one plot line to another seemingly unrelated to it are perceived as a sort of mystery. Moreover, the identification of the characters from various plot lines is postponed until we are well into the heart of the novel.

In recent times we have seen a revival of the mystery novel with a new interest in complicated and entangled plots. An original example of the mystery technique is offered by Andrej Belyj. He gives us a transformed version of the riddle technique which is quite interesting. In his *Kotik Letaev,* for example, two levels are presented, "heaven" and "order." Order is "real life which has already formed"; "heaven" is the swelling of life in flux, before its formation. "Heaven" is formed either through a series of metaphors or through puns. In this arrangement "heaven" first appears, then "order"—in other words, an inversion takes place. The puns usually take the form of a riddle.[4]

Belyj also supplies us with the mystery technique in its pure form. *Saint Petersburg* may serve as an example. Belyj's followers, in particular, Boris Pil′njak, have developed the device of parallelism to a high degree. This parallelism is one in which the connection between the parallel levels is obscured and moved to the background. Such novels create an impression of great complexity when they are, in fact, quite elementary. The connecting link between the parts is presented either through the most rudimentary device, such as the kinship of the characters, or else through the episodic participation of a character of one line in another line. See, for example, "A Petersburg Tale," "Rjazan′ Apple," or "The Snowstorm." It is interesting to observe in this connection Pil′njak's method of making separate stories take form as a novel.

In the mystery novel both the riddle and the solution are important. Such a novel offers the possibility of impeding the action, throwing it into strange perspective, and thus exciting the reader's interest. The main thing is not to give the reader an opportunity of recognizing the object. Once an object is recognizable, it no longer frightens us. For this reason, in Maturin's novel *Melmoth the Wanderer*, the author repeatedly conceals from us the proposals Melmoth makes to assorted people in terrible predicaments, prisoners of the Inquisition, people dying of hunger and selling their blood, inmates of a madhouse, people wandering lost in underground passageways, etc. Whenever the action reaches Melmoth's proposal, the manuscript breaks off—the novel consists of separate parts which have only a confused relationship to one another. The traditional duty to solve the mystery weighs heavily on many novelists, who nevertheless tend to avoid fantastic solutions. If fantasy is introduced at all, then it occurs at the end of the novel within the confines of the dénouement. The fantastic element is offered as a sort of final judgment, as a cause of the action, but rarely in the course of the action itself. And if fantasy is introduced, then it appears in a special form, as a premonition, for example, or a prediction, so that the novel will develop according to predetermined conditions.

The element of fantasy appears in Lewis's novel *The Monk*, in which the cast of characters includes a devil with a companion spirit and a phantom nun. In the last act the devil carries the monk away and reveals the whole intrigue to him. Such revelations, of course, do not occur in the novel accidentally. Dickens with his many involved plot constructions constantly had to resort to this type of device. This explains the "mystery of the watch" in *Little Dorrit*, in which it again becomes necessary to gather all the people together in one room—a device common to many novels and parodied over and over in V. Kaverin's novel *A Chronicle of the City of Leipzig*. In Dickens people are literally dragged together by the scruff of their necks. In *Little Dorrit* Pancks and Baptist dragged Rigaud to Clennam's mother in such a way.

"And now," said Mr. Pancks. . . I've only one other word to say before I go . . . If Mr. Clennam was here, he would say, 'Affery, tell your dream!' "

The dénoument is achieved in the following way: Affery tells her dreams. Dreams function here as a new type of ironic motivation and deformation of the old device of eavesdropping. In Dickens, eavesdropping is usually performed by office clerks (as in *Nicholas Nickleby*) and sometimes by the main characters. There is a renovation of this device in Dostoevskij's *A Raw Youth*, in which the eavesdropping occurs as if by accident.

The main reason for the artificiality of the dénoument in *Little Dorrit* is the fact that it takes place without the presence of outsiders and that people tell one another things that they themselves already know quite well.[5]

How does one explain the success of the mystery novel from Radcliffe to Dickens?

I see the matter in this light. The adventure novel had outlived its day. It was revived by satire. Elements of the adventure novel in Swift's *Gulliver's Travels* played a purely subordinate role. A time of crisis had arrived. In *Tom Jones*, Fielding parodied the old novel form in his depiction of the main character's amorality. Instead of the traditional lover's fidelity, sustained through various trying adventures, we are presented with Jones's carefree adventures.

Sterne wrote an even more radical parody and parodied the very structure of the novel, mustering all of its devices for review. Simultaneously, the younger genres began to rise and strive for canonization. Richardson canonized the genre of the epistolary novel. According to legend, he intended to write a collection of edifying letters, but instead wrote an epistolary novel. At the same time the Gothic tales appeared (the Pinkertons of that day), as did Anne Radcliffe and Charles Maturin with their mystery novels.

The old novel form attempted to increase the effectiveness of its devices with the introduction of parallel plot intrigues. The technique of the mystery novel offered a convenient means of connecting several parallel intrigues. Dickens's complicated plot constructions were a result.

The mystery novel permits the author to incorporate into a work large passages of local-color description which, while serving the goal of retarding the plot, themselves undergo pressure from the plot and are perceived as belonging to the work of art. The descriptions of the debtor's prison, the Ministry of Circumlocution, and the Bleeding Hearts Yard are incorporated into *Little Dorrit* in such a way. Thus we see how the mystery novel came to be used by the social novel.

Translator's Notes

1. Šklovskij's example of the Russian song has been omitted here.

2. The Russian Formalists distinguished between *fabula* and *sjužet* in discussing plot construction. Fabula refers to the raw material of a story, the story stuff, the basic causal-temporal relationships. Sjužet refers to the presentation and manipulation of this basic story stuff—what we would call plot. Šklovskij's discussion here is an excellent example of these two concepts. The fabula consists of the three main relationships: Clennam-Dorrit, the Dorrit family, and Mrs. Clennam-Rigaud—but not in any particular order, nor even clarity. In fact, because of their ordering by sjužet, they appear cloudy and mysterious until the very end of the novel.

3. Pages 119-129 of the Russian text have been omitted.

4. Pages 131-132 of the Russian text have been omitted.

5. Pages 133-137 of the Russian text have been omitted.

O. Henry and the Theory of the Short Story*

Boris M. Èjxenbaum

1

In the history of twentieth-century Russian literature, special allowance for a period of translated fiction will probably have to be made, just as had to be done for Russian literature at the beginning of the nineteenth century, when a work by a Russian author (in prose, at any rate) was a rarity. Perhaps, though, one should speak of this not so much in the context of the history of literature as in that of the history of the Russian reader and publisher, granted the possibility of such a history. Russian literature has always been in very close contact with Western literature, it is true. Still, translated novels ten or fifteen years ago would have been modestly tucked away in periodicals, and the pages they covered would not infrequently have been left uncut. Now, translated fiction fills a vacuum which has come about in our native literature—only a seeming vacuum perhaps, but for the reader one unquestionably there. The reader is no historian of literature. All these problems of crises, turnabouts, shifts have little interest for him. What he needs is to have an absorbing book on hand for leisurely reading. He needs a finished product, one ready to use; interest in raw materials is for professionals only. If, in answer to the reader's complaints, you explain that Russian literature is now searching out new directions, assuming a new shape, and has yet to overcome a whole series of enormous difficulties, that the trouble is not lack of talent or know-how but the complexity of the historical situation, he might nod his head approvingly, but he is unlikely to do any reading: Russian literature can go ahead and search and reshape itself . . . he'll wait.

And so what happened was that, beginning in 1919-1920, the bookstore shelves and stalls broke out in arrays of translations. By 1923-1924, the flood of translations had reached extraordinary force. Russian literature yielded its place, as it were, to world literature.

The flood of translated fiction, torrential at first, came gradually to be contained within shorelines. Shallows, alluvia, and islets of a sort formed. The bed of this verbal river came into focus. I do not mean at all to say that there was something "watery" about that entire literature from beginning to end; I am simply more interested in shorelines and islands than in waters flowing off into obscurity. Many pages of French and German writers did flow through our midst without leaving a trace. The English and Amer-

*"O. Genri i teorija novelly" (1925), *Literatura* (Leningrad, 1927), pp. 166-209. Translated by I. R. Titunik.

ican writers took firmer hold. To pursue the metaphor, I might say that the flood of translated fiction came to be contained primarily within American shores.

Certain contemporary American authors were well known in Russia even earlier. Jack London, for instance, had been included in the series of little yellow-cover editions of the *Universal'naja Biblioteka* [Universal Library] published sometime before World War I. But at that time, against the background of "great" Russian literature, such fiction was looked upon as nothing more than travel or vacation reading. Only the writers of the North, the Swedes and the Norwegians (Hamsun, Lagerlöf, Jakobsen, and others), enjoyed any serious popularity during those years. One must also bear in mind that all the attention then was absorbed by verse; prose, generally speaking, stood in the background.

For some reason we were completely unaware of O. Henry's name until 1923, although he died back in 1910 and during the years preceding his death was one of the most popular and beloved authors in America. During the years O. Henry was publishing in his own country (1904-1910), his stories would hardly have attracted the Russian reader's attention. Their success in our day is all the more characteristic and significant: they obviously satisfy some literary need. Of course, for us O. Henry is only a foreign guest artist, but one who has appeared on call, by invitation, not accidentally.

There was a moment in the history of Russian fiction when readers were provided with something on the order of O. Henry's short stories—and not without a link with the American short story of the time (Washington Irving). In 1831 Puškin published his *Povesti pokojnogo Ivana Petroviča Belkina* [Tales of the Late Ivan Petrovič Belkin]. Their basic literary meaning (essentially that of parody) lay in surprise, in pointedly happy endings. Sentimental and romantic naïveté, calculated to bring the reader to tears or trepidation, was done away with—instead, the smile of the master toying ironically with his reader's expectations. Russian criticism was nonplussed by these "antics": suddenly, after sublime romantic poems, anecdotes and vaudevilles with costume disguises! Gogol''s "It's dreary in this world, ladies and gentlemen!" proved more pertinent than Puškin's "So it was you?" ("Metel'" [The Snowstorm]). Later, and not without difficulty, Čexov's name was added to the list of the Russian "classics" and, at that, mostly in recognition of his "sense of despair."

The short story generally has made its appearance in Russian literature only from time to time, as if by chance and solely for the purpose of providing a transition to the novel, which we here are accustomed to consider the higher or more dignified species of fiction. In American fiction the cultivation of the short story runs throughout the nineteenth century, not, of course, as an orderly, consecutive evolution, but as a process of incessantly elaborating the various possibilities of the genre. "One might say," writes one critic, "that with the history of the genre designated by the general term of short story, the history of verbal art in America, if not the history of its literature, is exhausted."

It goes from Washington Irving, himself still tied to the tradition of manners-and-morals sketches in England, to Edgar Allan Poe, to Nathaniel Hawthorne; after them come Bret Harte, Henry James, and later Mark Twain, Jack London, and finally O. Henry (I have listed, of course, only the most prominent names). O. Henry had good reason to begin one of his stories ("The Girl and the Habit") with complaints at the critics' constant reproaches for his imitating this or that writer: "Henry George, George Washington, Washington Irving, and Irving Bacheller. . ." he quips. The short story is the one fundamental and self-contained genre in American prose fiction, and the stories of O. Henry certainly made their appearance in consequence of the prolonged and incessant cultivation of the genre.

On Russian soil O. Henry showed up minus those national and historical connections, and we of course regard him as something other than do the Americans. Tolstoj's *Voskresenie* [Resurrection] is read in Japan as a typical love novel, the ideological part being taken as the setting. Thus literature coming from another country undergoes a curious and often far from invalid refraction when it passes through local national traditions. O. Henry in Russia is preeminently the author of picaresque stories and clever anecdotes with surprise endings—an aspect that for the American reader apparently seems a secondary or traditional feature. It is enough to compare the Russian and the American editions of O. Henry's works. Of the thirty-three stories in a Russian edition and the twenty-five in an American one only five coincide.[1] Picaresque stories and stories with humorous plots predominate in the Russian edition, while primarily sentimental slice-of-life stories are collected in the American one, with only those of the picaresque stories which show the criminal repenting or on his way to reform. The stories about which American critics and readers rave pass unnoticed in Russia or cause disappointment. (Tender stories about New York shopgirls have more appeal for the American reader.) Frequently Theodore Roosevelt is quoted: "The reforms I attempted on behalf of the shopgirls of New York were suggested by the stories of O. Henry." So the old schoolroom legend goes: the influence of Turgenev's *Zapiski oxotnika* [Sportsman's Sketches] on the abolition of serfdom, the influence of Dickens's novels on the reform of the English courts, and so on. Statesmen and presidents think they are paying literature and themselves a great compliment when they make a statement of that sort. Actually, they are only testifying to their own gross naïveté. American critics have been trying to "elevate" O. Henry (as the Russian critics have Čexov) to the level of classical traditions. They eloquently argue a resemblance between O. Henry and, for instance, Shakespeare, on the basis of their common sympathies and frame of mind. "He was," writes one of them, "the large-hearted born democrat who, with utmost sincerity, can lay his hand upon his breast and say: *Humani nihil a me alienum puto.*"

Very likely O. Henry was a large-hearted man and doubtless, under the conditions of American civilization, he himself frequently suffered and was appalled by the sufferings of others. Still, it was not for statesmen that he wrote his stories, and he prized them somewhat higher than the compliments of Roosevelt. The laws of the short story dictated that he distort reality over and over again; for instance, that he make not himself but a detective magnanimous, because otherwise he would have had to end with the hero's downfall. The real-life James Valentine was promised his freedom if he would agree to open a safe with a tricky lock but was put back in jail when the job was done.[2] In the story, Valentine opens a locked vault door to save a little girl who is trapped inside. The detective, who is on his trail to arrest him for his previous robberies, abandons his intention at the sight of this deed. In real life, Valentine usually opened the locks of safes with the aid of no tools other than his own sandpapered finger tips, whereas a set of tools does figure in the story. When asked by a friend why he had done it that way, O. Henry answered: "It chills my teeth to think of that gritting operation. I prefer the set of tools. I don't like to make my victims suffer. And then, you see, the tools enable Jimmy to make a present to a friend. The gift illustrates the tolerance of the man who has been in prison."[3] It would also be to the point here to recall another story told by a friend of O. Henry's, Al Jennings, about O. Henry's not wanting to make use of a plot which he had passed on to him, a story about a girl who had been seduced by a banker and who afterward killed him because he refused her money for their dying child. Jennings was almost outraged by O. Henry's indifference and asked: " 'Don't you think Sally's story has the real heartthrob in it?' 'The pulse beats too loud,' Henry answered. 'It's very commonplace.' "

The real O. Henry is found in the irony pervading all his stories, in his keen feeling for form and tradition. Americans cannot help wanting to prove a resemblance in outlook between O. Henry and Shakespeare—it is their way of expressing national pride. As for the Russian reader, he in this instance does not care about comparisons. He reads O. Henry because it is entertaining to read him, and he appreciates in O. Henry what is so lacking in our own literature—dexterity of construction, cleverness of plot situations and dénouements, compactness, and swiftness of action. Torn from their national tradition, the stories of O. Henry, as is true of the works of any writer on foreign soil, give us the feeling that they are a finished, complete genre, and they contrast in our minds with that fluidity and vagueness now so evident in our literature.

2

The novel and the short story are forms not only different in kind but also inherently at odds, and for that reason are never found being developed simultaneously and with equal intensity in any one literature. The novel is a syncretic form (whether it develops directly from collections of stories or is complicated by the incorporation of manners-and-morals material); the short story is a fundamental, elementary (which does not mean primitive) form. The novel derives from history, from travels; the story, from fairy tale, anecdote. The difference is one of essence, a difference in principle, conditioned by the fundamental distinction between big and small form. Not only individual writers but also individual literatures cultivate either the novel or the short story.

The story must be constructed on the basis of some contradiction, incongruity, error, contrast, etc. But that is not enough. By its very essence, the story, just as the anecdote, amasses its whole weight toward the ending. Like a bomb dropped from an airplane, it must speed downward so as to strike with its warhead full-force on the target. I am speaking here, of course, of the story of action, leaving aside stories of the sketch or *skaz* type, typical, for instance, of Russian literature. "Short story" is a term referring exclusively to plot, one assuming a combination of two conditions: small size and the impact of plot on the ending. Conditions of this sort produce something totally distinct in aim and devices from the novel.

An enormous role is played in the novel by the techniques of retardation (*texnika tormoženija*) and of linking and welding together disparate materials, by skill in deploying and binding together episodes, in creating diverse centers, in conducting parallel intrigues, and so on. With that sort of structuring, the ending of the novel is a point of letup and not of intensification. The culmination of the main line of action must come somewhere *before* the ending. Typical of the novel are "epilogues"—false endings, summations setting the perspective or informing the reader of the *Nachgeschichte* of the main characters (as in *Rudin*, or *Vojna i mir* [War and Peace]). It is only natural, then, that surprise endings should be a very rare occurrence in the novel (if encountered, then they most likely testify to the influence of the short story); a big form and a multiformity of episodes preclude that sort of construction. The short story, on the contrary, gravitates expressly toward the maximal unexpectedness of a finale concentrating around itself all that has preceded it. In the novel there must be a descent of some kind after the culmination point, whereas it is most natural for a story to come to a peak and stay there. The novel is a long walk through various localities, with a peaceful return trip assumed; the short story, a climb up a mountain, the aim of which is a view from on high.

Tolstoj could not end *Anna Karenina* with Anna's death. He had to write an entire extra section, however difficult, with the novel largely centered on Anna's fate. Otherwise the novel would have had the appearance of a drawn-out story rigged with completely superfluous characters and episodes. The logic of the form required a continuation. It was a sort of tour de force to kill off the main heroine before the fate of the other personages had been decided. There is good reason why heroes usually do manage somehow or other to hang on till the end (the supporting roles fall by the wayside) or manage to save themselves after having been a hair's breadth from death. What helped Tolstoj was the parallelism of the construction—Levin's competing with Anna from the very beginning for the central position. Quite on the other hand, Puškin in *Tales of Belkin* aims expressly at making the ending of the story coincide with the high point of the plot, thus creating the effect of a surprise dénouement (see his "Metel′" [The Snowstorm], and "Grobovščik" [The Coffin-maker]).

The story presents the problem of posing a single equation with one unknown; the novel presents a problem involving various rules, soluble with the aid of a whole system of equations with various unknowns in which the intermediary steps of positing are more important than the final answer. The story is a riddle; the novel is something on the order of a charade or a rebus.

The story, precisely because it is a *small form* (short story), has nowhere been so consistently cultivated as in America. Until the middle of the nineteenth century, American literature, in the minds of both its writers and its readers, was inseparable from English literature and was largely incorporated into it as a "provincial" literature. Washington Irving in the preface to his sketch of English life (*Bracebridge Hall*), says not without bitterness: "It has been a matter of marvel . . . that a man from the wilds of America should express himself in tolerable English. I was looked upon as something new and strange in literature; a kind of demi-savage, with a feather in his hand, instead of on his head; and there was a curiosity to hear what such a being had to say about civilized society." Nevertheless, he himself acknowledges that he had been brought up on English culture and literature, and his sketches have unquestionably very close affinity to the tradition of English manners-and-morals sketches. "Having been born and brought up in a new country, yet educated from infancy in the literature of an old one, my mind was early filled with historical and poetical associations, connected with places and manners and customs of Europe, but which could rarely be applied to those of my own country . . . England is as classic ground to an American, as Italy is to an Englishman; and old London teems with as much historical association as mighty Rome." True, in his first book of sketches there are attempts to use American material ("Rip Van Winkle," "Philip of Pokanoket"); "Philip of Pokanoket" begins with Irving's expressing regret that "those early writers, who treated of the discovery and settlement of America, have not given us more particular and candid accounts of the remarkable characters that flourished in savage life." However, the very type of sketches he wrote remained traditional in manner and language; there was nothing "American" about them in the contemporary meaning of the word.

The 1830s and 1840s brought out with full clarity the tendency of American prose to develop the genre of the short story. At the same time English literature cultivated the novel. By mid-century various types of magazines had begun to play a sizable role both in England and America and to increase in numbers. But it is characteristic that the big novels of Bulwer-Lytton, Dickens, Thackeray were primarily printed in the English magazines, while the main position in American magazines was held by short stories. This, incidentally, is a good illustration of the contention that the development of the short story in America cannot be regarded as a simple consequence of the appearance of magazines. In this instance, as in many others, there is no simple causality. The consolidation of the short-story genre was associated with, not engendered by, the propagation of magazines.

It was only natural that American criticism at this period should have shown special interest in the story and, coupled with it, a marked disinclination toward the novel. The views of Edgar Allan Poe, whose stories testify to the consolidation of the genre, are especially noteworthy and revealing in this connection. His article on the tales of Nathaniel Hawthorne reads as a sort of treatise on the specific characteristics of story structure. "There has long existed in literature," writes Poe, "a fatal and unfounded prejudice, which it will be the office of this age to overthrow—the idea that the mere bulk of a work must enter largely into our estimate of its merit. I do not suppose even the weakest of the quarterly reviewers weak enough to maintain that in a book's size or mass, abstractly considered, there is anything which especially calls for our admiration. A mountain, simply through the sensation of physical magnitude which it conveys, does indeed affect us with a sense of the sublime, but we cannot admit any such influence in the contemplation even of 'The Columbiad.' " Poe further develops his own particular theory, which consists in the fact that, in terms of artistry, the "rhymed poem," not exceeding in length what can be read in an hour, stands highest of all: "The unity of effect or impression is a point of greatest importance." The long poem, from Poe's point of view, is a paradox: "Epics were the offspring of an imperfect sense of Art, and their reign is no more." Closest of all to the poem as the ideal type stands the "prose tale." With prose Poe considers it possible to increase the time limit, "from the very nature of prose itself," to two hours of reading aloud (in other words, up to thirty-two printed pages). As for the novel, he considers it "objectionable" because of its size, to begin with: "As it cannot be read at one sitting, it deprives itself, of course, of the immense force derivable from totality."

Finally, Poe passes on to a characterization of the story genre: "A skillful literary artist has constructed a tale. If wise, he has not fashioned his thoughts to accommodate his incidents; but having conceived, with deliberate care, a certain unique or single *effect* to be wrought out, he then invents such incidents—he then combines such events as may best aid him in establishing this preconceived effect. If his very initial sentence tends not to elicit this effect, then he has failed in his first step. In the whole composition there should be no word written of which the tendency, direct or indirect, is not the one pre-established design. And by such means, with such care and skill, a picture is at length painted which leaves in the mind of him who contemplates it with a kindred art, a sense of the fullest satisfaction. The idea of the tale has been presented unblemished, because undisturbed; and this is an end unattainable by the novel." Poe has said of his own stories that he was in the habit of writing them from back to front, as the Chinese write their books.

Poe thus ascribes particular importance in a story to a central effect to which all the details must gravitate and to a finale which must account for everything which preceded. An awareness of the particular importance of the final impact runs throughout the cultivation of the story in America, whereas for the novel—especially the Dickens or Thackeray type of novel—the finale plays the role not so much of a dénouement as of an epilogue. Stevenson wrote a friend of his in 1891 apropos of one of his stories: "What am I do do? . . . Make another ending to it? Ah, but that's not the way I write; the whole tale is implied; I never use an effect, when I can help it, unless it prepares the effects that are to follow; that's what a story consists in. To make another end, that is to make the beginning all wrong. The dénouement of a long story is nothing . . . it is a coda, not an essential member in the rhythm; but the body and the end of a short story are bone of the bone and blood of the blood of the beginning."

Such is the general conception of the specific characteristics of the story in American literature. All American stories, beginning with Edgar Allan Poe, are more or less constructed on these principles. Hence the particular attention paid to the unexpected in the finale and, connected with it, a story structured on the basis of a riddle or an error which holds back the significance of the plot mainspring until the very end. This kind of story is at first completely serious in character; in the case of some writers, the effect of the unexpected is vitiated by moralistic or sentimental tendencies, but the principles of construction remain the same. This is so, for instance, in the case of Bret Harte: the posing of the riddle is usually more interesting than its solution. Take his story "An Heiress of Red Dog." There you have a riddle or even two riddles at its base: why did the old man will his money to that particular plain and ignorant woman and why was she so stingy about making use of it? But the solution is disappointing. The first riddle remains entirely unsolved, and the solution to the second one—the old man had forbidden her to give the money to anyone with whom she fell in love—seems insufficient, feeble. The same impression is produced by the sentimental-moralistic solutions of such pieces as "The Fool of Five Forks," "Miggles," or "The Man Whose Yoke Was Not Easy." Bret Harte seems almost afraid to give the finale point in order not to forego the sentimental naïveté with which he imbues the tone of his narrator.

In the evolution of every genre there are stages when the genre, once utilized as an entirely serious or "high" one, undergoes regeneration, coming out in parodic or comic form. Such was the case with the lyric poem, the adventure novel, the biographical novel, and so forth. Local and historical conditions bring about the most diverse variations, of course, but the process itself, as a sort of sui generis law of evolution, maintains its effect: the initially serious treatment of the fable, with its painstaking and detailed motivation, gives way to irony, joke, parody; motivational connections grow slack or are laid bare as conventions, and the author himself steps to the forefront, time and again destroying the illusion of genuineness and seriousness; the plot construction takes on the character of a play on the fable, while the fable turns into riddle or anecdote. It is in this way that the regeneration of a genre comes about—by a transition from one set of possibilities and forms to another.

The American story passed through its first stage of development in the hands of Irving, Edgar Allan Poe, Hawthorne, Bret Harte, Henry James, and others, changing in style and construction but remaining serious and "high." The appearance in the 1880s of the humorous stories of Mark Twain, who switched the story over onto the track of anecdote and who augmented the role of the narrator-humorist, was therefore an entirely natural and logical consequence. This affinity with the anecdote is even in some instances pointed out by the author himself. Take, for example, "About Magnanimous-Incident Literature," where Mark Twain says: "All my life, from boyhood up, I have had the habit of reading a certain set of anecdotes. . . . Many times I wished that the charming anecdotes had not stopped with their happy climaxes, but had continued the pleasing history of the several benefactors and beneficiaries. This wish rose in my breast so persistently that at last I determined to satisfy it by seeking out the sequels of those anecdotes myself." Three anecdotes with special "continuations" or "sequels" follow.

The novel retreats to the background and continues to exist primarily in the form of the dime detective novel. In connection with this, a fashion for parodies develops. Among Bret Harte's works, alongside his own unsuccessful novels, there is a series of parodies on novels by others which, in the form of condensed sketches illustrates the manner of various writers–Cooper, Miss Braddon, Dumas, Brontë, Marryat, Hugo, Bulwer-Lytton, Dickens, and others. It is no wonder that Poe so vehemently attacked the novel–the principle of structural unity serving as his point of departure discredits big form in which different centers and parallel lines are inevitably constructed and descriptive material brought to the fore, etc. In this regard Poe's critical essay apropos of Dickens's novel *Barnaby Rudge* is very significant. Among other things, Poe criticizes Dickens for inconsistencies and factual errors, seeing the reason for this in "the present absurd fashion of periodical novel-writing . . . [whereby] . . . our author had not sufficiently considered or determined upon *any* particular plot when he began the story."

Novels come on the scene which by their entire character are manifestly oriented toward the story (with their small number of personages, their one central effect consisting of some secret, and so on). Such a work is, for example, Hawthorne's *The Scarlet Letter*, the remarkable structure of which American theoreticians and historians of literature are forever pointing out. The novel has only three characters, bound to one another by a single secret which is disclosed in the last chapter. There are no parallel intrigues, no digressions or episodes; there is complete unity of time, place, and action. This is something different in principle from the novels of Balzac or Dickens, writers who take their origin not from the story but from sketches of manners and morals or so-called "physiological" sketches.

In sum, it is characteristic of American literature to present that type of story built on the principle of structural unity with a centralization of the basic effect and a strong accentuation on the finale. Until the 1880s this kind of story kept changing within its type, now approaching the sketch, now moving away from it, but maintaining a serious (moralistic, sentimental, psychological, or philosophical) character. Beginning in the 1880s (Mark Twain), the American story takes a decided step in the direction of the anecdote, bring the narrator-humorist to the fore or introducing elements of parody and irony. The feature of the surprise finale takes on the character of a play on the plot scheme and on the reader's expectations. Structural devices are purposely laid bare in their purely formal meaning, motivation becomes simpler, psychological analysis disappears. It is on this foundation that the stories of O. Henry are developed, stories in which the principle of an approximation to the anecdote is carried, it would seem, to the limit.

3

O. Henry's literary beginnings were extremely characteristic of the 1890s: the feuilleton, parody, anecdote—such were his first ventures published in the little humor magazine the *Rolling Stone* (1894). Among these pieces, incidentally, there are parodies on the Sherlock Holmes detective mysteries ("Tracked to Doom or the Mystery of the Rue de Peychaud," "The Adventures of Shamrock Jolnes," and "The Sleuths"). These stories are something like Bret Harte's *Condensed Novels*—detective mysteries carried to the absurd: instead of arresting the criminal whom he encounters in a saloon, the detective hastens to jot down in his notebook the details of the place, the time of the encounter, etc.; horrors come thick and fast; situations, surprises, and transformations are of the most improbable sort—in short, all the stereotypes hyperbolized. Alongside these pieces we find an anecdote ("A Strange Story") about a father who went out to get some medicine for his sick child and returned home with the medicine after a lapse of so many years that he had since become a grandfather: he kept missing the streetcar.

Prison brought this newspaper work of O. Henry's to an abrupt halt, cutting off his contact with the literary world. However, as may be seen from Jennings's memoirs, he continued to write, using material collected during his stay in Austin, Texas, and in South America. One of his first stories written after prison was "A Retrieved Reformation" (about Jimmy Valentine), the details of which were mentioned above. To this same period belong "The Duplicity of Hargraves," "Roads of Destiny," and others. In these O. Henry is far from parody; he is sometimes even serious, sentimental, or emotional. Such is the general character of his first collection of stories, *The Four Million* (1906), which includes stories written between 1903 and 1905. Interestingly enough, O. Henry did not include in this collection certain stories written and published during this same period, considering them, evidently, unsuited to the collection as a whole. O. Henry apparently aimed at a certain cyclical organization when selecting stories for inclusion in collections. In certain instances, as will be seen later on, this cyclical organization is also supported by a unity of principal characters (Jeff and Andy in *The Gentle Grafter*) and sometimes the connection between the stories is underscored by their being called "chapters," as they are in the collections *Heart of the West* and *Whirligigs.*

O. Henry's first book, the novel *Cabbages and Kings*, published in 1904, is also constructed on the principle of cyclical organization. This book is not, in fact, a novel in our modern understanding of novel but something like the older novels which maintained their connection with collections of stories—"a patched comedy," as O. Henry himself says. In the novel there are seven separate stories of which one—the story of the president Miraflores and Goodwin (occupying chapters I, III-V, IX, XV and XVI) becomes the main story, expanded by interpolations into it of the remaining six stories (chapters II, VI-VII, VIII, X-XI, XII and XIII-XIV). These six stories are loosely hooked onto the events and characters of the main one. For example, the story about the consul Geddie and the bottle containing a letter (chapter II) constitutes a completely independent whole; its connection with the main story consists only in Geddie's being a friend of Goodwin's and living in the same city of Coralio. Once the whole novel is read, such interpolated stories and episodes easily drop off from the main story, but what matters is that the reader is not certain where precisely the solution of the main mystery lies until the very end. The novel is built on an error—it wasn't the president of the Republic of Anchuria, Miraflores, who met his end but the president of the Republic Insurance Company, Mr. Wahrfield.

This error is, moreover, the main mystery for the reader—he can see that some riddle lies at the basis of the novel, but where it is lodged and with which characters it is connected he doesn't discover until the end. Hence, the possibility of and justification for bringing in completely extraneous persons and speaking about completely extraneous events—their "extraneousness" is revealed only in the last chapters. The interpolated stories thus acquire a special kind of motivation justifying their presence—the motivation not only of "retarding" the riddle's solution but also of leading the reader off onto a false track, the motivation of a false solution or hints of such a solution; the finale not only solves the riddle but reveals the presence of the error itself and of the coincidence.

The novel lists at the outset all the facts of which the main story will consist: "They will tell you in Anchuria, that President Miraflores, of that volatile republic, died by his own hand in the coast town of Coralio; that he had reached thus far in flight from the inconveniences of an imminent revolution; and that one hundred thousand dollars, government funds, which he carried with him in an American leather valise as a souvenir of his tempestuous administration, was never afterwards recovered." At the conclusion of this list O. Henry declares: "It would seem that the story is ended, instead of begun; that the close of tragedy and the climax of a romance have covered the ground of interest; but, to the more curious reader, it shall be some slight instruction to trace the close threads that underlie the ingenuous web of circumstances. . . . Only by following out the underlying threads will it be made clear why the old Indian Galvez is secretly paid to keep green the grave of President Miraflores by one that never saw that unfortunate statesman in life or in death, and why that one was wont to walk in the twilight, casting from a distance looks of gentle sadness upon that unhonored mound."

That there is a riddle involved is therefore shown from the very beginning—the novel is in the nature of answers to questions posed at the outset of the novel. This "laying bare" of a mystery as the mainspring of the plot makes its whole construction somewhat ironic or parodic;[4] the mystery is presented not as something serious but only as an intriguing and teasing element, by which means the author plays with his reader. Sometimes the fact that there is a riddle involved is deliberately underscored—the author, who knows the solution, does not hide behind events as in the usual novel of mysteries; on the contrary, he reminds the reader of his presence. When mentioning that the mysterious Smith will not appear again until the end of the novel (chapter III), O. Henry adds: "This he must do; for, when he sailed away before the dawn in his yacht *Rambler*, he carried with him the answer to a riddle so big and preposterous that few in Anchuria had ventured even to propound it."

Psychological motivation is completely absent—the focus of the novel is not on inner experiences but on events. Therefore the reader easily passes through the scene of the president's suicide. O. Henry does not try to bring his reader close enough to his characters to achieve the illusion of living people. The characters of the novel are marionettes: they say and do what the author commands them to say and do, and say nothing that must be kept undisclosed in order to retain the secret, because that is the way the author wants it.

The motivational basis of the novel is, in this sense, completely transparent and simple: the fact that the president of the Republic of Anchuria was confused with the president of the Republic Insurance Company made the whole novel possible. Thus the whole riddle is built upon a kind of pun—a device typical of O. Henry. A simple coincidence, which in itself in such a novel requires no motivation, turns out to be the cause of all the events that take place.

The ending gives a threefold solution: the president, the one whom Goodwin caught and who committed suicide, was not Miraflores but Mr. Wahrfield; Goodwin's wife was not the actress Isabel Guilbert but Wahrfield's daughter; Goodwin did not appropriate the money (as "Beelzebub" Blythe is convinced and as the reader is inclined to think) but returned it to the insurance company. Of these three solutions only the last is definitely expected by the reader, and, at that, not on the basis of context but because that was the right thing to do. The other two turn out to be complete surprises. True enough, there are tiny hints—as always in O. Henry—beginning with the "Proem," where mention is made of the strange grave and of "that one" (i.e., Goodwin) who for some reason takes care to see that the grave is kept neat and often comes to this place. Still, while reading the novel, the reader is inclined to see the riddle at any point except where it actually is.

However, the most important consideration for us in this novel is the fact that it is a unified collection of stories—a novel with "patched" construction and based on the principle of cyclical organization. This is underscored even by the title itself—

Cabbages and Kings— which originates from Lewis Carroll's well-known ballad in which the Walrus proposes that the oysters listen to his tale of many things, of shoes, of ships, of sealing wax, of cabbages and kings. The novel is written in a way similar to that in which verses are sometimes written on rhymes given in advance; the artistry in such an instance consists in cleverly joining the most surprising and seemingly unjoinable things together. The formal and game-like basis of the novel, if not its parodic basis, is seen clearly enough in the opening "Proem by the Carpenter," which ends with the autocritique: "So, there is a little tale to tell of many things. Perhaps to the promiscuous ear of the Walrus it shall come with most avail; for in it there are indeed shoes and ships and sealing-wax and cabbage-palms and presidents instead of kings. Add to these a little love and counterplotting, and scatter everywhere throughout the maze a trail of tropical dollars—dollars warmed not more by the torrid sun than by the hot palms of the scouts of Fortune—and, after all here seems to be Life itself, with talk enough to weary the most garrulous of Walruses." Here O. Henry himself indicates the construction of his novel, singling out love, plots, and so forth, as the motivation for the joining together of "many things."

In connection with what I have said above about the American story and about Poe's views on the novel, the appearance of a novel such as *Cabbages and Kings* is extremely characteristic. Its kind of cyclical organization, which brings us back to the older forms of the novel, brings us back by that same token to the story as the basic, elementary, and natural form of prose fiction. It is entirely predictable that with such an understanding of the novel O. Henry was to write stories which could easily be arranged in cycles with respect to various of their features. Big form as such, based on the welding together of diverse material, on the technique of deploying and linking episodes together, the creation of varied centers, parallel intrigues, etc., was absolutely outside of O. Henry's dimension.

4

However consistent and homogeneous—and, in many people's opinion, even monotonous—O. Henry's work might appear, there are noticeable vacillations, transitions, and a certain evolution to it. Sentimental stories—stories about New York shopgirls or others of the type of "Georgia's Ruling"—predominate in the years immediately following his imprisonment (though they do also appear later). Generally speaking, the comic or satiric and the sentimental do very often go together in the poetics of one and the same writer in just their function of correlated contrasts; this is what we find in the work of Sterne, of Dickens, and, to some extent, in the work of Gogol′. In O. Henry this combination stands out with particular relief owing to the fact that his basic orientation toward the anecdote with its unexpected and comically resolved ending is so extremely well-defined. His sentimental slice-of-life pieces, therefore, give the impression of experiments—the more so because they are all, in terms of technique and language, much weaker than the others. Usually they are drawn-out, wishy-washy, with endings which disappoint the reader and leave him feeling unsatisfied. The stories lack compactness, the language is without wit, the structure without dynamism. American critics, it is true, would seem ready to place these stories higher than all the others, but that is an evaluation with which we find it difficult to agree. An American, in his leisure time at home, readily gives himself over to sentimental and religious-moralistic reflections and likes to have appropriate reading. That is his custom, his tradition, a feature of national history conditioned by the peculiarities of his way of life and civilization. Traditional for the American to the same degree is, for instance, his fear of any kind of "pornography" in literature, be it even something in the spirit of Maupassant. O. Henry, in many respects himself a typical American, protested at being compared with Maupassant, calling the latter, not without disdain, a pornographic writer. To the Russian reader these traditions of the American way of life are alien, and the sentimental stories of O. Henry that earned the appreciation of President Roosevelt have had no success among us.

Leaving these pieces aside, I shall first of all consider one of O. Henry's first stories, one which calls for attention owing to the oddity of its construction, which furnishes evidence of the nature of O. Henry's first explorations in this field. I have in mind "Roads of Destiny," first published in 1903 and printed again only in 1909 (in the collection of the same name). The action takes place not in America but in eighteenth-century France, during the era of the Revolution. It consists of three chapters, which are in fact three independent stories. The peasant poet, David Mignot, leaves his village and sets out for Paris; the way leads to a crossroads: "Three leagues, then, the road ran, and turned into a puzzle. It joined with another and a larger road at right angles. David stood, uncertain, for a while, and then took the road to the left." A separate story follows ("The Left Branch"), ending with a shot from the pistol of the Marquis de Beaupertuys from which David dies. Immediately after this comes the second part, entitled "The Right Branch" and beginning with the same words: "Three leagues, then the road ran, and turned into a puzzle. It joined with another and a larger road at right angles. David stood, uncertain, for a while, and then took the road to the right." The second story follows, again ending with David's death—under different circumstances but with the same Marquis de Beaupertuys and his pistol taking part. Next comes the third part ("The Main Road"), which has the same opening but which goes on with David, after a moment's thought, turning back to the village. The third story follows. David ends by committing suicide, using a pistol he had obtained by chance, a pistol once belonging to the Marquis de Beaupertuys.

At the basis of the story is the "three roads" motif of folklore illustrating the inevitability of fate. This thesis is also underscored by the epigraph in verse (the only such instance in O. Henry, it appears), which raises the question whether it is possible "To order, shun, or wield, or mold My Destiny?" It is not, of course, the idea itself that is original, but the fact that the story consists of three independent tales left as variants not only without motivational connection but even without any possibility of being joined together into one consecutive whole. The plot is presented straight off in its three possible versions—in the form of pure parallels, without their being brought together, as is usually done, into a single whole with the aid of one or another motivational device. For comparison, one may take, for instance, Tolstoj's "Three Deaths," in which the parallelism (the lady, the peasant, the tree) is presented in a specially motivated, consecutive order of events (the halt on the road, the driver, and the boots of the dying peasant, the promise to erect a cross, etc.). O. Henry offers his readers the type of construction in which each new part is an independent whole: the hero begins his life over again each time, as if forgetting that in the preceding part he had lost it. We have here three tales joined together, but the joining is done not on the principle of the consecutive order of the hero's adventures (as it would be in the adventure novel) but on the principle of comparison and contrast. The unity of the hero, conditioned by the thesis, moreover, is not joined together with the unity of his fate.

If one were to change the endings of the first two parts (David is spared), we would have a sort of adventure novel. Or the other way around—we need only eradicate the "helpers" in any adventure novel and the hero would die several times over (something of the sort happened, apparently, in one of Dumas's novels).

However, the originality of the structure does not end there. The main line of action, that of the main hero, David Mignot, is twice cut off by his death and begun over again, and, consequently, there is none of the usual consecutiveness or connection here. The secondary level of the action, however, does proceed in regular fashion—in straightforward chronological order: the Marquis de Beaupertuys travels to Paris ("The Left Branch"); the Marquis de Beaupertuys participates in a conspiracy against the king ("The Right Branch"); the Marquis de Beaupertuys is exiled because of the conspiracy, all his property is sold, the pistol turns up in a secondhand shop and from there falls into David's hands ("The Main Road"). We get a second hero, whose story, though episodic and in the background, is nevertheless presented in the form of consecutive events, one taking up where the other left off. Even the pistol is a hero of sorts, passing as it does from hand to hand and each time encountering David on its way. Thus, a curious collision or crisscrossing of two levels of action takes place in the story: the one is represented by the story of the marquis and his pistol, and it evolves in time normally; the other is represented by the three tales about the same hero, without any temporal interconnection but, as it were, interpolated three times into the secondary level of action, with each new interpolation liquidating the one preceding it. The conditions of "verisimilitude" are broken down, artistic motivation is cast aside, and replaced by a "thesis."

We have here a very special type of a collation of stories. If one calls to mind that O. Henry was at this time working on his novel *Cabbages and Kings*, one can argue that at this period O. Henry was concerned precisely with the problem of the combination and cyclical organization of stories, devising complex and original constructions such as the one in the story analyzed. It was as if, having sought a way out of the stereotypes of the adventure and detective novel, he gave up these experiments in the end and began to write separate stories, combining them later in collections on the basis of unifying features of one sort or another. A certain role in this rejection of further experimentation in cyclical organization might have been played by the literary working conditions in which O. Henry was placed: it was just at this time, December 1903 (*Roads of Destiny* had been published in April), that O. Henry signed a contract with a New York newspaper to do weekly stories. Apparently, the idea of a new transition to forms of larger caliber never forsook him. His biographer quotes him as saying not long before his death that writing short stories had ceased to satisfy him and that he had conceived an idea for a big novel. "Everything I have written up till now will amount to mere whimsicality, a trial of the pen, in comparison with what I shall have written in a year's time."[5]

Traces of partial cyclical organization, as I noted above, may be observed in O. Henry's collections of stories, such as *Heart of the West* and *The Gentle Grafter*. In the latter, there is even a constant narrator, Jeff Peters. Many of the stories begin with the author's preambles, of a kind typical for cycles in the style of the *Decameron*, which motivate the stories that follow. Sometimes, over and above that, a specific thematic connection is established between adjacent stories (as is done in the preamble to *The Exact Science of Matrimony*—the preamble is usually missing in Russian translations). One need only expand these preambles into a special framework and we would have something on the order of a "picaresque" novel with the figures of Jeff and Andy at the center: now we see them in the liquor business, now duping the mayor, now setting up a marriage bureau, and so on.

In the course of its development, the story of action (*sjužetnaja novella*) naturally gravitates toward cyclical organization—such is the history of the formation of the old adventure novel (Lesage's *Gil Blas*). Later on, a redistribution of elements takes place; secondary, motivational elements come to the foreground and play an organizing role: the hero is transformed from an element of the motivational apparatus (a device for threading and binding events together) into a form-organizing element—the structural function of the hero changes. What we get is a novel with a weakened plot and a developed descriptive aspect (descriptions of a way of life, the psychology of characters, etc.), the kind of novel typical of nineteenth-century Russia. We have already passed beyond this novel and are confronted with the task of organizing new genres. In this sense, O. Henry is something of extreme interest to us. He terminates the process of development of the nineteenth-century American story and brings it up as far as cyclical organization. O. Henry's collected stories are a kind of *Thousand and One Nights*, lacking a traditional framework.

5

Working in the literary trade and tied down by the conditions of his contract and the need to make his writing pay off, O. Henry was obliged to write stories to suit a variety of tastes, including those of newspaper editors and readers. Any story writer could have produced "Georgia's Ruling," "Blind Man's Holiday," or "A Fog in Santone." The genuine, original O. Henry is found in his comic, picaresque, and parodic stories, stories with surprise endings, with clever dialogue and ironic author commentary. They are the ones brimful of literary irony arising as a consequence of his sensitivity to clichés both of language and of story structure. Unlike Mark Twain, O. Henry does not deal in straight humor; in his hands anecdote constantly turns into parody, into play on form, into material for literary irony—precisely the shape the regeneration of a genre takes. O. Henry often stands on the brink of parodying the short story itself, reminding one of Sterne's devices in his novel-parody *Tristram Shandy.*

Let us begin with his language, although for the Russian reader this aspect of O. Henry's stories is, of course, largely lost. His language was about the most important thing for O. Henry. The stories, on being read, may appear to have been written swiftly and effortlessly, without any particular care taken to work them over or revise them, without any special selection of words. Jennings, who remained on friendly terms with O. Henry after his imprisonment, recounts how O. Henry worked. A whole night was spent writing "The Halberdier of the Little Rheinschloss," and the story was finished by noon the next day:

> At about ten minutes after twelve he called me up. "You're late. I'm waiting," he said..
>
> When I got to his room, the big table where he did his writing was littered with sheets of paper. All over the floor were scraps of paper covered with writing in longhand.

In response to Jennings's question whether he always worked that way, O. Henry opened a desk drawer and said, "Look at those," pointing to "a crammed-down heap of papers covered with his long freehand." He did not usually make preliminary drafts; he would start writing only when the story was completely finished in his mind. But the work over his language was an involved process:

> O. Henry was a careful artist. He was a slave to the dictionary. He would pore over it, taking an infinite relish in the discovery of a new twist to a word.
>
> One day he was sitting at the table with his back to me. He had

been writing with incredible rapidity, as though the words just ran themselves automatically from his pen. Suddenly he stopped. For half an hour he sat silent, and then he turned around, rather surprised to find me still there.

"Thirsty, colonel? Let's get a drink."

"Bill," my curiosity was up, "does your mind feel a blank when you sit there like that?" The question seemed to amuse him.

"No. But I have to reason out the meaning of words."

Elsewhere Jennings recalls having spent several hours in O. Henry's room waiting for him to finish writing a story: "He was writing with lightning speed. Sometimes he would finish a page and immediately wrinkle it into a ball and throw it on the floor. Then he would write on, page after page, with hardly a pause, or he would sit silent and concentrate for half an hour at a stretch."

Thus the construction of the story from beginning to end (rather, it would be better to say in this case, from end to beginning) had already formed in O. Henry's mind before he sat down to write, which is, of course, a characteristic feature of the short story (see the remarks of Poe and Stevenson quoted above) and also of O. Henry. What he did at his desk was to work out the details of language and narration. What sort of work was that, what principles guided him, what procedures did he use? The basic principle was to get rid of stylistic clichés, to come to grips with bookishness, with the slick middle style and to subject the high style to irony. This opened the way for his extensive use of slang in crime stories, his express avoidance of artiness, his unfailingly downgrading images, their humor stemming from their oddity and unexpectedness, and so on. Frequently we find in O. Henry an attitude of outright irony toward one or another literary style, an irony which has the effect of bringing his own principles into the open. In "Let Me Feel Your Pulse," he even refers to names. After giving an account of the doctor's examination of his patients, O. Henry says: "I'll bet that if he had used the phrases: 'Gaze, as it were, unpreoccupied, outward—or rather laterally—in the direction of the horizon, underlaid, so to speak, with the adjacent fluid inlet,' and 'Now, returning—or rather, in a manner withdrawing your attention, bestow it upon my upraised digit'—I'll bet, I say, that Henry James himself could have passed the examination" (referring to the complexity and ornateness of James's style); or in the same story, on a description of mountains: "It was about twilight, and the mountains came up nobly to Miss Murfee's[6] description of them."

At those points in his stories where the need to advance the narrative or tradition would have made a special description requisite, O. Henry turns the occasion to literary irony. Whereas another story writer would have used the opportunity to wax eloquent or to transmit detailed information about his characters—their personalities, outward appearances, dress, past history—O. Henry is either exceedingly terse or ironic: "Old Jacob Spraggins came home at 9:30 P.M., in his motor car. The make of it you will have to surmise sorrowfully; I am giving you unsubsidized fiction; had it been a street car I could have told you its voltage and the number of flat wheels it had" ("A Night in New Arabia"). There you have a typical O. Henry twist. Another instance of the same kind, a description of the hero: "Overlooking your mild impertinence in feeling a curiosity about the personal appearance of a stranger, I will give you a modified description of him. Weight, 118; complexion, hair and brain, light; height, five feet six; age, about twenty-three; dressed in a $10 suit of greenish-blue serge; pockets containing two keys and sixty-three cents in change. But do not misconjecture because this description sounds like a General Alarm that James was either lost or a dead one" ("What You Want"). Sometimes the irony is underscored by parody. O. Henry simulates verbosity:

> Ileen was a strictly vegetable compound, guaranteed under the Pure Ambrosia and Balm-of-Gilead Act of the year of the fall of Adam. She was a fruitstand blond—strawberries, peaches, cherries, etc. Her eyes were wide apart, and she possessed the calm that precedes a storm that never comes. But it seems to me that words (however much is paid per word) are wasted in an effort to describe the beautiful. Like fancy, 'It is engendered in the eyes.' There are three kinds of beauties—I was foreordained to be homiletic; I can never stick to a story ("A Poor Rule").

The parodic device of substituting the language of an official report for literary description, as in the example above, is systematically employed in the story "A Municipal Report." Broadly speaking, the story is a polemic, an answer to Frank Norris's assertion that only three cities in the United States were "story cities," New York, New Orleans, and San Francisco, whereas Chicago, Buffalo, or Nashville held out nothing for a story writer. The story takes place, as a matter of fact, in Nashville, but instead of describing the city, O. Henry interpolates into the text quotations from a guidebook which clash with the style of the usual literary description. The very fact of inserting such quotations carries with it the character of parody. The narrator arrives in the city on a train:

All I could see through the streaming windows were two rows of dim houses. The city has an area of 10 square miles; 181 miles of streets, of which 137 miles are paved; a system of waterworks that cost $2,000,000, with 77 miles of mains.

Further on, in a conversation between the narrator and one of the characters:

"Your town," I said, as I began to make ready to depart (which is the time for smooth generalities), "seems to be a quiet, sedate place. A home town, I should say, where few things out of the ordinary ever happen." It carries on an extensive trade in stoves and hollow ware with the West and South, and its flouring mills have a daily capacity of more than 2,000 barrels.

It is an interesting fact that this parodic or playful use of quotation—one of O. Henry's most constant stylistic devices—was noted long ago by American critics. O. Henry quotes Tennyson, Spenser, and others, informing their words with new meaning, inventing puns, deliberately misquoting parts, and so on. Russian readers, unfortunately, miss all of this, as they also do, for the most part, those instances of play on words in O. Henry's crime stories which are motivated by the speaker's illiteracy (for example, a confusion of scientific words as in the case of "hypodermical" instead of "hypothetical").

O. Henry's characters often behave in a way not usual in books, and this oddity of behavior is also sometimes underscored by the author himself. The hero of "A Technical Error," Sam Durkee, is preparing himself to commit an act of blood revenge ("feuding" is one of the traditional motifs in American fiction):

Sam took out and opened a bone-handled pocket-knife and scraped a dried piece of mud from his left boot. I thought at first he was going to swear vendetta on the blade of it, or recite "The Gypsy's Curse." The few feuds I had ever seen or read about usually opened that way. This one seemed to be presented with a new treatment. Thus offered on the stage, it would have been hissed off. . . . During the ride Sam talked of the prospect for rain, of the price of beef, and of the musical glasses. You would have thought he had never had a brother or a sweetheart or an enemy on earth. There are some subjects too big even for the words in the "Unabridged."

It is curious that this last notion, encountered constantly in the old romanticists (cf. the ending of Turgenev's *Dvorjanskoe gnezdo* [A Nest of Gentlefolk]) and used to motivate reticence, serves in O. Henry's case to motivate the unexpectedness of what his characters say or do in an excited state—an unexpectedness of a literary nature.

The general observation should be made that O. Henry's basic stylistic device (shown both in his dialogues and in the plot construction) is the confrontation of very remote, seemingly unrelated and, for that reason, surprising words, ideas, subjects, or feelings. Surprise as a device of parody thus serves as the organizing principle of the sentence. It is no accident that he goes out of his way to avoid orderly and scrupulous descriptions and that his heroes sometimes speak in a completely erratic way; the verbiage in these instances is motivated by a special set of circumstances or causes.

O. Henry has provided us with a sort of treatise on how characters should speak when undergoing emotional stress. Such a "treatise" is the story "Proof of the Pudding," which brings us back to the old genre of "conversations" between the editor or journalist and the writer. O. Henry was very apt to express himself ironically with regard to editors and editorial boards. In the story cited above ("A Technical Error") we read: "Sam Durkee had a girl. (If it were an all-fiction magazine that I expected to sell this story to, I should say 'Mr. Durkee rejoiced in a fiancée')." In "Proof of the Pudding" the editor and the story writer meet in a city park. The editor has persistently rejected the writer's manuscripts because the latter followed the French and not the English manner in his stories. They join in a theoretical dispute. The editor reproaches the writer for spoiling his pieces at their very point of climax: "But you spoil every dénouement by those flat, drab, obliterating strokes of your brush that I have so often complained of. If you would rise to the literary pinnacle of your dramatic scenes, and paint them in the high colors that art requires, the postman would leave fewer bulky, self-addressed envelopes at your door." The story writer counters by expounding his own theory:

You've got that old sawmill drama king in your brain yet. When the man with the black mustache kidnaps golden-haired Bessie, you are bound to have the mother kneel and raise her hands in the spotlight and say: 'May high heaven witness that I will rest neither night nor day till the heartless villain that has stolen me child feels the weight of a mother's vengeance!' . . . I'll tell you what she'd say in real life. She'd say: 'What! Bessie led away by a strange man? Good lord! It's one trouble after another! Get my other hat, I must hurry around to the police station. Why wasn't somebody looking after her, I'd like to know? For God's sake, get out of my way or I'll never get ready. Not that hat—the brown one with the velvet bows. Bessie must have been crazy; she's usually shy of strangers. Is that too much powder? Lordy! How I'm upset!' That's the way she'd talk, continued Dawe. People in real life don't fly into heroics and blank verse at emotional crises. They simply can't do it. If they talk at all on such occasions, they draw from the same vocabulary that they use every day, and muddle up their words and ideas a little more, that's all.

The editor is indignant because the heroine in one of the stories they are discussing, after having discovered from a letter that her husband had run off with a manicurist, says: "Well, what do you think of that! Absurdly inappropriate words. . . . No human being ever uttered banal colloquialisms when confronted by sudden tragedy." The writer argues to the contrary that "no man or woman ever spouts high-falutin talk when they go up against a real climax. They talk naturally and a little worse." The special humor of the story consists in the fact that, immediately after their conversation, both simultaneously find themselves in identical "dramatic predicaments." Having failed to resolve their argument, they go off to the writer's apartment, where they find a letter from which they learn that their wives have left them. Their response "in practice" turns out to be the opposite of what each had expounded in theory. The writer "dropped the letter, covered his face with his trembling hands, and cried out in a deep, vibrating voice: 'My God, why hast Thou given me this cup to drink? Since she is false, then let Thy Heaven's fairest gifts, faith and love, become the jesting bywords of traitors and fiends!' " The editor "fumbled with a button on his coat as he blurted between his pale lips: 'Say, Shack, ain't that a hell of a note? Wouldn't that knock you off your perch, Shack? Ain't it hell, now, Shack, ain't it?' " The ironic meaning of the story is wholly directed against references to "real life," where things are always supposedly "not that way," the sort of references with which, one must suppose, editors had regaled O. Henry and brought him to a state of exasperation; in real life, it turns out, anything goes.

It is highly characteristic of O. Henry's general parodic bent that he frequently takes problems having to do with literary practice as themes for his stories, making theoretical and ironic comments on matters of style and now and again having his say about editors, publishers, readers' demands, and so on and so forth. Some of his stories remind one of the once very popular sonnet parodies in which the subject matter was the process of composing a sonnet. These pieces disclose a very keen awareness on O. Henry's part of forms and traditions and confirm the view of his work as a sort of culmination point reached by the American short story of the nineteenth century. He was a writer of fiction no less than he was a critic and theorist—a feature very characteristic of our age, which has completely dissociated itself from the naïve notion that writing is an "unconscious" process in which all depends on "inspiration" and "having it inside one." We haven't had a parodist with so subtle a knowledge of his craft, so inclined time and again to initiate the reader into its mysteries, probably since the time of Laurence Sterne.

However, first a few words more about O. Henry's style. His narration is invariably ironic or playful. His writing is studded with metaphors but only for the purpose of disconcerting or amusing the reader with the unexpectedness of the comparisons—a surprise of a literary nature: their material is not traditional and usually runs counter to the "literary norm," downgrading the object of comparison and upsetting the stylistic inertia. This applies with particular frequency to descriptive passages, toward which, as we have seen above, O. Henry maintained an invariably ironic attitude. For instance, when describing a city, he says: "Though the dusk of twilight was hardly yet apparent, lights were beginning to spangle the city like popcorn bursting in a deep skillet" ("Compliments of the Season"). There is no need to multiply examples—the reader of O. Henry cannot fail to notice them. A detailed and serious literary description of anything whatsoever is the height of absurdity in O. Henry's eyes. When putting a novice writer to the test ("The Plutonian Fire"), O. Henry, who plays the role of his friend in the story, suggests: " 'Suppose you try your hand at a descriptive article . . . giving your impressions of New York as seen from the Brooklyn Bridge. The fresh point of view, the—.' 'Don't be a fool,' said Pettit. 'Let's go have some beer.' " Naturally enough, in the narrative and descriptive passages of his stories, O. Henry more often than not enters into conversation with his reader, making no point of arousing in him an illusion of direct contact or of reality but rather forever emphasizing his role as the writer and, therefore, conducting the story not from the standpoint of an impersonal commentator but from that of his own person. He brings in an outside narrator (as in his crime stories) in those cases in which there is occasion for using slang, for playing on words, or the like.

Given such a system of narration, his dialogue stands out in high relief and takes on a substantial share of the effect of plot and style. The terseness of the narrative and descriptive commentary is naturally compensated for by the dynamism and concreteness of speech in the dialogues. The conversations of the characters in O. Henry stories always have a direct connection with the plot and with the role the character in question plays in it; they are rich in intonations, fast-moving and often devious or ambiguous in some special way. Sometimes a whole dialogue will be built on an incomplete utterance or on mutual misunderstanding, with implications, in certain cases, not only for style but for the plot, as well. In "The Third Ingredient," one girl talks about her trip and its unhappy outcome (she had thrown herself into the river in despair), while at the same time the other girl is preparing beef stew and lamenting the fact that she has no onion to put in it:

"I came near drowning in that awful river," said Cecilia, shuddering.

"It ought to have more water in it," said Hetty. "The stew, I mean. I'll go get some at the sink."

"It smells good," said the artist.

"That nasty old North River?" objected Hetty. "It smells to me like soap factories and wet setter dogs—oh, you mean the stew. Well, I wish we had an onion for it."

A curious fact in this connection is that there is a kind of submerged analogy in the story between the role of the onion in the dish being prepared (meat and potatoes) and the role of the young man who appears at the end of the story (with onion in hand). The analogy comes out explicitly in Hetty's line with which the story ends. In another story ("The Ransom of Mack"), two friends carry on a conversation from which it is possible to conclude that Mack is getting married (a conclusion that Mack's friend does make). Taking his words in that meaning, the friend undertakes a whole complicated scheme designed to prevent the marriage from happening, only to find out at the end of the story that Mack's words, "I'm going to marry the young lady who just passed tonight," plus his and the bride's subsequent words, meant only that Mack, no other suitable person being available, was going to perform the marriage rites himself.

Thus, in O. Henry's hands the short story undergoes regeneration, becoming a unique composite of literary feuilleton and comedy or vaudeville dialogue.

6

I return to O. Henry's penchant for parody in order to show, with the help of that material, what his general structural devices and principles were. I have already mentioned O. Henry's use of literature—the building of a story on a discussion of the theoretical problems connected with it—as the subject matter of certain of his stories. These pieces may be taken as sui generis treatises in which O. Henry himself reveals his principles, criticizes all the possible stereotypes, and so forth. However, even in his most ordinary things, O. Henry often enough annotates the progress of the plot, taking each instance as an opportunity for introducing literary irony, for destroying the illusion of authenticity, for parodying a cliché, for making palpable the conventionality of art, or showing how the story is put together. The author time and again intrudes into the events of his own story and engages the reader in literary conversation, turning the story into a feuilleton. All the component parts of the story are commonly fitted out with commentary of that sort.

Let us go through all of one story to see the whole of his system of literary play and irony, a system built on an awareness of traditional devices of structure and the laying bare of these devices. "A Night in New Arabia"[7] opens with a long introduction, in which a parallel is drawn between Al Rashid of the *Thousand and One Nights* and American philanthropists (a frequent O. Henry theme): "But now [O. Henry concludes his introduction], there being ten sultans to one Sheherazade, she is held too valuable to be in fear of the bowstring. In consequence the art of narrative languishes." A story under the special title "The Story of the Caliph Who Alleviated His Conscience" follows. It begins abruptly: "Old Jacob Spraggins mixed for himself some Scotch and lithia water at his $1,200 oak sideboard." Right at the start, however, the author himself appears with a comment: "Thus, by the commonest article of the trade, having gained your interest, the action of the story will now be suspended, leaving you grumpily to consider a sort of doll biography beginning fifteen years before." After the brief biography of Spraggins, the author's voice sounds again: "There now! it's over. Hardly had time to yawn, did you? I've seen biographies that–but let us dissemble." There follow a few more details of Spraggins's past, which prompt a short digression on the topic of quarrels between husbands and wives ending with the words: "After all, we are all human–Count Tolstoj, R. Fitzsimmons, Peter Pan, and the rest of us. Don't lose heart because the story seems to be degenerating into a sort of moral essay for intellectual readers." The rest of Jacob's biography follows–the events of his life immediately preceding the one with which the story opens.

Thereupon Jacob's daughter makes her entrance: "Celia is the heroine. Lest the artist's delineation of her charms on this very page humbug your fancy, take from me her authorized description." Celia feels attracted to a grocery store clerk and speaks of this to her maid Annette, who is well read in romantic fiction: " 'Oh, marshmallows!' cried Annette. 'I see. Ain't it lovely? It's just like "Lurline the Left-Handed"; or "A Buttonhole Maker's Wrongs." I'll bet he'll turn out to be a count.' " Instead of describing the process of courtship, O. Henry declares: "The processes of courtship are personal, and do not belong to general literature. They should be chronicled in detail only in advertisement of iron tonics and in the secret bylaws of the Woman's Auxiliary of the Ancient Order of the Rat Trap. But genteel writing may contain a description of certain stages of the progress without intruding upon the province of X-ray or of park policemen."

Finally, O. Henry resumes the story from the point at which it began: "Which justifies the reflection that some stories, as well as life, and puppies thrown into wells, move around in circles. Painfully but briefly we must shed light on Jacob's words." The words uttered at the very outset—" 'By the coke ovens of hell, it must be that ten thousand dollars! If I can get that squared, it'll do the trick!' "—are now explained: Jacob wants to return the money to the heirs of a miner whom he had once duped: "And now must come swift action, for we have here some four thousand words and not a tear shed and never a pistol, joke, safe, nor bottle cracked." Jacob institutes a search for the heirs of the miner, Hugh McLeod; meanwhile, we know from what was said at the start that the grocer's name is Thomas McLeod: "Get the point? Of course I know as well as you do that Thomas is going to be the heir. I might have concealed the name; but why always hold back your mystery till the end? I say, let it come near the middle, so people can stop reading there if they want to."

The whole story is constructed out of this sort of incessant ironic play and underscoring of devices—just as if O. Henry had taken up the "Formal method" in Russia and had often had his ear bent by Viktor Šklovskij. But the fact is that he had actually been a pharmacist, a cowboy, a bank teller, had spent three years in jail—all ingredients for the making of a garden variety slice-of-life writer who would have, more ingenuously than ingeniously, spoken about how much injustice there was on earth. O. Henry did indeed value art above the compliments of Roosevelt.

And what we have just examined is not the exception, not a rare occurrence, but O. Henry's customary system. So generally essential a component part of a story as reportage of a character's past (*Vorgeschichte*) appears in O. Henry usually accompanied by literary irony, as a static factor, one bringing the action to a halt.

Here is another example: "First, biography (but pared to the quick) must intervene. I am for the inverted sugar-coated quinine pill—the bitter on the outside" ("Thimble, Thimble"). In this connection O. Henry revitalizes, but in a pointedly comic way, the naïve manner of interpolating biography so familiar to us from the models of the past: "And now for Hetty's thumbnail biography while she climbs the two flights of stairs" ("The Third Ingredient").

For all the instances of literary irony and play on form which I have extracted from "A Night in New Arabia," analogous illustrations can be produced from other of his stories.

The opening:

There are no more Christmas stories to write. Fiction is exhausted; and newspaper items, the next best, are manufactured by clever young journalists who have married early and have an engagingly pessimistic view of life. Therefore, for seasonable diversion, we are reduced to two very questionable sources—facts and philosophy. We will begin with—whichever you choose to call it" ("Compliments of the Season").[8]

The initiation of the intrigue: In "The Third Ingredient" the intrigue is initiated by the fact that the price of meat had suddenly gone up, and the salesgirl, who had lost her job, had only enough money to buy meat: "That fact is what makes this story possible. Otherwise, the extra four cents would have—[9] But the plot of nearly all good stories in the world is concerned with shorts who were unable to cover; so, you can find no fault in this one." The transition from the announced intrigue to action is ironically underscored in "Thimble, Thimble," in which the intrigue is initiated by the receipt of a letter: "As soon as Blandford had finished the reading of this, something happened (as there should happen in stories and must happen on the stage)."

Love: The passage cited above, in which O. Henry declines to describe in detail the process of courtship, is very characteristic. The stereotype of the love story built on "psychological analysis" revolts him, and he avoids that type completely, relegating love complications to the background or shifting them to a special setting and hedging them round with special details (as in "Heart of the West"). In "The Plutonian Fire" there is a digression on this score analogous to the one cited above: (The character in question is a novice writer.)

He wrote love stories, a thing I have always kept free from, holding the belief that the well-known and popular sentiment is not properly a matter for publication, but something to be privately handled by the alienists and florists. But the editors had told him that they wanted love stories, because they said that the women read them.

Now, the editors are wrong about that, of course. Women do not read the love stories in the magazines. They read the poker-game stories and the recipes for cucumber lotion. The love stories are read by fat cigar drummers and little ten-year-old girls. I am not criticizing the judgment of editors. They are mostly very fine men, but a man can be but one man, with individual opinions and tastes. I knew two associate editors of one magazine who were wonderfully alike in almost everything. And yet one of them was very fond of Flaubert, while the other preferred gin.

Most of O. Henry's love stories are built on the most traditional kind of situation: two men love the same woman (the conventionality of this is underscored by O. Henry himself in one of his stories). But some detail is always added, usually a comic detail not directly connected with love but which, at the same time, turns out to be the fundamental detail for the plot. Love supplies the simple motivation for creating the intrigue. So, for example, in "Psyche and the Pskyscraper," love serves as the reason for contrasting the "inhospitable" universe to the cozy store whose owner vies with the "philosopher." The love theme takes on unexpected concreteness via a shift onto another plane. In another story, "Cupid à la Carte," the tale of the conquest of the heroine by one of her suitors is built on her aversion to men when they are eating. One is also reminded of "The Handbook of Hymen," in which the heroine is won over by the "encyclopedic" knowledge of one of the rivals who charms her with his learning, expressed in statements of the following type: " 'In this very log we sit upon, Mrs. Sampson . . . is statistics more wonderful than any poem. The rings show it was sixty years old. At the depth of two thousand feet it would become coal in three thousand years. The deepest coal mine in the world is at Killingworth, near Newcastle. A box four feet long, three feet wide, and two feet eight inches deep will hold one ton of coal. If an artery is cut, compress it above the wound. A man's leg contains thirty bones. The Tower of London was burned in 1841.' " This story is a sort of antithesis to "Psyche and the Pskyscraper" where the "philosopher's" efforts end in fiasco. As these examples make clear, O. Henry's love stories have nothing in common with tales "about love" and are parodies of a special type on the very genre of the love story itself.

Mystery and dénouement: A mystery as the plot motif, the mainspring of the action, must have struck O. Henry as no less hackneyed than the "love story." And indeed, O. Henry almost never employs the device of a simple mystery or puzzle, but he does sometimes deliberately make a game of it, giving the secret away just at the moment the reader thinks it is going to be the central issue. As a parallel to what was done in "A Night in New Arabia," I shall take an example from the story "Compliments of the Season." A little girl, a millionaire's daughter, has lost her favorite rag doll. But the reader is mistaken in thinking that the disappearance of the doll is going to serve as the motive for a mystery; on the very next page O. Henry fills the reader in on what happened: "The Scotch pup had ravished the rag doll from the nursery, dragged it to a corner of the lawn, dug a hole, and buried it after the manner of careless undertakers. There you have the mystery solved, and no checks to write for the hypodermical wizard or fi'-pun notes to toss to the sergeant." Elsewhere, even when the mystery or riddle is retained as such, it either turns out to be not where the reader expected it or its very presence is disclosed only in the dénouement, as was the case, for instance, with *Cabbages and Kings.* Play on the dénouement is one of O. Henry's customary devices. In one story ("The Country of Elusion"), he suddenly aborts what was supposed to have been the mystery and was supposed to have brought the story to a climax—fixing, instead, on a different, unexpected ending to the story and accompanying this with a special commentary: "Mary has robbed me of my climax; and she may go. But I am not defeated. Somewhere there exists a great vault, miles broad and miles long—more capacious than the champagne caves of France. In that vault are stored the anticlimaxes that should have been tagged to all the stories that have been told in the world. I shall cheat the vault of one deposit."

On the basis of the examples cited, examples which illustrate O. Henry's pervasive tendency to lay bare the construction of a story and to subject the plot to parodic play, the "unexpectedness" of his endings acquires special meaning. The unexpectedness of the ending is the most striking and consistently commented on feature of his stories, the unexpectedness, moreover, being almost invariably of the "happy ending" variety. I have already spoken of the short-story ending in connection with Edgar Allan Poe and the American short story, but that is insufficient for an understanding of the role of the final accent in O. Henry. The reason is that the O. Henry story is parodic or ironic through and through—not only where the author himself interferes with the story in progress but also where nothing of the sort takes place. His stories are parodies on a certain, commonly accepted, short-story logic, on the usual plot syllogism. In itself, the surprise effect is a common feature of both the novel and the short story, and the American short story in particular. But for O. Henry this quality of the unexpected constitutes the very heart of the construction and bears a perfectly specific character. His endings are not merely a surprise or contrary to expectation, they appear in a sort of lateral way, as if popping out from around the corner; and it is only then that the reader realizes that certain details here and there had hinted at the possibility of such an ending. This is the surprise of parody, a trick surprise which plays with the reader's literary expectations, throwing him off center and very nearly mocking him. Frequently the story is so constructed that it is not clear until the very end where the riddle actually lies or what, in general, all the events portend—the ending not only serves as the dénouement but also discloses the true nature of the intrigue, the real meaning of all that has occurred. Therefore it often happens in O. Henry that not only the reader but also one of the characters in the story is fooled. "It takes a thief to rob a thief"—that's the situation typical of O. Henry's system (see "The Ethics of Pig," or "The Man Higher Up"). He does not even lay "false tracks," as is commonly done in mystery stories, but operates with the help of ambiguities, half-statements, or barely noticeable details which turn out at the end to have been highly significant (such as the ring "Mammon and the Archer," the mole near the left eyebrow in "The Furnished Room," the button in "A Municipal Report," the half of a silver dime in "No Story").

In "Jeff Peters as a Personal Magnet," everything leads up to Peters's falling into a trap—expect what he will, the reader cannot question this fact. But the situation turns out to be quite different: "When we got nearly to the gate, I says: 'We might meet somebody now, Andy. I reckon you better take 'em off, and—' Hey? Why, of course it was Andy Tucker. That was his scheme; and that's how we got the capital to go into business together." The finale completely changes what had seemed a perfectly clear-cut situation. The reader, it turns out, had been led astray, not because the author had insinuated a false lead, but simply because the author had said nothing. The conversation of the characters had been reported without commentary.

In "Friends in San Rosario," the situation seems perfectly clear:

the bank president is unable to produce the securities for six notes to show the examiner; his long account is obviously supposed to clear up the mystery of their disappearance. The reader, even one accustomed to O. Henry's surprise dénouements, expects something unexpected along precisely this axis, the very fact of the disappearance of the securities seeming beyond doubt. Instead, the dénouement comes from a completely different angle, sidewise, and alters the whole situation: the bank president had launched into his long story solely for the purpose of prolonging the examiner's visit, thus giving his friend (a fellow banker) the chance to put his affairs in order before the examiner's visit to him; the story he tells has nothing to do with the securities (they were safely tucked away in his coat pocket). In retrospect, the reader sees that certain casually mentioned details (the note, the window, the shade) were hidden hints that had prepared the ground for the unexpected turn of the whole story. The reader is fooled, and at the same time the examiner is fooled. In the story, "The Ransom of Mack," mentioned above, Mack's friend is also fooled, because Mack's words meant something other than what he, and the reader along with him, took them to mean.

No wonder "crime" material should have come in so handy for O. Henry. It was, of course, not so much a matter of the crooks in themselves but rather the fact that the picaresque story supplies excellent motivation for his plot devices. His crooks have not so much an American as an Arabian-Spanish-French origin, of a tradition going back to the early picaresque stories and novels. What he had to have for the most part was motivation via some piece of trickery or cleverness, or via a misunderstanding of the kind that supplied the basis for the well-known and truly typical O. Henry story "The Gift of the Magi" (the husband sells his watch to buy his wife a set of combs while his wife sells her hair to buy him a watch chain). This almost amounts to a plot scheme in pure form, a kind of algebraic problem, under the signs of which one could substitute any other facts one likes.

The principle of the surprise dénouement makes it obligatory that the dénouement be a happy or even a comic one. So it was in Puškin's *Tales of Belkin* (parodies, fundamentally), and so it is with O. Henry (compare Puškin's "Grobovščik" [The Coffinmaker] and O. Henry's "The Head-Hunter"). In the affairs of everyday life, we are much accustomed to surprise of a tragic nature, but, at the same time, it brings in its wake an outcry against fate. In art, there is no one against whom to cry out. No one forces the writer to vie with fate, even if only on paper. A tragic dénouement requires special motivation (guilt, nemesis, and "character" are the usual ones in tragedy), and that is why it is more natural in a psychological novel than in a plot-oriented short story. The reader has first to come to terms with the tragic dénouement, to understand its logical necessity, and for that reason it must be carefully prepared, so that the force of it does not strike on the *result* (in other words, does not come at the very ending) but on the *progression* toward the ending. Happy endings in O. Henry stories, as in *Tales of Belkin*, are by no means a response to the pressure of the American reading public's "demands," as is customarily claimed, but the natural outcome of the principle of the surprise dénouement, a principle incompatible in a plot-oriented story with detailed motivation. And it is also for this reason that tragic endings are so rare and so paradoxical on the screen—psychological motivation is altogether too foreign to the nature of the motion picture. In the O. Henry short story, with its parodic focus on the finale, a tragic outcome is possible only in the case of a *double* dénouement, as in "The Caballero's Way," in which Tonia is killed but, on the other hand, the Kid remains alive and celebrates his revenge. To put it more strongly, O. Henry's stories are so far from any psychology, any ambition to foster in the reader an illusion of reality and bring him into contact with his heroes as people, that the very categories of the tragic and the comic may be said to be inapplicable to his works.

As a general rule, O. Henry does not address himself to his readers' emotions. His stories are intellectual and literary through and through. Stories in which he tries to introduce an emotional tone (in the effort, perhaps, to attune himself to the tastes of his editors and the reading public) inevitably take on a sentimental character and simply fall out of his system. He has no "characters," no heroes; he works on the imagination of his readers by picking out and juxtaposing incisive and unexpected particulars which, by reason of their being very concrete, are striking. In this way, he compensates, as it were, for the schematic structuralism of his stories (a device connected with the art of parody: cf. details in Sterne). No wonder that the structures of his stories were habitually fully formed in his mind, as Jennings bears witness, and no wonder that he could so easily change the facts—he thought in schemes, in formulas, like an expert theoretician. The work of writing went into details of language and delineation. That explains one's impression of a certain monotony, about which O. Henry's Russian readers often remark. Despite his popularity and his supposed lightness and readability, O. Henry is a very complex and subtle writer. He is so good at deceiving his reader that the latter more often than not even fails to notice where it is the author has led him to—into what milieu of literary parody, irony, and play on form he has turned up in O. Henry's company. It would be useful, therefore, after all that has been said above, to stop and consider those pieces in which he himself lays bare the essential O. Henry. These are stories "for the few," but it is precisely in them that the genuine O. Henry is lodged—O. Henry, the parodist, almost overcome by his own awareness of literary things, by his own wittiness, and by the irony of his position vis à vis the reader and vis à vis even the craft of fiction.

7

I have in mind such stories as "A Dinner at . . . (The Adventures of an Author with His Own Hero)," "Tommy's Burglar," and "The Plutonian Fire." A number of other stories might also be included here (e.g., "No Story," "Best-Seller"), but for the sake of brevity I shall concentrate only on the most important ones.

"A Dinner at . . . " (in the posthumous collection, *Rolling Stones*) provides a sort of theoretical commentary to the story "The Badge of Policeman O'Roon," a commentary with an ironical point directed at those custodians of banality, the editors.[10] In it the author enters into a conversation with his character, Van Sweller, who is supposed to be the hero of a story in progress. The plan of the story-to-be is expounded in an ironic-rhapsodic tone: "And then the clatter and swoop of Mounted Policeman Van Sweller! Oh, it was—but the story has not yet been printed. When it is, you shall learn how he sent his bay like a bullet after the imperiled victoria. A Crichton, a Croesus, and a Centaur in one, he hurls the invincible combination into the chase. When the story is printed you will admire. . . ." The reader witnesses, as it were, the staging of this scenario: the author instructs the hero how to act, what to do. The author's attention is focused on keeping his hero from committing banalities for which the latter displays a marked inclination: "Once or twice we had sharp, brief contentions over certain points of behavior; but, prevailingly, give and take had been our rule. His morning toilet provoked our first tilt." The hero has it in mind to begin his role by taking breakfast and a bath during one or the other of which he proposes to receive a guest. The author rejects both: " 'Neither,' I said. 'You will make your appearance on the scene when a gentleman should—after you are fully dressed, which indubitably private function shall take place behind closed doors.' "

Evidently what we have here is a spoof on those traditional opening scenes which have nothing to do with the plot. The hero feels "a trifle piqued": " 'Oh, very well, . . . I rather imagine it concerns you more than it does me. But the "tub" by all means, if you think best. But it has been the usual thing, you know.' " As things go on, the author is compelled to make to his adamant hero a concession or two; banalities of style now come in for their share of ridicule: "But he worsted me when I objected to giving him a 'coat unmistakably English in cut.' I allowed him to 'stroll down Broadway,' and even permitted 'passers-by' (God knows there's nowhere to pass but by) to 'turn their heads and gaze with evident admiration at his erect figure.' I demeaned myself, and as a barber, gave him a 'smooth, dark face with its keen, frank eye and firm jaw.' " At the club Van Sweller addresses someone as "dear old boy"; the author grabs him by the collar: " 'For heaven's sake talk like a man,' I said, sternly. 'Do you think it is manly to use those mushy and inane forms of address? That man is neither dear nor old nor a boy.' " The hero this time agrees: " 'I used those words because I have been forced to say them so often. They really are contemptible. Thanks for correcting me, dear old boy.' "

However, the author is aware that his hero is up to some chicanery, and he begins keeping track of him:

> I suppose that every author must be a valet to his own hero. . . . When he had reached his apartments he said to me, with a too patronizing air: "There are, as you perhaps know, quite a number of little distinguishing touches to be had out of the dressing process. Some writers rely almost wholly upon them. I suppose that I am to ring for my man, and that he is to enter noiselessly, with an expressionless countenance."
>
> "He may enter," I said with decision, "and only enter. Valets do not usually enter a room shouting college songs or with St. Vitus's dance in their faces; so the contrary may be assumed without fatuous or gratuitous asseveration."

The author makes himself a source of constant disillusionment as to his hero by pointing out to the latter useless tautologies in his speech and turning down his suggestions. A serious quarrel breaks out over the question as to whether the hero should dine at a restaurant: " 'You intend deliberately to make me out a tout for a restaurant. Where you dine tonight has not the slightest connection with the thread of our story.' " The hero protests: " 'Even a character in a story has rights that an author cannot ignore. The hero of a story of New York social life must dine at . . . at least once during the action.' " In answer to the author's question, why he "must" do so, the hero declares that it is what magazine editors require in order to please out-of-town subscribers:

"How do you know these things?" I inquired, with sudden suspicion. "You never came into existence until this morning. You are only a character in fiction, anyway. I myself created you. How is it possible for you to know anything?"

"Pardon me for referring to it," said Van Sweller, with a sympathetic smile, "but I have been the hero of hundreds of stories of this kind."

I felt a slow flush creeping into my face.

"I thought . . ." I stammered; "I was hoping . . . that is . . . Oh, well, of course an absolutely original conception in fiction is impossible in these days."

The hero explains that he has acted in much the same way in all the stories he has been in: " 'Now and then the women writers have made me cut some rather strange capers, for a gentleman; but the men generally pass me along from one to another without much change.' " Despite these arguments, the author does not allow his hero to go to the restaurant, no matter how hard the latter tries to convince him of the absolute necessity for it: " 'The authors all send me there. I fancy many of them would have liked to accompany me, but for the little matter of the expense.' " Thereupon the hero goes off in a cab, and the author hires a hansom for two dollars, to follow after him: "If I had been only one of the characters in my story instead of myself, I could have easily offered $10 or $25 or even $100. But $2 was all I felt justified in expending, with fiction at its present rates." The story is returned to the author with a letter from the editor suggesting, among other changes, that the hero dine at some restaurant.

Against the background of all this parodic commentary, O. Henry's own system comes clearly into focus—plot dynamism, the absence of detailed descriptions, compact language—and his wariness of any sort of cliché is amply borne out. "Tommy's Burglar" is a story within a story, providing excellent commentary to his tales of "crime." It is a parody on sentimental stories having repentant criminals. The author of "A Dinner at. . . " is replaced here by the boy Tommy, and the thief is analogous to Van Sweller. The difference consists in Tommy's teaching the burglar what he must do and how he must act, according to the literary canon, as Tommy is a person experienced in such matters (his father "writes books"). Together they, so to speak, stage a traditional scene and behave as if some writer had made them up; the planes of the "real" and the "imagined" are interwoven: "And mamma and papa have gone to the Metropolitan to hear De Reszke. But that isn't my fault. It only shows how long the story has been knocking around among the editors. If the author had been wise, he'd have changed it to Caruso in the proofs." When the burglar asks: " 'Aren't you afraid of me?,' " the boy answers: " 'You know I'm not. . . . Don't you suppose I know fact from fiction? If this wasn't a story, I'd yell like an Indian when I saw you; and you'd probably tumble downstairs and get pinched on the sidewalk.' " When the burglar explains that he robs people's houses because he has " 'a little brown-haired boy Bessie at home,' " Tommy, wrinkling his nose, remarks: " 'Ah . . . you got that answer in the wrong place. You want to tell your hard-luck story before you pull the child stop.' " The boy directs the construction of the scenario: " 'After you finish your lunch,' said Tommy, 'and experience the usual change of heart, how shall we wind up the story?' " The burglar, investing himself in the role of a character, begins to plan out a sequel: on his return home, the father will recognize in him an old college classmate and will give the college yell: " 'Rah, rah, rah!'. . . . 'Well,' said Tommy wonderingly, 'that's the first time I ever knew a burglar to give a college yell when he was burglarizing a house, even in a story.' " Further on, the burglar complains about his earnings: " 'Why, in one story, all I got was a kiss from a little girl who came in on me when I was opening a safe,' " but when he expresses himself as having a notion to tie a tablecloth over the boy's head and get about his business with the silverware, Tommy firmly declares: " 'Oh, no, you haven't. . . .Because, if you did, no editor would buy the story. You know you've got to preserve the unities. . . . But it's tough on both of us, old man. I wish you could get out of the story and really rob somebody.' " Having done everything that a criminal was supposed to do in stories "for family reading" and having intoned the traditional, "Bless you, young master!" the burglar adds: " 'And now hurry and let me out, kid. Our 2,000 words must be nearly up.' "

The story "The Plutonian Fire" is interesting in a different respect. It is not straight parody, as are "A Dinner at . . . " and "Tommy's Burglar," but something on the order of a feuilleton on literary topics. The beginning resembles the conversation between the editor and the story writer in "Proof of the Pudding." It is all about editors and their attitudes toward novice writers. The writers, when submitting manuscripts, consider it their duty to note that the content is taken directly from life: "The destination of such contributions depends wholly upon the question of the enclosure of stamps. Some are returned, the rest are thrown on the floor in a corner, on top of a pair of gum shoes, an overturned statuette of the Winged Victory, and a pile of old magazines containing a picture of the editor in the act of reading the latest copy of *Le Petit Journal*, right side up—you can tell by the illustration. It is only a legend that there are waste baskets in editors' offices." In this context, O. Henry's words about his own story have an unmistakably ironic ring: "This preamble is to warn you off the grade crossing of a true story. Being that, it shall be told simply, with conjunctions substituted for adjectives wherever possible, and whatever evidence of style may appear in it shall be due to the linotype man." The hero of the story is the novice writer, Pettit. He writes love stories: "They were well constructed, and the events were marshalled in orderly and logical sequence. But I thought I detected a lack of living substance—it was much as if I gazed at a symmetrical array of presentable clamshells from which the succulent and vital inhabitants had been removed." A conversation between Pettit and the author follows, during which the story writer attempts to defend himself:

"You sold a story last week," said Pettit, "about a gun fight in an Arizona mining town, in which the hero drew his Colt's .45 and shot seven bandits as fast as they came in the door. Now, if a six-shooter could—"

"Oh, well," said I, "that's different. Arizona is a long way from New York. I could have a man stabbed with a lariat or chased by a pair of chaparreras if I wanted to, and it wouldn't be noticed until the usual error-sharp from around McAdams Junction isolates the erratum and writes in to the papers about it. But you are up against another proposition. This thing they call love is as common around New York as it is in the Sheboygan during the young onion season."

Taking the author's advice, Pettit falls in love—and writes even worse than before: "The story was sentimental drivel, full of whimpering soft-heartedness and gushing egoism. All the art that Pettit had acquired was gone. A perusal of its buttery phrases would have made a cynic of a sighing chambermaid." Then the situation changes: Pettit becomes the object of affection for a girl who "worshipped him, and now and then bored him"; he writes a story that sends the author into raptures: "I broke into Pettit's room and beat him on the back and called him names—names high up in the galaxy of the immortals that we admired. And Pettit yawned and begged to be allowed to sleep." The story ends with Pettit tearing up his manuscript and deciding to go back home.

"You can't write with ink, and you can't write with your own heart's blood, but you can write with the heart's blood of someone else. You have to be a cad to be an artist. Well, I am for old Alabam' and the Major's store. Have you got a light, Old Hoss?"

I went with Pettit to the depot and died hard.

"Shakespeare's sonnets?" I blurted, making a last stand. "How about him?"

"A cad," said Pettit. "They give it to you, and you sell it—love, you know. I'd rather sell ploughs for father.

"But," I protested, "you are reversing the decision of the world's greatest. . . ."

"Goodby, Old Hoss," said Pettit.

"Critics," I continued. "But—say, if the Major can use a fairly good salesman and bookkeeper down there in the store, let me know, will you?"

Here O. Henry's irony has touched upon the craft of literature itself. From this story a certain amount of light is shed on what I have already spoken of—the absence of any emotional intimacy (including that of love) in O. Henry's stories. O. Henry's rejection of the canon of the "love story" is here motivated overtly and expressly.

Parody is a road that leads to something else, and O. Henry hoped to find that something else. A manuscript of an unfinished story, "The Dream" (published in the posthumous collection, *Rolling Stones*, 1912), was found on his desk after his death. It was meant, apparently, to be a completely serious and even harrowing story. Prison, convicts condemned to death—the time comes for one of them to be led off to the death chamber, where about twenty people have already assembled (the prison officials, newspaper reporters, and spectators). At this point the manuscript breaks off, but it is known that O. Henry had it in mind to evoke later the picture that arises in a condemned man's imagination and completely screens out reality—the picture of family life: a little cottage, a wife, a little child. "The accusation, the trial, the conviction, the sentence to death in the electric chair—all a dream. He takes his wife in his arms and kisses the child. Yes, here is happiness. It was a dream. Then—at a sign from the prison warden, the fatal current is turned on. Murray had dreamed the wrong dream."

Concerning this story, O. Henry's commentor informs us: "He had planned to make this story different from his others, the beginning of a new series in a style he had not previously attempted. 'I want to show the public,' he said, 'that I can write something new—new for me, I mean—a story without slang, a straightforward dramatic plot treated in a way that will come nearer to my idea of real story writing.' " And so O. Henry came up against the problem of "something new," the necessity of evolution. He even thought of abandoning short stories and of writing a novel instead. Fate had it her own way. O. Henry's name is forever linked with the comic short story—with what he came to call "child's play" and a "trial of the pen." But the evolution of the American short story is proceeding, in fact, along the road O. Henry had conceived in his mind. In contemporary American fiction (Dreiser, Sherwood Anderson, Waldo Frank, Ben Hecht, and others), there is a marked movement toward the story of manners and morals and the psychological story, in which the choice of material has greater formal significance than does the construction of the story. Carefully worked out, thorough-going motivation receives the focus of attention. The O. Henry story, with parody at its core, opened the way for this regeneration.

Notes

1. *Blagorodnyj žulik i drugie rasskazy* (*The Gentle Grafter and Other Stories*). Edited and with an introduction by Evgenij Zamjatin and K. I. Čukovskij. Moscow-Leningrad: Gos, Izd., "Vsemirnaja Literatura," 1924. *Selected Stories from O. Henry*. Edited by C. Alphonso Smith. New York, 1922.

2. See the article, "Žizn´O. Genri" [O. Henry's Life] by K. I. Čukovskij in *Blagorodnyj žulik i drugie rasskazy*, p. 14.

3. Al Jennings, *Through the Shadows with O. Henry* (London, 1924), pp. 159-160. (The Russian translation of this book is *O. Genri na dne* [O. Henry Down and Out], translated and edited by V. Azov. Leningrad, 1925.) We see, then, that the burglar tools and suitcase, despite everything, were put in to motivate the ending—they were invented to replace finger tips because that is what the "central effect" required.

4. The material of the main story—a farcical revolution in Anchuria—recalls Mark Twain's story, "The Great Revolution in Pitcairn."

5. K. I. Čukovskij, "Žizn´O. Genri," *Blagorodnyj žulik i drugie rasskazy*, p. 17.

6. A woman writer famous for her descriptions of nature, who published under the pseudonym of G. Egbert Craddock.

7. A connection with Stevenson is evident here. See his *New Arabian Nights,* which O. Henry mentions at the end of "While the Auto Waits."

8. In the introduction to another Christmas story, O. Henry quips on the same score: "So far has this new practice been carried that nowadays when you read a story in a holiday magazine, the only way you can tell it is a Christmas story is to look at the footnote, which reads 'The incidents in the above story happened on December 25th'—Ed." ("An Unfinished Christmas Story.")

9. From what follows, it is clear that O. Henry means to say here: ". . . would have purchased an onion." It is the missing onion on which the whole story is built—an example of how he could take the merest trifle and construct an ingenious story out of it.

10. It is likely that "The Badge of Policeman O'Roon" had once been rejected by an editor and that O. Henry wrote "A Dinner at—" by way of reaction.

11. Cf. similarly constructed things: Ambrose Bierce's "An Occurrence at Owl Creek Bridge," and L. Perutz's *Master of the Day of Judgement.*

Part VI

Russian Formalism in Retrospect
Krystyna Pomorska

The Formal Method and Linguistics
Ladislav Matejka

Russian Formalism in Retrospect

Krystyna Pomorska

273

The best way to understand what our anthology is would be first to ask ourselves: what is it not? This is a reasonable question, when we realize how many anthologies and studies in recent years have been devoted to the topic of "Russian Formalism."[1] All of them are valuable, and each one, of course, offers a certain principle according to which the selections were made.

Our anthology does not present a meticulous development of the trend, with all its characteristic exaggerations, which frequently were the result of its polemical nature. Boris Èjxenbaum comments on this point in his fundamental study, "The Theory of the Formal Method," included in this selection. We therefore do not offer the early and purely theoretical works of Šklovskij whose role is becoming overrated; nor do we present any of the highly interesting and, indeed, controversial studies by the young Èjxenbaum (see, for example, "How Gogol′'s 'Overcoat' Is Made"). Very few studies which could be considered typical for the *development* of the trend have been included.

Our task is to offer those works not solely of historical or polemical interest but also valuable for modern theoretical thought. It has been our idea to present theoreticians who "rounded up" and transformed the works of the *Opojaz* (Baxtin, Vološinov, Jakobson). We might use the words of T. Todorov in maintaining that we wished to show the "methodological heritage of Formalism,"[2] for the heritage of the so-called Formalist School is particularly valuable today, when the very same, or very similar, questions concerning science arise: what is science? Which phenomena of our world can be subjected to real scientific scrutiny? The question which follows from this is: should or could the humanities be considered the domain of science? And, if so, what is the proper method for scrutinizing such products as works of art in order to know them with a satisfactory degree of probability? Should the student of the humanities use methods identical, or similar, to those of physics, biology, and mathematics? Or should these methods be as diverse as the student's subjects of study? The fundamental problem is this: does the subject of the scrutiny of the humanities differ so greatly from that of "the sciences proper"?

These very questions were posed by the young students of literature when they created the famous *Opojaz*[3] (founded between 1914 and 1916), later called the "Formalist School" by their opponents. Their efforts, their heritage, must be considered from two points of view: first, as polemics against and a struggle with the tradition of Positivism, the tradition which is widely adhered to even today; second, as the prestructural phase, that is, as preparation of the field for contemporary, modern, literary studies.

The so-called "anti-Positivist revolt" began, both in philosophy and sociology, sometime before the young Russian scholars had made their contribution. This struggle has been identified with the names of three German thinkers: W. Dilthey, W. Windelband, and H. Rickert. Around the turn of the century they reestablished the basic division between the natural sciences and the humanities, a separation which was effaced and actually obscured by the theoreticians of Positivism.

The *Opojaz* members concerned themselves with the same problem. In attempting to occupy themselves with literature, they were first and foremost obliged to redefine the very subject of literary studies. "Literariness," or those features which *make* a work literature, was proclaimed the material for investigation. A concentration on "literary fact" itself was carefully observed against the sociological fallacy of Positivism, with its offshoots of biographism and psychologism. The primary features of a literary work were sought; these were found in poetic language. Everything which did not fit into the category of poetic language was considered to be a secondary feature and was therefore dismissed from the field of investigation. In his pioneering study *Novejšaja russkaja poèzija* [*Modern Russian Poetry*, 1921], R. Jakobson compares the adherents of the "cultural school" in literary studies to those detectives who, when looking for a real perpetrator of a crime, arrest everyone around, "just in case." In other words, instead of grasping the primary features, they have contented themselves with secondary ones, various heterogeneous factors which do not explain the uniqueness of literature among other cultural phenomena.

The question posed now regarding works of literature was not "What is it about?" or "Why and how did it appear?" but "*How is it made?*"[4] Thus, the literary work was now defined, not in terms of its subject matter nor its origin, but in terms of its construction.

Many brilliant studies, particularly those on verse structure, resulted from such a tendency. During the early and later periods of the *Opojaz*, the works of O. Brik, such as "Zvukovye povtory" [Sound Repetitions, 1919] or "Ritm i sintaksis" [Rhythm and Syntax], Jakubinskij's "O zvukax stixotvornogo jazyka" [On Sounds in Verse Language, 1916], B. Tomaševskij's *Russkoe stixosloženie* [Russian Versification, 1923], and his articles later published as a book, *O stixe* [On Verse, 1929], Žirmunskij's *Vvedenie v metriku* (Introduction to Metrics, 1925)—all these studies showed not only how poetic language was constructed but also they simultaneously proved how poetic language differed from the nonpoetic, or, as they phrased it, "practical language."[5]

In prose, or in any nonlyrical work, the problem was solved similarly. The decisive factor for the structure of a prose piece was found in its *sujet* (plot), the element of construction, in contradistinction to the story itself, which was recognized as and equated with the subject matter (or the "material," as Šklovskij called it).

Thus, for example, the *sujet* in *Evgenij Onegin* was not the love story between Tatjana and Onegin, but rather the very manner in which this particular story was used, with its systematic parallelism and symmetry of situations, its inversions of time, its retardations, etc.

Such a procedure may lead to the conclusion that it is the construction itself that makes literature "art." This controversial point has been frequently attacked, mainly because it does not endow the investigator with a sufficiently strong criterion for discerning what is and what is not "artistic." In other words, it does not permit us to evaluate. But the *Opojaz* members never introduced the problem of evaluation into their system; to put it more categorically, they did not think that scholarly procedure should be an evaluative one at all. Indeed, they seem to accept silently the principle enounced by Croce: that our evaluation of art is always and necessarily intuitive.[6] This point may also be made in different terms (although the essence is the same), namely, that in every culture artistic phenomena objectively (or, in Husserlian terms, intersubjectively) are accepted as such owing to the common background of the criteria created by this culture. The last interpretation is closer to the thought of the *Opojaz*, especially in its later period, and may be seen indirectly in works such as Èjxenbaum's "Literaturnyj byt" [Literary Environment, 1929], in this volume.

The essential task for the *Opojaz* scholars was to prove the difference between poetic and nonpoetic language (literature and nonliterature, respectively) in terms of the material from which it is "made," that is, in terms of *language* in its various interrelations. Their point proved to be correct and also topical. Contemporary structural (or semiotic) studies demonstrate without much controversy, by statistical methods and computations, that there exists an important distinction between artistic and non-artistic prose in the very structure of the language, on its various levels.[7]

Consequently, the other merit of the Formalists was their rejection of the genetic approach to literature and their fruitful descriptive-functional investigations. Classification and typology developed as the main methods of exploration, especially in the earlier stages of the *Opojaz*'s studies. Propp's work on the fairy tale (incorporated into this volume) is a masterful demonstration of how typology itself can aid in grasping historical changes. Furthermore, it proves that the purely historical (or genetic) approach may cause misinterpretations when applied to a work of art. No matter how specific folklore is as a subject for analysis, Propp's study, nevertheless, is one of the most valuable because of the very scholarly method it represents, for it incorporates the two operations to which a work of art is subjected: the synchronic (descriptive) and the diachronic (historical). Moreover, it shows that the synchronic procedure should precede the diachronic, and that synchrony is not static but *dynamic*.

The question of the sequence in investigatory procedure proved to be methodologically essential. In order to know our subject intimately, we must make this subject the starting point of our study. Only then can we move outward and set up further relations. If we proceed in the opposite direction, from the environment toward the subject, we always run the risk of applying ready-made theories to something not suited to them. The history of literature supplies us with numerous examples of such a deductive fallacy. How many studies, for instance, have tried to fit Gogol′ into "environmental" categories, such as Romanticism or Naturalism? The scholars who made these attempts forgot, however, that the term "Romanticism" was forged against a background of very heterogeneous factors, and that these factors often had no direct connection to a particular work itself.

The principle of primacy for synchrony was an effort toward a systematization of the scholarly procedure—not at all an exercise in isolationism and "formalism." A literary work represents a complex phenomenon whose *process* is as significant as is its ontological nature. But it seems impossible to study the process before knowing the nature of the product.

Returning to Propp's study, we observe that synchrony is characterized by the dynamic quality. Propp classifies fairy tales in transformational terms. From one basic type of tale, he discerns several variations, the result of a transformational process which is dynamic by nature. The transformations occur among diverse extraliterary factors. Nonetheless, the very transformation is of an immanent character and deals with the commutation and permutation of structural components within the text. Our main interest here is to note precisely the immanent nature of this phenomenon. Thus synchrony is not static, but is applicable specifically to immanent processes. Devoting a study to an immanent process does not imply its isolation, but rather the delimitation of scholarly procedures.

The terms used above (synchrony and diachrony) are well known to general linguistics. Their distinct formulation and fruitful application belong to the leading linguists of the last century, Jan Baudouin de Courtenay and Ferdinand de Saussure. This fact casts light on an important problem: the close connection between the methodology of the *Opojaz* and modern linguistics.

We shall not develop this thesis from the viewpoint of its background, but shall note only several of the more striking aspects and evident results of such a relationship. Much has been written about the treatment of a literary work in terms of the relation between parts and wholes,[8] a relation which was basically influenced by phonological studies in linguistics. Such is Tynjanov's method, initiated in his famous works, *The Problem of Verse Language* (see the anthology) and "The Ode as an Oratorical Genre."[9] Another interesting example showing a similar influence is Èjxenbaum's "O'Henry and a Theory of The Short Story" (see the present anthology). The study is based on the principle of an immanent evolution of literary genres, which change according to the law of contrast. From a "high style" of the sentimental and romantic story, one which brings the reader to "tears and trepidation," the genre evolves toward "self-debasement": the parody of sentimental plots, toward anecdotes, and vaudevilles (Puškin's *Tales of Belkin*), or the "dreariness of the world" (Gogol′). As Jakobson outlined it earlier in his *Modern Russian Poetry*, so Èjxenbaum proceeds in his analysis of concrete material: parodies and "debased" genres within the process of literary evolution play a role similar to that of *dialects* in language development, in the domain of linguistic investigation. Dialects may be treated both as "debasements" of the standard language and also as the sources of its future development. They are the subcodes of a standard language and, at the same time, its large reservoir of creative energy. Similarly, the "secondary" or "younger" genres may be again recognized, just as the canonized ones may undergo the process of debasement and be shifted away under the pressure of new necessities.

The theory of literary evolution as elaborated by the *Opojaz* was an important contribution to the modern knowledge of literature and to cultural history alike. It brought about the revision of a widely accepted concept of history as a progressive evolution. This concept, built up by the Positivists (such as Spencer or Buckle) was often challenged by puzzling facts and questions. For example, why should we call a contemporary novel a "higher" form in comparison to, say, *Evgenij Onegin?* Or, why do we still consider Gothic cathedrals an embodiment of architectural perfection yet at the same time call the Middle Ages "ages of darkness"? The theory of evolution, taken as changes of artistic forms according to their own immanent laws, largely refuted the question of "progress" and showed the impossibility of applying it to art.

There is one more fundamental point, one which constituted the basis for much discussion: the problem of meaning in verbal art. The *Opojaz* scholars were often attacked for having (allegedly) neglected or rejected this point. In fact, they approached it in a new and different way. Having shown that every work of art creates a *system*, the "Formalists" proved by that very fact that every sign in the system is a meaningful one. The problem of meaning, therefore, is not to be approached in a traditional way, one in which every separate *signans* was supposed to fit some *signatum*, and in which such a unity was regarded as steady and universal. In this kind of operation, in a number of signs of various art systems, the "meaning" was simply guessed and thus misunderstood, or, a number of signs were considered "meaningless" (cf. in "supraconscious" poetry or in surrealistic literature). To the contrary, in a new approach by the *Opojaz*. the sign acquired meaning only *within the system* in which it played a part.[10] This principle allows us to consider as signs the smallest units within a system of verbal art, for example, separate sounds and distinctive features (specifically, in a verse structure) as well as larger units, such as "heroes" in structures which deal with a plot.

Hence we may talk about the meaningfulness of "accumulations of similar liquid sounds" in certain poetic constructions, as Jakubinskij has traced them. In the first place, they play a distinctive role, one which permits us to distinguish a poetic text from a nonpoetic one. Depending on the particular structure to which they belong, we may talk about their further role, that is, meaningfulness. The "hero," being to a large extent also a "sign" in a work of art, has many levels on which his meaningfulness is manifested. Tynjanov, Jakobson, Tomaševskij and others proved the narrowness of such a treatment, in which the "hero" is regarded only as a copy of a real being. It is, then, fitted in psychological (and other) probabilities, and only this "meaning"–its characterological features–is ascribed to a "hero." Yet, it has many other roles in the entire system, such as paralleling (by either similarity or contrast) other characters, motivating certain situations which would otherwise not be understood, contrasting or paralleling the author's point of view in the narration, etc. Therefore, when Šklovskij discussed the role of a "hero" in terms of a pure "device,"[11] no matter how much he exaggerated, he did make a valuable contribution by examining some important aspects of this sign which were quite neglected before.

We find in the activity of the *Opojaz* group the challenge in their trying to make out of literary studies a homogeneous domain, or, as some scholars express it, in wishing to formalize such studies. As we observe, they succeeded to a very large extent. For this reason alone, it is important to accept the most enriching part of their heritage and to continue it, rather than to grasp its weak points and to criticize them. The latter is always the easiest task.

Notes

1. See these anthologies: Lee Lemon and Marion Reis, ed., *Russian Formalist Criticism; Four Essays,* University of Nebraska Press 1965; Tzvetan Todorov, *Théorie de la litérature. Textes des Formalistes russes, réunis, preséntés et traduits par T. Todorov.* Préface par Roman Jakobson, Paris, 1966; Jurij Stridter, *Texte der Russischen Formalisten* (Munich, 1963), 2 vols.

2. T. Todorov, "L'Héritage Méthodologique du Formalisme," *L'Homme,* Janvier-Mars, 1965.

3. Obščestvo po izučeniju poètičeskogo jazyka [Society for the Study of Poetic Language].

4. See the reflection of such an attitude in the very titles of the Opojaz people's studies: "Kak sdelana 'Šinel' Gogolja," by Boris Èjxenbaum or "Kak sdelan 'Don Kixot' " by Viktor Šklovskij.

5. Cf. L. Jakubinskij, "Skoplenie odinakovyx plavnyx v praktičeskom i poètičeskom jazykax," *Sborniki po teorii poètičeskogo jazyka* (Petrograd, 1916), Vol. 1.

6. Benedetto Croce, *Aesthetic as Science of Expression and General Linguistics,* Gloucester, Mass: Peter Smith, 1909; 1953.

7. See T. S. Lesskis, "K voprosu o grammatičeskix različijax naučnoj i xudožestvennoj prozy," *Semeiotiké. Trudy po znakovym sistemam* (Tartu, 1965), Vol. 2. Also, A. J. Syrkin, "Ob otdel'nyx čertax naučnogo i xudožestvennogo tekstov," *ibid.* See also: V. V. Ivanov, "Poètika," *Kratkaja literaturnaja enciklopedija,* Vol. 5.

8. See C. Lévi-Strauss, "L'analyse morphologique des contes russes," *International Journal of Slavic Linguistics and Poetics* III, 1960.

9. J. Tynjanov, "Oda kak oratorskij žanr," *Poétika,* III (Leningrad, 1927).

10. Regarding this, see Jurij Lotman, "O probleme značenija vo vtoričnyx modelirujuščix sistemax," *Semeiotiké,* Vol. 2.

11. See especially his *O teorii prozy,* from which an excerpt is translated in Lemon and Reis's anthology, *Russian Formalist Criticism.*

1

The Formal Method and Linguistics

Ladislav Matejka

Verbal art, whether oral or written, represents a challenge to every linguist who considers the correlation of sound and meaning as the cardinal issue of his analytic endeavors. The imaginative handling of formal means, their concatenation and superposition in a work of verbal art, puts forward compelling questions about the properties of a verbal sign, about its variable and invariable features, its physical and relational characteristics, and about the nature of the rules which govern semiotic usage. The arrangement of sound naturally enters into the foreground as a fundamental factor of the communicative system which finds in the work of verbal art its physical implementation.

In Russian scholarship, the investigation of the significant functions of sound in verbal communication had received an acute impetus from Jan Baudouin de Courtenay and Mikołaj Kruszewski, two illustrious representatives of the Kazan school. By the late 1870s they had already begun their search for the minimal significative components of utterance, and they had even used the term *phoneme.*[1] In a reaction to the causal, historically oriented generalizations of the neogrammarians, the Kazan school focused on the affective processes of verbal systems in their diverse roles, including those of aesthetics.

There is a direct link between the impact of the Kazan school and the preoccupation with sound arrangements which characterized the synchronically conceived inquiries of the early adherents of the Formal method, most of whom were either students of Baudouin de Courtenay or students of his students. Their analytic inquisitiveness found engaging targets in the "transrational" products of the linguistic alchemistry practiced by the literary avant garde, under the flag of Futurism in its Russian vintage.[2] The Futurists' poetic games disclosed unexplored aesthetic sound texture arranged so as to fascinate by its very physiognomy, and these games served as alluring examples of a linguistic usage capable of releasing the formal means of utterance from subordination to the semantic load. It became tempting to expect that an accurate, empirically disciplined analysis of sound was the safest step in the attack on the entire complex of semantic values displayed in verbal communication.

Baudouin de Courtenay's observation of the disregard of the nondistinctive properties of sound in casual discourse and of the supremacy of the semantic component of a verbal sign over its sound manifestation, enticed the Formalists to define the poetic usage of verbal signs conversely, as the supremacy of sound over meaning. In its early stage, the postulation of this converse role of sound and meaning in poetry prompted a series of attempts to isolate poetic language from practical language, rather than to consider their common properties and to seek the difference in distinct applications of the same inventory.

In the compendium published in 1916 by the Society for the Study of Poetic Language (Opojaz), E. D. Polivanov pointed out that Japanese poetry made use of certain sounds not found in conversational Japanese, thus suggesting the existence of two Japanese languages, each with its own distinct inventory of sound.[3] In the same volume, Lev Jakubinskij singled out certain phonetic peculiarities of Russian, implying that they occur only in conversation, not in poetry.[4] This implication, embraced by Šklovskij in his "Art as Device,"[5] was subsequently challenged by Roman Jakobson, who restated the difference between Russian in poetry and Russian in everyday life in terms of distinct functions, and who thus shifted attention from the inventory of its elements to the functional aspects of the language.[6] This shift, however, did not imply any change in the fundamental awareness of the dominant role played by sound in poetic usage. The degree of analytic precision, however, was heightened.

These observations of the role of sound in a work of verbal art naturally provoked interest in various types of sound symmetry, involving vowels, consonants, and syllables, as well as morphemes, words, and more comprehensive syntagmatic formations. The sound symmetry manifested in rhymes had played an important role in the phonemic inquiries of Baudouin's student Lev Ščerba, who most effectively interpreted the teaching of the Kazan school to the adherents of the Formal method, whether they were members of *Opojaz*, or the *Moscow Linguistic Circle*, or both. In connection with rhyme, it became essential to deal with sound, both in its articulatory and acoustic aspects, and with the reproductive as well as the recognitive processes in communication. Moreover, the prominent problem of sound and its orthographic representation entered the picture, together with questions concerning recitation, on the one hand, and silent reading on the other. An acceptability of rhyme was unveiled as a complex process because of its changeability and striking relativeness, involving not only the physical manifestations of identifying sound but also the intricate constraints imposed by morphological patterns and by various traditional values, such as orthography. It became necessary to consider the problem of sight rhymes, the discrepancy between homophony and homography in their relevance to rhyming, and in general the entire set of conditions determining the acceptability of rhymes and the degree of their value, whether good or bad, full or partial, etc. Accurate inquiries into the intrinsic characteristics of rhyming clearly revealed that a consideration of the phonological arrangement of the sound system was crucial for both synchronic and diachronic studies of rhyme. Subsequently, the phoneme in its relation to sound implementation began to serve as an underlying concept, not only in the studies of rhyme but also in the analysis of the sound texture in poetry in general. At the same time, an increased awareness of the role of extralinguistic factors in the acceptability of rhyme served as a warning not to neglect the system of cultural norms controlling euphony and other aesthetic values. This, of course, required a deep penetration into the territory of literary scholarship, in which linguistics could properly serve only as an auxiliary discipline. It was characteristic, however, that the adherents of the Formal method considered such a crossing from the domain of linguistics into the domain of literary scholarship as a vital strategy for both disciplines, provided that in cooperating, each retained its identity.

And, in fact, the distributional studies of rhyme and other types of sound parallelism naturally strengthened knowledge, not only knowledge of the elements and their patterns, but also of their relationship to other components of the work of art, particularly to the properties delimiting it as a unit. Characteristic of this trend was the term "structure" (*struktura*) appearing several times in Osip Brik's study of sound repetition, published in 1917 with the subtitle, "Analysis of the Sound Structure of Verse."[7] Patterns of sound were viewed as the components making the poetic "structure" strikingly unique, so that a precise study of patterns appeared as the most reasonable strategy for seizing the work of art in its essentials. The patterns in Brik's interpretation of sound were laid bare as subtle devices endowed with the power to elevate sound from its subordinate status in communication to an autonomous system of values. According to Brik's exposition, the creative usage of the sound system coexists synchronically with the creative usage of imagery in such a way that each individual work of art represents, in fact, a resultant of two distinct domains of creativity. This analytic demarcation suggested the possibility of approaching the complex structure of a work of art by observing, on the one hand, the variability within each participating system and, on the other, the variability in their mutual relationship.

Although Brik considered the interaction between sound and meaning as the most crucial operation observable in the work of verbal art, many among the early adherents of the Formal method showed a compulsive predilection for the concreteness of the physical implementation of art and a distrustful attitude toward the problem of meaning. Some of them were apparently convinced that a rigorous segmentation and stratification of the literary text and a classificatory ingenuity in describing the inventory would provide direct access to the mystery of verbal art without involvement in the web of semantics. Their contemptuous scorn for the definition of poetry as "thinking in images" was coupled with exaggerated expections about the data directly derivable from the physical manifestation of a work of verbal art.

The promotion of sound as an autonomous source of creative potentials naturally found itself faced by the problem of evaluation. The role of sound arrangement in attracting attention to the formal means of verbal signs provoked questions about the "psychophonetic phenomena" in their relationship to the "physiophonetic facts," to use the terms of Baudouin de Courtenay, whose impact on this psychological stream in the early stages of the Formal method is clearly detectible. Both Jakubinskij and Viktor Šklovskij began to speculate about the general laws of perception, and both found it of particular interest to quote William James on the physical basis of emotions and other related matters; but Karl Vossler and his brand of psycholinguistics certainly played an important role as well.

Psychological observations about sound in poetry prompted Jakubinskij to assume that sound in practical language does not fully enter into the consciousness of the human mind, whereas the systematic recurrence of sound in poetry becomes significant in its own right by its ability to capture one's mind. In developing his mentalistic excursus, Jakubinskij found sound in poetry closely linked with emotional surrender to the sublime magic of euphony. The confessions of poets about their emotive involvement with sound was brought in as circumstantial evidence. Jakubinskij's psychological exploration of aesthetic values even scrutinized the articulatory enjoyment of sound, "the dance of the organs of speech," in its correlation with acoustic delight.

Thus the inquiry into sound in poetry began to tiptoe into the obscure territory of kinaesthetics.[8]

The fascination exerted by the psychological vistas also overpowered Viktor Šklovskij's investigation. He found the fundamental mission of verbal art in its technical ability to release sound from the status automatized by everyday language.[9] In Šklovskij's view, the poetic arrangement revitalizes sound by preventing its retreat into the area of unconsciousness; by making forms unusual and difficult, art prolongs perception so that it is possible to experience artfulness. Thus the aesthetic values of verbal art were revealed by Šklovskij as a process triggered by the manipulation of formal properties of the verbal sign: the poetic language was assumed to impose special constraints on the verbal means, in order to obstruct their causal usage and to provoke intensified participation which ultimately would give aesthetic joy as a reward for overcoming difficulties. Paraphrasing Aristotle, Šklovskij proclaimed that "poetic language must appear as strange and wonderful."[10]

In Šklovskij's view, however, the defamiliarizing of the familiar and de-automatization of the automatized does not apply solely to the domain of sound. It applies also to the lexical selection, to the distribution of words, and even to the referential aspect of the total utterance. Accordingly, verbal art is expected to de-automatize and "make strange" not only language but also the objects referred to, the semantic buildup, the very perception of things and life. "Art is with us," Šklovskij says, "to enable things to be felt, to make stone stony."[11]

Šklovskij's probe into the depths of verbal creation virtually obliterated the importance of a careful distinction between the referential means and the referent, the designator and the designated. Accordingly, Šklovskij, in his polemic article about the Russian linguist Potebnja and his followers, claims that:

> Poetic language is distinguished from prosaic language by the palpableness of its construction. The palpableness may be brought about by the acoustic aspect, or the articulatory aspect, or the semasiological aspect. Sometimes what is palpable is not the structure of the words but the use of words in constructions, their arrangement. One of the means for creating a palpable construction, the very fabric of which is experienced, is the poetic image, but it is only one of the means.[12]

Thus, rather than to clarify the delicate relationship between sound and meaning, Škloviskij's generalization tended to obscure it. A revision in terms of analytic precision and methodological lucidity became unavoidable. Subsequently, in the process of solidifying the methodological basis, the theoreticians of the Formal method had, on the one hand, to resist the lure of intuitive insights, and, on the other hand, to expose the fallacies of classificatory descriptivism concealed under the guise of scientific vigor.

2

As early as in 1917, the impact of the Kazan school on the fermentation of the Formal method was decisively strengthened by the teaching of Ferdinand de Saussure, brilliantly transmitted by Sergej Karcevskij, who returned to Moscow after his scholarly apprenticeship in Geneva.[13] Thus, long before the concept of the phoneme began to dominate the entire field of linguistics, the young Russian theoreticians were exposed to functional linguistics in its two most fundamental versions. Moreover, they were faced by the provoking but not entirely clear Saussurian distinction between language as a system (*la langue*) and the concrete implementation of language in speech (*la parole*). There were other stimulating designs to think about, as, for example, the interlocking model of paradigmatic and syntagmatic procedures, the new projection of the classical correlation of *signans* (the designator) and *signatum* (the designated), the antinomy in the basic mode of any verbal communication, manifested by the profoundly distinct roles of two participants in dialogue, and, above all, the concept of synchrony and diachrony in language studies.

It became apparent that the systematic nature of verbal art may considerably benefit by applying a consistent phonological approach. This was convincingly demonstrated by Roman Jakobson's study of Czech verse (1923), dealing with the difference between Czech and Russian phonological systems in their fundamental connections with their respective systems of versification.[14] The study discloses that word stress, which has phonological status in Russian but not in Czech, plays a decisively different role in each of the two systems of versification, so that the distinct character of Russian poetry as compared with Czech poetry is fundamentally determined by the differences in their phonological systems. With the help of examples from other languages, it was possible to conclude that the analysis of the phonological system should be a mandatory step of every inquiry into the system of versification.

The systematic nature of poetry also became the main target of Osip Brik's study "Rhythm and Syntax" outlined as a lecture in 1920 and published in 1927.[15] In this penetrating essay rhythm is interpreted as the structural interaction of the meter with the prosodic and grammatical systems of the language. In Brik's view:

> If we take by way of experiment a random sequence of meaningless syllables and try to read them as iambs, trochees, dactyls, anapests, or amphibrachs, the result will be completely even, uniform systems of syllables, the systems differing from one another only by virtue of the basic distribution of stressed and unstressed elements. But as soon as we begin to read, using one of the five possible patterns, a series of meaningful words, we quickly discover that the initially regular curve of intensives becomes increasingly complex.

Hence, Brik argues, "the complex system of rhythmic intensives in the poetic line cannot be understood without reference to semantics and syntax."[16] He adds:

> We can turn any line of poetry into a transrational one if, instead of meaningful words, we insert sounds which express the rhythmico-phonic arrangement of these words. But, in depriving the line of its semantics, we go beyond the limits of poetic language; further variations of this line will be conditioned not by its verbal composition but by its tonality. In particular, the system of stress and intonation will be independent of the stress and intonation of ordinary speech and will imitate the stress and intonation of a musical phrase. In other words, by depriving the line of its semantic meaning, we transfer it from the domain of language to a new domain—that of music. The poetic line thus ceases to be a verbal fact.[17]

In Brik's view, the rhythmico-semantic complex does not imply a subordination of one domain to the other: "They originate simultaneously, creating specific rhythmico-syntactic structures different both from that of ordinary speech and that of a transrational sequence of sounds."[18]

The patterning of sound repetition, emphasized in Brik's earlier studies as a design to attract attention, had been discerned as one of the components integrated into the structure. The gradual elaboration of the structural concept shifted emphasis from components and levels to the process of structural interlocking displayed within the contours of the work viewed as a whole. According to Brik, "The correct point of view sees in poetry a specific verbal complex created on the basis of special laws which are not identical with those of ordinary speech."[19]

It is noteworthy that Brik's inquiry into the rhythmico-syntactic problems of verbal art conspicuously avoids a separation of the synchronic and diachronic aspects; the system is considered in its evolution, which, in Brik's view, is prompted by two basic attitudes toward verse: one emphasizing the rhythmic aspects and the other, the semantic. "At various times in poetic culture," he explains, "various aspects have dominated, first one thing, then another, first the rhythmic aspect, then the semantic aspect; the development of poetry may be characterized as a struggle against the prevailing norms of the moment."[20]

The divorce of synchrony from diachrony, implied in Saussure's views and rigorously executed by some of his followers, became one of the matters which the development of the Formal method submitted to profound revision. It was Jakobson, in fact, who in his linguistic studies most convincingly disclosed the dangerous fallacy in separating synchronic and diachronic approaches to verbal communication. In the synopsis of Jakobson's lecture delivered in the Prague Linguistic Circle in 1927, the claim is made that "the antinomy between synchronic and diachronic linguistic studies should be overcome by a transformation of historical phonetics into history of the phonemic system."[21] In the field of literary scholarship, the transformation of synchrony and diachrony entirely dominated Jurij Tynjanov's inquiry into literary evolution. In Tynjanov's view, "tradition, the basic concept of the established history of literature, has proved to be an unjustifiable abstraction of one or more literary elements of a given system, within which they are on the same plane and play the same role."[22] Therefore, according to Tynjanov:

> If we agree that evolution is the change in interrelationships between the elements of a system, i.e., between functions and formal elements, then evolution may be seen as the "changing" of systems. These changes vary from epoch to epoch, sometimes occurring slowly, sometimes rapidly. They do not entail sudden and complete renovation or replacement of formal elements, but rather the new function of these formal elements. Thus, the very comparison of certain literary phenomena must be made on the bases of functions as well as of forms.[23]

The literary system is explained by Tynjanov as being organically interrelated with other systems and conditioned by them so that it becomes mandatory to consider the correlation of systems.

Tynjanov especially emphasizes the fact that the literary system does not display an equality of all its elements, so that certain factors in the hierarchical arrangement of the system acquire a controlling position by the subordinating of other factors. "Since a system," Tynjanov asserts, "is not an equal interaction of all elements, but involves the foregrounding of a group of elements— the *dominant*— and the deformation of the remaining elements, a work enters into literature and takes on its own literary function through this *dominant.*"[24]

The dominant, defined as the focusing component which rules, determines, and transforms the remaining components, was gradually developed into one of the crucial concepts in the period when the Formal method was restated in terms of Structuralism. The concept of the dominant and of foregrounding was expanded so as to be relevant not only to the hierarchy in an individual work of art, viewed as a system, but also to higher structures viewed as a system of systems.

A new approach to the Saussurian distinction between static synchrony and dynamic diachrony received prominent attention in Tynjanov and Jakobson's joint programmatic article concerning problems in the study of literature and language (1928). "Pure synchronism," they claimed, "proves to be an illusion: every synchronic system has its past and its future as inseparable structural elements of the system."[25] Thus many decades before synchronic descriptivism in linguistics reached its zenith, it was rejected by that brand of Structuralism which evolved from the Russian Formal method. In Tynjanov and Jakobson's words, "The opposition between synchrony and diachrony lost its importance in principle as soon as it was recognized that every system necessarily exists as an evolution, whereas, on the other hand, evolution is inescapably of a systematic nature."[26]

The theses proposed by Tynjanov and Jakobson also posit in a restated version the Saussurian assertion distinguishing *la langue* from *la parole.* The authors point out that the distinction outlined by Saussure was exceedingly fruitful for linguistic science, and therefore its application to literature should be elaborated to permit the analysis of the immanent laws underlying the history of the literary system and its correlation with other systems—the system of systems.

Neither Saussure nor his editors have ever presented the opposition between abstractness of language *(la langue)* and concreteness of speech (*la parole*) in terms of all its possible implications. It has remained unanswered whether linguistics should deal with two objects of possible investigation or with only one of them; in the latter case the question was whether the object of investigation should be exclusively the system or perhaps only the corpus of recorded data. The linguistic mechanists and the Marxists were naturally tempted to concentrate on the physical manifestation while interpreting the system essentially as a scientific result of rigorous classification and description of the corpus. On the other hand, the mentalistic trend in linguistics tempted one to see only the underlying system as being worthy of scientific effort, while the implementation of the system was regarded with an obvious lack of interest, even with scorn. Thus the Saussurian design was dissolved in favor of one of its poles, either the material or the purely relational one. The theoreticians of the Formal method in its transition into Structuralism were consistent, however, in their emphasis on the complementary, inseparable nature of the two conjoined aspects subsequently termed *message* and *code.*

In their concise outline of the boundary between studies of folklore and literary scholarship (1929), Jakobson and Petr Bogatyrev compare the essential relationship between message and code with the relationship between the individual implementation of folklore work and its extra-individual existence in the memory of the cultural community, where it appears only potentially as a complex of established norms and stimuli.
The extraindividual existence of a work of oral art is viewed as "a skeleton of actual traditions which the implementers embellish with the tracery of individual creation, in much the same way as the producers of a verbal message (*la parole* in the Saussurian sense) act with respect to the verbal code (*la langue*)."[27]

Jakobson's insistence on transforming the Saussurian antinomy into an indivisible correlation of two aspects connects his earliest linguistic studies with his mature work and consistently distinguishes him from the mechanists as well as from the mentalists. In 1957 in his study *Shifters, Verbal Categories, and the Russian Verb,* the Saussurian antinomy is restated as the relationship between two vehicles of linguistic communication functioning in a dual manner: "They may at once be utilized and referred to (pointed at); thus a message may refer to the code or to another message, and, on the other hand, the general meaning of a code unit may imply a reference (*renvoi*) to the code or to the message."[28] In the use of language, according to Jakobson, duality plays a cardinal role. In fact, the awareness of duality characterizes not only the early Structuralists but also other followers of the Russian Formal method, as Baxtin and particularly Vološinov, to whom Jakobson gives special credit in his *Shifters.*

Baudouin de Courtenay and his Kazan school as well as Ferdinand de Saussure and his Geneva school regarded dialogue as a principal mode of verbal communication; necessarily, therefore, they had to consider the roles of two distinct participants, the speaker and the hearer.

The continuous tradition of the Formalists' inquiries into dialogue supplied the necessary prerequisites for a new approach to the problem of prose in verbal art. It became possible to reveal the techniques of stylization, parody, and represented narration, and to analyze from a new viewpoint various types of reported speech in their subtle application in literature.

In his important contribution to the study of dialogue, Jakubinskij suggests that "every interaction between people tends by its very nature to avoid a one-sided monologue and to become a two-sided dialogue."[29] In his view, "dialogue is natural because, like action and reaction, it corresponds to the social facts of interaction, in which the social aspects most nearly approach the biological (psycho-physiological) aspects."[30] He points out that "dialogue, while it is doubtless a phenomenon of 'culture,' is at the same time to a larger extent than monologue a phenomenon of 'nature,' "[31]

The observations about dialogue skillfully applied by Mixail Baxtin to the domain of verbal art opened a new path in literary scholarship. In Baxtin's view:

> Any literary discourse more or less keenly senses its listener, reader, or critic, and reflects anticipated objections, evaluations, and points of view. Besides, literary discourse senses alongside it other literary discourse, other style. An element of the so-called reaction against a previous literary style, present in every new style, is just such an internal polemic; it is a hidden antistylization (so to speak) of another style, which often unites with an outright parody of it.[32]

Moreover, according to Baxtin:

> Hidden dialogue is especially significant and important; it does not coincide with the hidden polemic. Imagine a dialogue between two persons in which the statements of the second speaker are deleted, but in such a way that the general sense is not disrupted. The second speaker's presence is not shown; his actual words are not given, but the deep impression of these words has a determining effect on all the utterances made by the only one who does speak. We feel that this is a conversation of the most intense kind, because each uttered word in all its fiber responds and reacts to the invisible partner, referring to something outside itself, beyond its limits, to the unspoken word of the other speaker. In Dostoevskij's works, this hidden dialogue occupies a very important place and is subtly and profoundly elaborated.[33]

In contrast to Baxtin, V. Vološinov in his lucid exposition on reported speech sharply distinguishes between dialogue and the reaction of one utterance to another utterance, reported and viewed as another person's message. According to Vološinov, "A productive study of dialogue presupposes a more profound investigation of the forms used in reported speech, since these forms reflect basic and constant tendencies in the active reception of other speakers' speech, and it is this reception, after all, that is fundamental also for dialogue."[34]

In Vološinov's definition of the dual role quoted by Jakobson in his *Shifters*, "Reported speech is speech within speech, message within message, and at the same time it is also speech about speech, message about message."[35] The manipulation of reported speech in various constructions provides, as Vološinov demonstrates, delicate devices which serve in the literary language as vehicles of interaction between the auctorial context and the speech of the participants of the narrated event. In Vološinov's view:

> Earlier investigators of the forms of reported speech committed the fundamental error of virtually divorcing reported speech from the reporting context. That explains why their treatment of these forms is so static and inert (a characteristic applicable to the whole field of syntactic study in general). Meanwhile, the true object of inquiry ought to be precisely the dynamic interrelationship of these two factors: the speech being reported (the "other person's" speech) and the speech doing the reporting (the "author's" speech). After all, they do in actual fact exist, function, and take shape only in their interrelationship, not independently, the one apart from the other.[36]

Vološinov's observations about dialogue and the role of the participants involved in both reporting and reported language were advanced by the Structuralists of the Prague variety. However, the entire scheme of interaction between the verbal system and its users acquired new dimensions in several of Jakobson's studies on poetics. His consistent interest in the characteristics distinguishing the addresser from the addressee, the speaker from the hearer, the writer from the reader, or, to use later terminology, the encoder from the decoder, had a paramount importance in the development of his analytic approach, not only to the verbal system, but to the other systems of signs and to semiotics in general.

As early as 1921, Jakobson was applying his observations about dialogue to the problems of realism in art, whether verbal or visual.[37] His consideration of the roles played by the encoder and the decoder brought into focus the distinction between realism conceived and realism perceived, and, by implication, the importance of norms controlling aesthetic values in semiotic processes.

It was shown that the knowledge of the normative code is fundamental for any treatment of aesthetic values, either in the creative process or in the process of interpretation. "The methods of projecting three-dimensional space onto a flat surface," Jakobson asserts, "are established by convention; the use of color, the abstracting, the simplification of the object depicted, and the choice of reproducible features are all conventional."[38] Hence it is concluded that it is impossible to understand the picture without learning the conventional language of painting, just as it is impossible to understand what is said without knowing the language. Since our perception of visual art is conditioned to a great extent by the normative code, the artist-innovator in Jakobson's view "must impose a new form upon our perception if we are to detect in a given thing those traits which went unnoticed the day before."[39] Innovations in the domain of verbal art are in many respects of the same nature. An unexpectedness of usage contrasts with the expected usage, whether it is one of selection or of combination, so that the aesthetic value of innovation is viewed in terms of the relation between the actual manifestation of verbal usage and the code controlling it.

The interpretation of art as a kind of language, verbal or nonverbal, implies, of course, a considerable expansion of the territory to which the model of dialogue is applicable. In this way, we can view verbal communication together with other systems of signs and observe the common denominators as well as the *differentiae specificae*. We are compelled to note the differences between a verbal sign and a nonverbal sign, between a verbal system and other semiotic systems, between verbal art and other arts.

Both the Formalists and Structuralists paid close attention to Saussure's observations about the paradigmatic and syntagmatic usage of verbal signs, although they did not apply it without modifications. Eventually, the concept had to be substantially redefined, so that Saussure's syntagmatic procedure could embrace two varieties of combination, concurrence and concatenation, both distinguishable from the selection characterizing Saussure's paradigmatic procedure.

In Jakobson's studies, the opposition between paradigmatic and syntagmatic procedures was early recognized as being connected with the two fundamental poles dominating the verbal operation: the metaphoric pole, making use of similarity, and the metonymic pole, making use of contiguity. In his study of Pasternak's prose (1927), Jakobson applied the binary concept of the metaphoric and metonymic poles as a classificatory device of two profoundly different types of poetic creation. The opposition of the metaphoric and the metonymic, exemplified in the domain of verbal art, was linked in Jakobson's subsequent investigation with the very bases of human capacity in using verbal signs. Nevertheless, consistent references to verbal art continued to play an important role even within the framework of Jakobson's studies on aphasia, focused on the pathology of speech: the disorder of similarity and the disorder of contiguity. The fact that the discussion of verbal art constitutes Jakobson's closing chapter in the *Fundamentals of Language* demonstrates that the author, in the tradition of the Russian Formalists and the Prague Structuralists, considered the exploration of verbal art among the most basic tasks of the inquiry into human dialogue at its foundations.[40]

In such a framework, the investigation of verbal art is far from being self-contained: it is used to shed light on other aspects of semiotics; and, vice versa, various aspects common to general semiotics are used to illuminate the nature of verbal art. Thus the crossing of the boundaries between literature and other related systems becomes an essential part of the analytic strategy concerned with the structural interconnection of scientific exploration.

Notes

1. Roman Jakobson, "Kazańska szkoła polskiej lingwistyki i jej miejsce w światowym rozwoju fonologii," *Biuletyn Polskiego Towarzystwa Językoznawczego*, 19 (1960), pp. 1-34.

2. Krystyna Pomorska, *Russian Formalist Theory and Its Poetic Ambiance*, The Hague, 1968.

3. E. D. Polivanov, "O zvukax poètičeskogo jazyka," *Poètika. Sborniki po teorii poètičeskogo jazyka* (Petrograd, 1919), pp. 27-36. First published in *Sborniki po teorii poètičeskogo jazyka*, 1, 1916.

4. Lev Jakubinskij, "O zvukax poètičeskogo jazyka," *Poètika. Sborniki po teorii poètičeskogo jazyka* (Petrograd, 1919), pp. 37-49. First published in *Sborniki po teorii poètičeskogo jazyka*, 1, 1916.

5. Viktor Šklovskij, "Iskusstvo kak priem," *Poètika. Sborniki po teorii poètičeskogo jazyka* (Petrograd, 1919), pp. 101-114. First published in *Sborniki po teorii poètičeskogo jazyka*, 2, 1917.

6. Jakobson, *O češskom stixe preimuščestvenno v sopostavlenii s russkim* (Berlin, 1923), p. 17. [Republished in Brown University Slavic Reprint VI]

7. Osip Brik, "Zvukovye povtory. Analiz zvukovoj struktury stixa," *Michigan Slavic Materials*, 5 (Ann Arbor, 1964), pp. 3-45. First published in *Sborniki po teorii poètičeskogo jazyka*, 2, 1917.

8. Jakubinskij, "O zvukax. . . ," pp. 45-49.

9. Šklovskij, "Isskustvo," pp. 103-114.

10. *Ibid.*, p. 112.

11. *Ibid.*, p. 105.

12. Šklovskij, "Potebnja," *Poètika. Sborniki po teorii poètičeskogo jazyka* (Petrograd, 1919), p. 4.

13. Jakobson, "Retrospect," *Selected Writings*, 1 (The Hague, 1962), p. 631.

14. Jakobson, *O češskom stixe*, p. 41.

15. Brik, "Ritm i sintaksis," *Michigan Slavic Materials*, 5 (Ann Arbor, 1964), p. 58. First published in *Novyj Lef*, 1927.

16. *Ibid.*, p. 58.

17. *Ibid.*, p. 72.

18. *Ibid.*, p. 72.

19. *Ibid.*, p. 72.

20. *Ibid.*, p. 59.

21. Jakobson, "The Concept of the Sound Law and the Teleological Criterion," *Selected Writings*, 1 ('s-Gravenhage, 1962), p. 2.

22. Jurij Tynjanov, "O literaturnoj èvolijucii," *Arxaisty i novatory* (Leningrad, 1929), p. 32.

23. *Ibid.*, p. 46.

24. *Ibid.*, p. 41.

25. Tynjanov and Jakobson, "Problemy izučenija literatury i jazyka," *Michigan Slavic Materials*, 2 (Ann Arbor, 1962), p. 101. First published in *Novyj Lef*, 12, 1927.

26. *Ibid.*, p. 102.

27. Jakobson and Petr Bogatyrev, "K probleme razmeževanija fol'kloristiki i literaturovedenija," *Selected Writings*, 4 (The Hague, 1966), p. 16.

28. Jakobson, *Shifters, Verbal Categories, and the Russian Verb* (Cambridge, 1957), p. 1.

29. Jakubinskij, "O dialogičeskoj reči," *Russkaja reč'*, ed. L. V. Ščerba, (Petrograd, 1923), p. 133.

30. *Ibid.*, p. 139.

31. *Ibid.*

32. Mixail Baxtin, "Tipy prozaičeskogo slova," *Michigan Slavic Materials*, 2 (Ann Arbor, 1962), p. 59. First published in *Problemy tvorčestva Dostoevskogo.* (Leningrad, 1929).

33. *Ibid.*, p. 60.

34. V. V. Vološinov, "Èkspozicija problemy 'čužoj reči' " *Michigan Slavic Materials*, 2 (Ann Arbor, 1962), p. 74.

35. *Ibid.*, p. 72.

36. *Ibid.*, p. 76.

37. Jakobson, "O xudožestvennom realizme," *Michigan Slavic Materials*, 2 (Ann Arbor, 1962), pp. 30-36.

38. *Ibid.*, p. 31.

39. *Ibid.*, p. 31.

40. Roman Jakobson and Morris Halle, *Fundamentals of Language* (The Hague, 1956), pp. 55-82.

Name Index

Subject Index